THE PENGUIN POETS

THE PENGUIN BOOK OF
SCOTTISH VERSE

TOM SCOTT, the son of a Clydeside boiler-maker, was born in Glasgow in 1918. After leaving school (the family moved to St Andrews in 1931) he was apprenticed to the building trade, but was drawn to singing and poetry irresistably. He served during the war, in Nigeria, and at home, and settled in London after he was demobbed, freelancing, odd-jobbing, reading and living. On the invitation of Edwin Muir, and backed by T. S. Eliot, he went to Newbattle Abbey College near Edinburgh, after which he took an honours M.A. and Ph.D. at Edinburgh university. He has published a dozen or so books and widely in magazines and anthologies, but has suffered much from the publishing barriers raised against Scottish language and literature.

THE PENGUIN BOOK OF

SCOTTISH VERSE

INTRODUCED
AND EDITED BY
Tom Scott

PENGUIN BOOKS

PENGUIN BOOKS

Published by the Penguin Group
Penguin Books Ltd, 27 Wrights Lane, London W8 5TZ, England
Viking Penguin, a division of Penguin Books USA Inc.
375 Hudson Street, New York, New York 10014, USA
Penguin Books Australia Ltd, Ringwood, Victoria, Australia
Penguin Books Canada Ltd, 2801 John Street, Markham, Ontario, Canada L3R 1B4
Penguin Books (NZ) Ltd, 182–190 Wairau Road, Auckland 10, New Zealand

Penguin Books Ltd, Registered Offices: Harmondsworth, Middlesex, England

First published 1970
5 7 9 10 8 6

Printed in England by Clays Ltd, St Ives plc
Set in Monotype Modern No.1

Contents

JOHN BARBOUR (c. 1320–95)

Barbour was archdeacon of Aberdeen and attached to the court of
Robert II and Robert III. He seems to have written *The Bruce* in
1375, by royal request, and his sources are in traditions of powerful
families around the court.

JAMES I (1394–1437)

The best of all the Stewart monarchs, James was piratically abducted
by the English while journeying to France, and kept a prisoner for
some eighteen years in England, from 1406 to 1424. *The Kingis Quair*
is believed to have been written shortly before release.

SIR RICHARD HOLLAND (?1420–?1485)

Holland was a cleric in the entourage of the Douglas family, and with
some of them he was exiled in England. The poem was written for

Elizabeth Dunbar, Countess of Moray, and is a unique example of a sustained 'beastie' allegory in parody of the old alliterative stanza.

from The Book of the Howlat

ROBERT HENRYSOUN (*c.* 1420–*c.*1490)

All that can be asserted confidently is that he was associated with Dunfermline, perhaps as notary, perhaps as music-master, or in some such capacity. That he was a cleric well versed in law (one of the earliest of the lawyer-writers so common in Scottish literature) is obvious, and he shows a greater range and accuracy of knowledge than any writer of his time, except perhaps his junior, Gawin Douglas. He is arguably the best Scottish poet before Burns, and if surpassed at all, only by Dunbar, and only in technique and range of forms and kinds. *The Testament of Cresseid* is the finest original long poem in the Scots language.

BLIN HARY THE MINSTREL (*fl. c.* 1460–90)

Even less is known about Hary than the other middle Scots poets. He had no lack of as much poetic education as a popular poet needed to achieve major work. He is a true bard of the people, reasserting patriotic feeling at a time when national morale was low.

from The Wallace

ANONYMOUS (? early 16th Century)

WILLIAM DUNBAR (?1460–?1520)

Dunbar seems to have been a younger son of the Dunbar family, and to have been brought up for the Church. He was a Master of Arts, probably went to St Andrews University, seems to have been a far-travelled Franciscan novice, hoped to become a bishop, served in various unknown capacities at the court of James IV, which he hated, and spent most of his life trying to escape from it to that serenity of life Henrysoun enjoyed in Dunfermline. Like all the Scottish poets of the age, he is steeped in the great European traditions, particularly French. His nearest affinity in Europe is Villon, and no man could have been more unlike Chaucer than Dunbar: which underlines the idiocy of calling him a 'Scottish Chaucerian'. Like all the great, and most of the lesser, poets of his time, he was a European, and that meant belonging to the cultural empire of France. In range and variety of lyric form he has no equal in either Scots or English during this period, and is of universal stature.

GAWIN DOUGLAS (c. 1475–1522)

Third son of Archibald Douglas, Earl of Angus, Gawin was born to power. He graduated at St Andrews in 1494, studied and travelled in Europe, like most educated Scots, and rose in Church preferments to become Bishop of Dunkeld. He had a turbulent life because of his family's fortunes, close to the crown and violent, and died of the plague in exile in London. His greatness was worldly rather than saintly.

SIR DAVID LYNDSAY (?1490–1555)

Born probably at the family seat of the Mount, near Cupar, Fife, he studied at St Andrews and travelled abroad. He attended the court of James IV and was a tutor to the young James V, and ever after on close terms with him. In his courtly capacity he developed his powers of entertaining with plays and such, both before and after becoming Lyon King of Arms, and the skill which made the *Satyr of the Thrie Estaitis* possible.

SIR RICHARD MAITLAND (1496–1586)

Maitland of Lethington became Lord Privy Seal, and turned to versifying only in age; he leans heavily on Dunbar.

ANONYMOUS

ANONYMOUS (mid-16th Century)

ALEXANDER SCOTT (*c.* 1520–*c.* 1590)

Nothing at all is known of Scott apart from the few poems that have come down to us. He has been associated with Dalkeith, near Edinburgh.

ALEXANDER MONTGOMERIE (?1545–?1610)

He was a captain of horse, close to the court of James VI, but seems to have been involved in a Catholic intrigue which wrecked his career.

MARK ALEXANDER BOYD (1563–1601)

Son of Robert Boyd of Pinkhill, Ayrshire, Mark was of a goliardic temper, a bit of a picaresque character in Europe in youth, but became one of the finest Latin poets of his day.

SIR ROBERT AYTOUN (1569–1638)

A minor versifier of mediocre talent and taste, he is seen at his best in the light verse I have chosen.

BALLADS

The Scottish ballads of oral tradition belong as much to music as to literature – the tune is half the work. They have been the object of too much discussion this century for me to say much about them here. Only a small selection is given, but a Penguin *Book of Border Ballads* was done a few years ago edited by Dr William Beattie. The indispensable book for students is the collection by F. J. Child.

SIR ROBERT SEMPILL OF BELTREES (?1595–?1660)

After the comparative silence following the sweeping away of the great tradition of the Makars by the Reformation, the age of great cleric-poets is replaced by that of the rhyming laird and gentry. Sempill, Laird of Beltrees, ushers in the new day with his comic elegy on Habbie Simson, the stanza of which was to become so famous that we now call it 'Standard Habbie'.

FRANCIS SEMPILL OF BELTREES (?1616–?1685)

Son of Sir Robert, Francis followed his father in rhyming as in estate, and the best of his few poems is the one given here. It has an excellent tune, one of our best songs.

JAMES GRAHAM, Marquis of Montrose (1612–50)

Little need be said here of the great Montrose, 'perverse and brave' according to Edwin Muir, and his heroic stand for Charles I. He means every word of the noble poem on his execution, and lived it out on the gallows. The sentence for treason was: to be hanged by the neck, cut down, disembowelled, beheaded and quartered. This butchery Montrose contemplates in the poem.

ANONYMOUS (17th Century)

LADY GRIZEL BAILLIE (1665–1746)

Daughter of Patrick Hume, Earl of Marchmont, Grizel was involved in his intrigues against the government and suffered exile in Holland for a year or two. She married George Baillie in 1692, the son of a friend of her father's who had been executed in 1684.

WILLIAM HAMILTON OF GILBERTFIELD (?1665–1751)

The Laird of Gilbertfield was a retired army officer when he was drawn into the company and influence of Allan Ramsay. Not only was his *Bonnie Heck* the beginning of a craze for mock elegies on animals, but he and Ramsay began the craze for epistles between poets: both were taken up by Burns to some effect. He also produced a version of Hary's *Wallace* which had a deep influence on Burns's patriotic feeling.

ALLAN RAMSAY (1684/5–1758)

Born at Leadhills, Lanarkshire, son of a lead mines superintendent who died in Allan's infancy. His mother also died when he was only fourteen, and the boy was apprenticed to a wig-maker in Edinburgh. His passionate love of poetry soon led him into the book trade, and so to one of the most fertile careers in all Scottish letters. He was a one-man revolution, a Jacobite, anti-Calvinist, anti-philistine, and even set up an early attempt to revive theatre, which was soon suppressed by the Kirk. Without him neither Fergusson nor Burns could have done so much.

ALEXANDER ROSS (1699–1784)
An early disciple of Ramsay, he was born in Aberdeenshire, son of a farmer, graduated M.A. at Aberdeen, became a teacher and settled in Lochlea, Forfar, as schoolmaster. He published a lengthy pastoral, *Helenore*, in his seventieth year, but is best remembered for one or two songs.

JAMES THOMSON (1700–1748)
Thomson was born in Ednam, Roxburghshire, son of a minister there. He attended Edinburgh University, but in 1725 took the road to London where he wrote *Winter*, the first of his *Seasons* quartet. New to English, this was a traditional theme in Scots poetry, as witness Gawin Douglas's *Seventh Prologue*, Dunbar's *Meditatioun in Winter*, and the opening of Henrysoun's *Cresseid*. Thomson met most of the Pope circle, found himself patrons, and held minor political posts. He is an important example of the influence of the Scottish tradition on English poetry.

ADAM SKIRVING (1719–1803)
Skirving was a gentleman farmer in the Haddington area.

WILLIAM WILKIE (1721–72)
Wilkie was a 'lad o' pairts', at one time minister of Ratho, then Professor of Natural Philosophy at St Andrews. He wrote a six-thousand line epic, the *Epigoniad*, once much admired, but is now best known for his fables, of which I choose one in Scots.

JOHN SKINNER (1721–1807)

John Skinner was an Episcopal minister in an age when the Scottish 'piskies' were as persecuted as the Papists, with a church in Longside, Aberdeenshire. He produced one or two goodish songs, but the one here given is by far the best of them, and was Burns's favourite song.

JEAN ELLIOT (1727–1805)

Jean was third daughter of Sir Gilbert Elliot, Bart, of Minto. Her famous version of the *Flowers of the Forest* is a re-working of an older song unhappily no longer identifiable. These song-cobblings often merely corrupt where they think they improve.

ANONYMOUS (Pasquils on the Treaty of Union 1707)

Scottish poetry has its share of satires and popular broadsides. James Maidment collected many of these in his *Book of Scottish Pasquils*. I give two of them here showing the popular mind about the Treaty of Union of 1707.

JAMES BEATTIE (1735–1803)

Beattie was professor of Moral Philosophy in Aberdeen, and did much versifying in English, notably his Spenserian poem *The Minstrel*. But to my mind none of it has the vitality and genuineness of his one *tour-de-force* in Scots, which shows what was hidden by his anglicizing.

ROBERT GRAHAM OF GARTMORE (c.1735–97)

An ancestor of R. B. Cunninghame-Graham, Robert inherited the estate of Gartmore in 1774. He was educated at Glasgow University, of which he was elected Rector in 1785, defeating Burke, was M.P. for Stirling and a friend of Fox. His sympathies were Whig and he approved the French Revolution. He lent MSS to Walter Scott when he was writing *Rob Roy*, and Scott seems to have discovered this poem, which understandably he thought to be by the greater Graham, Montrose. But apparently this best of Scottish cavalier songs is by Robert and not by the likelier Montrose.

ALEXANDER GEDDES (1737–1802)

Geddes was a Catholic priest of first-rate scholarship, a great linguist, and of no mean poetic ability. He has had a number of poems attributed to him, but the authorship is often uncertain. But there is no doubt about the extract given here. His theories and practice of the Scots language are still of linguistic interest.

ROBERT FERGUSSON (1750–74)

Greatest poet of an Edinburgh which still neglects him, Fergusson attended St Andrews University till forced to leave by poverty following the death of his father. He scraped up a bare existence copying documents in the Commissary Office, but got involved in the club-life of better-off and stronger men. Ruddiman's *Weekly Magazine* evoked and published most of his best, if too hastily produced, work between 1771 and 1773, in which year he fell ill and went into a deep religious melancholy. A fall seems to have brought on the manic outburst which, because of his poverty, led to his being incarcerated in the local Bedlam. On discovering where he was (he had been tricked into it by friends) his agony of mind and spirit, plus the appalling conditions of his imprisonment, seem to have precipitated his death a few months later. His fate led to a reformation of treatment of the mad in Scotland.

LADY ANNE LINDSAY (or Barnard) (1750–1825)

Daughter of the Earl of Balcarres, Anne wrote her famous tear-jerker to an older tune, *The Bride-groom greets when the sun gaes doun*, when she was twenty-two. She married Andrew Barnard with whom she saw colonial life in South Africa.

ROBERT BURNS (1759–96)

Born in Alloway, Ayrshire, son of a cottar, biographies of this most famous Scots poet abound. The philistine Edinbourgeoisie treated him but little better than they did Fergusson, and Burns's lines on Fergusson apply even more aptly to himself:

14

My curse upon your whunstane hearts,
Ye E'nbrugh gentry!
The tythe o' what ye waste at cartes
Wad stow'd his pantry!

They toyed with him as a plaything, then cast him out to a life of
poverty and overwork leading to an early death, while fat sinecures
could be found for all manner of nonentities and sycophants. Burns,
like most men of genius, had a prodigious capacity for hard work
and prolific output of high quality: he can't have spent much time
sleeping. His conviviality was probably less than average in that
age, if only because of lack of average cash and opportunity. He was
plagued by illness, nervous depression, insecurity, anxieties of all
sorts, the harassing of exploiting landowners and others. He died
worn out with the unequal struggle, an old man at thirty-seven, of
rheumatic fever caught on long rides in drenching rain round his
territory as an exciseman. The dignity and pathos of his great and
noble life need rescuing from the drunken myth of 'Rabbie'. It is
unfortunate that his influence on Scottish poetry, apart from his
own achievement, has been almost wholly bad, leading to the de-
generation of Scots poetry against which MacDiarmid successfully
set his face.

from **THE MERRY MUSES** (Attributed to Burns)

These folk-songs are not to be confused with pornography or self-conscious, deliberate bawdry like the *Ball o Kirriemuir* or *The Irish Tinker*. They are innocent, frank, earthy songs that speak with the tongue of an age which was less hypocritical and puritanical than the eighteenth-century drawing-room, and of a class less affected and inhibited. They must be heard with the innocent ear of the uncorrupted peasantry which produced them, and not as bawdry at all. It is out of such material that Burns fashioned many of his songs, often improving in some ways, but worsening and corrupting in others. They are 'dirty' only to the dirty-minded.

CAROLINA OLIPHANT (Lady Nairne) (1766–1845)

Daughter of the Jacobite laird of Gask, in Perth, she married her second cousin William Nairne in 1806. In 1824 he became sixth Lord Nairne on the restoration of the 'attainted' Scottish peerages. About eighty-seven songs carry her signature, originals and cobblings alike, and her range is very wide. Her Jacobite ones are sentimental yet sincere, and among her best liked. It was only after her death that the songs appeared in her own name instead of the pseudonym 'Mrs Bogan of Bogan'.

ANONYMOUS (18th Century)

JAMES HOGG (1770–1835)

Born in Ettrick Forest, Hogg spent his early days as a shepherd, but he was discovered by Scott while collecting material for his *Border Minstrelsy*, and taken under that ample wing. He had almost no formal education, certainly much less than Burns's admirable father had afforded his boys, but he soon became famous among the famous of his time – helped by his magnificent personality. He farmed much of his life and left a variety of notable works, most importantly a novel, *Confessions of a Justified Sinner*.

WALTER SCOTT (1771–1832)

Born in Edinburgh where he attended the university and was apprenticed in his father's law firm. He was called to the bar in 1792. His literary career is well enough known, but it is worth stressing that he was rejected in love by a beautiful girl, and the wound left a psychological hurt as bad as his lame leg. He never quite rose above his age and its distorted values, and worked himself to death paying off the usurous claims of creditors against him and his publisher: a waste of man, of genius, and of work; for work produced in such conditions from such motives is unlikely to be of the best. There is a sense, therefore, in which this master of his age was the victim of his age.

ROBERT TANNAHILL (1774–1810)

Born in Paisley, Tannahill became a weaver. He was a frail, shy person, morbidly sensitive. His 1807 volume of poems met with considerable success, but when Constable felt unable to print a collection of new songs, temporarily, he fell into a deep depression, burned the MSS of a hundred new songs, and his body was found in a nearby canal.

ALLAN CUNNINGHAM (1784–1842)

Born on the Blackwood estate near Thornhill, Dumfries, Cunningham was a gardener's son. The family moved to Ellisland where the boy, aged six, heard (it is claimed) Burns read *Tam o' Shanter* while visiting the Cunninghams. Allan served with his stonemason brother for many years, but left for London in 1810, and the literary life. He was secretary to Chantrey the sculptor till near his death, and published various works of verse and prose.

ALEXANDER RODGER (1784–1846)

A mini-poet of the execrable school of Burns' diluters who contributed to *Whistle Binkie*. But the poem here sings well, and is a star among the tinsel.

WILLIAM TENNANT (1784–1848)

Born in Anst(ruth)er, crippled from birth, Tennant is a remarkable example of the 'lad o' pairts'. He became a clerk, but studied with such effect in his spare time that he became a classics master at Dollar Academy, and finally professor of Oriental Languages in St Andrews University. His long poem *Anster Fair* (1812) anticipates Byron's *Beppo* and *Don Juan*: the source of this mock-serious verse would seem to be the Italians Pulci and Berni (Tennant was linguist enough to have read them) but nothing definite can be affirmed: there is also *Hudibras* to be considered.

GEORGE GORDON BYRON (1788–1824)

Son of Catherine Gordon of Gight and John Byron, Lord Byron succeeded to the title of 1798. He was educated in Aberdeen, Harrow and Cambridge. The tale of his works, loves, quarrels and death in the heroic Greek cause are well enough known. He and Walter Scott were men of a kind – a gigantic kind – and that fact alone is evidence of the essential Scottishness of his genius.

GEORGE MACDONALD (1824–1905)

Born in Huntly, Aberdeen, of Glencoe stock, MacDonald is best known as a novelist. He became a minister of the kirk, was critical of the harsh aspects of Calvinism, and had more than a little of the mystic in him.

ALEXANDER SMITH (1830–67)

Born in Kilmarnock, Smith became a pattern-designer. His first book published in 1853 won praise from such critics as George Henry Lewes, Herbert Spencer and George Meredith. He held a minor post in Edinburgh University, but had to augment his wage with hack work, and bad health sapped his vitality, and that and overwork brought him to his end at the same age as Robert Burns.

ROBERT LOUIS STEVENSON (1850–94)

Another Edinburgh man, Stevenson felt affinities with his greater and elder brother in the Muse, Fergusson, but did little to develop them. He attended Edinburgh University, studied engineering, gave it up for law and was called to the bar in 1875. T.B. had afflicted him from childhood, and most of his life was spent searching for health, the search leading him to Samoa, where he met his untimely end, not from his illness, but from a blood-clot on the brain. His great promise was never quite fulfilled.

JOHN DAVIDSON (1857–1909)

Davidson was brought up in Greenock, the scene of one of the examples of his work given here. He was a tormented soul, at war with himself and his background, and made his way to London, where he worked as a journalist. He never managed to reconcile his conflicts and became very withdrawn. An incurable disease led to his ending his life in the English Channel.

CHARLES MURRAY (1864–1941)

Murray was a native of Aberdeen who spent most of his life in the Transvaal. His work was very popular at one time, particularly his masterly character-sketches such as the one given here. His Scots is consistent dialect, but his range too constricted and local for him to rank as a national poet. He is the best of the dialect poets, before MacDiarmid restored Scots to its national and international stature.

MARION ANGUS (1866–1946)

Another of the 'regional' singers, Marion Angus is the best of one or two women poets of her time, just before the MacDiarmid period, though in the second poem given here she is of national rank.

LEWIS SPENCE (1874–1955)

A well-known anthropologist, Spence was something of a forerunner of MacDiarmid in his recognition of the need to redeem and intellectualize Scots and to revive the great pre-Reformation tradition. He did imitations of Dunbar, but lacked the genius to revitalize the tradition: yet his direction was right.

ALEXANDER GRAY (1882–1968)

Sir Alexander Gray was professor of Economics in the University of Edinburgh, but did many fine translations of Danish and other Nordic ballads. His original work was mostly in the Mearns dialect.

ANDREW YOUNG (1885–1971)

Canon Young has lived mostly furth of Scotland, but few English-writing Scots are more clearly identifiable as such than he is.

HELEN B. CRUICKSHANK (1886–1975)

Helen Cruickshank was a native of Angus. A life-long friend of Hugh MacDiarmid, among other Scots writers, she ploughed her own furrow. Her services to Scottish literature were many and various, and she was a much-loved and respected figure among us.

EDWIN MUIR (1887–1959)

Born in Orkney, Muir was transported to Glasgow in boyhood, a traumatic experience which affected the whole of his life, cost him his parents and others of the family and provides the best passages of his superb autobiography. He had very little formal schooling but I have never met a professor of English literature whose knowledge and quality of knowledge equalled his. He married Willa Anderson, who took brilliant, first-class degrees in Classics and Philosophy, in 1918. They settled in London at first, but soon became wanderers in Europe, and wanderers they remained, except from each other. No other Scotsman has achieved so much in the medium of English: his Orcadian dialect allowed him little choice of medium for his highly philosophical imagination.

HUGH MACDIARMID (1892–1978)

It is typical of Scottish philistinism that respectable persons should hide their disreputable literary activities under a pseudonym: but C. M. Grieve had other motives in inventing Hugh MacDiarmid, for he has never had anything but contempt for respectability. Born in Langholm, he went to school there, then attended Broughton School in Edinburgh, and was set to become a teacher when his father died in 1911. He gave up academe and went in for journalism. His radical working-class background prepared him for his left-wing career, and, unlike the left-wing English poets of the thirties, his socialism had real roots in working-class experience. He served in the R.A.M.C. during the 1914–18 war, was invalided home from Salonika, married, but was not demobbed till 1920. Then he took on the local paper in Montrose, became a socialist town councillor and a J.P., and lived there till 1929. At first an opponent of the Scots movement because of its decay, he became converted and at once began to revive the sick language, using the pen-name Hugh MacDiarmid till he assessed the worth of his earliest experiments in Scots, so getting stuck with the name. It was the beginning of a Herculean cleansing of the Scots stables, and in the first few years he produced work which put him among the greatest Scots poets of all time – Dunbar, Henrysoun, Douglas and Burns. A London residence for a year or two did not work out and led to the break-up of his first marriage. He married again in 1932, became involved in nationalist and communist politics (both parties too small to contain him, while he easily contained them), supported C. H. Douglas's Social Credit schemes, and was forced by an outraged Scotland to retreat temporarily to a life of terrible poverty and hardship in the Shetland Isles with his young wife, Valda Trevlyn, a Cornish girl, and son. His health broke down but he recovered well enough to serve the country that had so ill used him in the Second World War; not in the Ministry of Information but in an arms factory as a labourer, and as an engineer in the Merchant Service. He and his wife live now in a two-room ploughman's cottage in Lanarkshire, on a Civil List Pension, awarded in 1950. Edinburgh University honoured itself by giving him an LL.D. in 1957. His *Collected Poems* were not published until 1962, and then by the MacMillan Company, New York. His output is prodigious.

JOE CORRIE (1894–1968)

Corrie was a miner in the Fife and other coalpits, and his early poems became famous during the twenties largely through the old Glasgow socialist weekly, the *Forward*. He is a genuine poet, and had considerable success also as working-class playwright. The fashion has passed for his work, and he lived in his declining years in straitened circumstances, and in ill-health.

WILLIAM JEFFREY (1896–1946)

Jeffrey was for many years editor of the *Glasgow Herald* till his untimely death. His work has never had the appreciation it deserves.

WILLIAM SOUTAR (1898–1943)

Son of a Perth carpenter, Soutar was schooled in his native city and went to Edinburgh University, destined for school-teaching. He served in the navy during the First World War (he was a tall, strong man, fond of rugby) and contracted some form of food poisoning which affected his spine. He became paralysed and was confined to bed for his last fourteen years, able to move only his arms and hands. His father built a world of books round his bed, and thus he was able to give us the fine books of poems which make him one of the best lyric poets Scotland has ever had. He was a source of inspiration to his friends.

ROBERT GARIOCH (1908–)

Son of an Edinburgh house-painter, Garioch was for many years a teacher of English. The only wholly classical Scottish poet now living, he is the true heir of the neglected Edinburgh genius, Fergusson; and if his imaginative range is limited, his Scots is more naturally felt and intellectually cultivated than most poets'.

KATHLEEN RAINE (1908–)

Daughter of a Scottish mother and Northumberland father, Miss Raine was educated at Cambridge among such contemporaries as William Empson. She has quietly developed her own unique talent, (largely inspired by the countryside of Wester Ross), in a somewhat uncongenial atmosphere, her affinities being with Muir and Yeats rather than the fag-end of modern English poetry, whose anti-imaginative scientific humanism conflicts with her neo-Platonic vision.

GEORGE BRUCE (1909–)

A Buchan man, George Bruce was a school teacher for a time before joining the B.B.C. as a producer, in which capacity he has done much for and had some influence on Scottish literature. His own work is rooted in the Buchan of his boyhood, and he has cultivated it quietly and with some success.

NORMAN MACCAIG (1910-)

Norman MacCaig is the son of an Edinburgh chemist, was educated
at the Royal High School and Edinburgh University where he took a
degree in Classics. He taught school for many years but now lectures
at Stirling. His eye for natural phenomena borders on the mystical,
and he has affinities with certain English romantics, though less lush.

DOUGLAS YOUNG (1913-73)

A Fife man of international experience, Dr Young was professor of
Greek in an American university, but was mostly associated with St
Andrews. His approach to literature is mainly academic, which tends
to be quantitative rather than qualitative, with odd effects on critical
judgement: few would give a total dud like McGonagall a place in
any but a joky anthology. But his own verse, especially his trans-
lations of Aristophanes, is the work of a craftsman.

G. S. FRASER (1915-80)

An Aberdonian, George Fraser took his degree in English at St
Andrews, worked on an Aberdeen paper, served in the Army during
the last great war, and his fine critical gift made him the centre of a
wide literary circle in London when he was on *The Times Literary
Supplement*.

W. S. GRAHAM (1915-)

Graham grew up in Greenock on the mouth of the Clyde, and the
imagery of sea and shipping is rarely far from his poetry. He was an
engineer in his youth, but gave it up for the life of the dedicated poet,
which he is, and has lived in Cornwall for most of the last twenty
years or so: a home from home for a west-coast Scot.

SYDNEY GOODSIR SMITH (1915-75)

Born in Wellington, New Zealand, Smith went to Oxford and various
Continental universities. He was already a young man when he settled

in Edinburgh and experienced the conversion to Scots which became
the inspiration of his work. He published many volumes and was for a
number of years art critic on the *Scotsman*.

GEORGE CAMPBELL HAY (1915–)

Son of J. MacDougal Hay who wrote the superb novel *Gillespie*,
George was brought up in Argyll. He is a fine linguist and Gaelic
scholar, and one of the best Gaelic poets in two centuries. He saw
service in North Africa during the last world war, and his health was
seriously undermined as a result. He lives in Edinburgh and often
contributes learned articles to the *Scotsman*.

MAURICE LINDSAY (1918–)

Lindsay is a Glasgow man whose musical career was altered by the
war. He has done sterling work as a poetry editor, and was for many
years associated with George Bruce on the B.B.C., and to some extent
still is. He has published several volumes of verse, and other books.

TOM SCOTT (1918–)

Editor of the present anthology, he was born in Glasgow, son of a
boiler-maker on the Clyde. He left school at fifteen, was apprenticed
to the building trade, but after the war, in which he served in Nigeria
and elsewhere, he freelanced in London for several years. He went
to Newbattle Abbey College on the invitation of Edwin Muir for a
year, then on to Edinburgh University. He has published several
books, including four of verse.

MODERN FOLK SONGS

The folk tradition never stops, and many fine songs are still to be
heard among the people – including some by professional poets,
which I cannot include here.

ALEXANDER SCOTT (1920–)

An Aberdonian, Scott lectures in Scottish Literature at Glasgow University, and is a newspaper columnist and broadcaster. He has published several books, including some of verse of his own.

Continent o Venus   500

EDWIN MORGAN (1920–)

A Glasgow man, Morgan now lectures in the university there, and his academic bent shows in much of his literary work. His best work in verse is to be found in the occasional, unobtrusive to the point of diffidence, lyric, such as the one given here, which slips in among the more intellectual things.

The Sheaf   501

GEORGE MACKAY BROWN (1927–)

Born and brought up in Orkney, Brown spent a year at Newbattle Abbey College with Edwin Muir, and went on to take an honours M.A. in English at Edinburgh. Ill-health has prevented his teaching, and he has had ample opportunities to taste the mercies of the welfare state and its treatment of poets. His work, despite his circumstances, has grown in quality and public favour, and some slight financial recognition has come his way from the Arts Council.

The Old Women   502

BURNS SINGER (1928–64)

Singer was brought up in Glasgow but worked for many years in the Marine Laboratory in Aberdeen. His fine mind, quivering sensibility and linguistic gifts were capable of a poetry of lyrical quality and intellectual power beyond his actual achievement.

Still and All   503

IAIN CRICHTON SMITH (1928–)

Crichton Smith is a Lewisman who teaches English in Oban, Argyll. He is the best Scottish poet now writing in English, but he has deep concern for his Gaelic heritage. He is also an imaginative prose-writer of talent.

Introduction

THIS anthology begins with a small poem dating from the late thirteenth century: but the history of Scottish poetry really dates from a much earlier period – thirteenth century B.C. would be nearer the mark than the thirteenth century A.D. I am referring, of course, to the Gaelic origins of the Scots and their poetry, which are identical with those of the Irish. Scottish poetry, indeed, begins in Ireland, with the great Irish cycles of Deirdre, Cuchulain, Finn, Ossian and the others. The Scots are, like the Welsh, and even the English, not an Anglo-Saxon people but a Celto-Teutonic one. The word 'Scot' derives from the Gaelic tribes who overran Ireland before the beginning of the Christian era and were Christianized by the Strathclyde Briton, Patrick, and his associates and successors. The *Scots language* meant Gaelic until Gawin Douglas, acknowledging the dominance of the lowland tongue as the national language in his own day, applied it to what had hitherto been known as *Inglis*.

The literature of the Scottish people is written in at least four, if not five, languages: Gaelic, Latin, lowland Scots and English: the putative fifth is Welsh, or more correctly, Brithonic. The great 'Welsh' poets Aneurin and Taliessin were both natives of what is now Scotland – one from the Edinburgh area (which still has its Arthur's Seat overlooking the city), the other from what is now Ayrshire. Perhaps it is as well not to press the Scottish claims to Aneurin and Taliessin too closely. But we must remember that the south-west of Scotland, indeed the south-west of what is now Great Britain, was Welsh-speaking from the south bank of the Clyde down to Wales and beyond. The Patrick who converted Ireland was probably a Welsh-speaker (I use the term 'Welsh' here for convenience, meaning the early form of Brithonic, P-Celtic, which became Welsh), as was, most likely, Nynia, whose foundation of Candida Casa on the Solway in 397 was the beginning of Christianity in Scotland.

Narrowing down these cloudy Celtic beginnings of international Scots literature, we come to 563, the year in which the Ulster Gael, Columcill, or Columba, landed in Dalriada (modern Argyll). Columba was not only a great prince, a great saint, a great man, but also a great poet. With his Latin hymns, and some Gaelic poems more dubiously attributed to him, the real history of poetry in Scotland begins. His *Altus Prositer* is the first poem I know of which shows the use of rhyme. Between Columba and the earliest fragments of our verse in the lowland tongue a very fine and highly developed prose literature in Latin existed, a far better prose than Scots, alas, has ever developed, and a great deal of oral poetry in Gaelic was known widely and preserved in oral tradition. Ossian MacPherson drew upon this great oral tradition as late as the eighteenth century for the highly romanticized and original 'translations' which made him famous. He has been rather unfairly abused by the purists, but there is no doubt at all that his sources were genuine. He was neither quite an original genius, as he would have had to be to 'invent' such poems, nor a translator in the strict sense, but a bit of both. The worst that can be said of him is that he lacked artistic and academic conscience, and cashed in on what proved to be a literary gold-mine. But it should not be forgotten that he influenced the prophetic books of Blake and had more influence on the Continent than any other British writer except Shakespeare, Scott and Byron. Ossianic fragments have been collected from oral tradition among the Gaels as late as the nineteen-fifties.

I stress all this because in this anthology I shall, for obvious reasons enough, be confining my choice to Scottish poetry written only in Scots and English, or an amalgam of the two. The poetry in Latin and Gaelic I very much hope will be dealt with in other volumes, and by persons better equipped for that job than I am. But the reader must bear in mind that the corpus of verse of which the following is a small, but I hope enticing, selection, is only one part, and not necessarily

the best part, of the poetry which may fairly be claimed as
Scottish in the widest sense. Nor should we think of the earlier
poetry and prose in Gaelic and Latin, especially the latter, as
in any way inferior, less civilized, less highly developed
culturally than the later work in Scots or English: the con-
trary is true. The values reflected in the work of Columba and
his biographer, Adomnan, are in most ways more civilized
than and superior to those we, in our new scientific barbar-
ism, reveal. Moreover, our literature in the Teutonic tongues
has not yet produced tragedies like the Celtic Sorrows, such as
Deirdre and the Sons of Uisneach, nor love-stories like *Tristan
and Yseult*. Compared to the highly imaginative poetic
genius of the Celts, the Teutonic strain is earthbound, pedes-
trian, realistic.

The earliest poem in the Teutonic tongue to which Scotland
has some claim is the romance of *Sir Tristrem*. Here the debt
to the Celtic tradition is obvious, for the poem is another
version (a translation from the French) of the Tristan and
Yseult story. French romance is deeply rooted in Celtic
traditions, among others, and this romance is a case in point.
I have not included an excerpt from *Sir Tristrem* here be-
cause I no longer feel sure that this is truly a Scottish poem:
it is in, I believe, a north-English dialect, though it may be
a bit pedantic to draw the Anglo-Scottish border too de-
finitely in this period, the thirteenth century. There is an
excerpt from *Sir Tristrem* in the *Oxford Book of Scottish Verse*.

Whether or not *Sir Tristrem* is a Scottish poem, there is no
doubt about the fragment on the death of Alexander III,
with which this anthology opens. It strikes a note rarely
absent from Scottish poetry – elegiac, laconic, realistic,
deeply socially concerned, nation-centred rather than in-
dividualistic. The fragment of song deriding the maidens of
England after Bannockburn is necessarily in an English ver-
sion: it is recorded only by Robert Fabyan in his *Chronicles*,
and of course he gives it in his own dialect.

The first major poet in this book is John Barbour, and his
'factional' romance of Bruce dates from 1375. The form of
the poem is that of certain French romances, and much of

his technique derives from the same source. He quite deliberately sets out to tell us a factual history in romance form, asserting that, as fictional stories delight the reader, how much more so will a true history delight him. Barbour's Scots language is scarcely distinguishable from the Northumbrian dialect which was spoken from the Humber to Aberdeen, roughly; it derives from the Angles rather than the Saxons, and is therefore arguably a purer English than the midland-southern speech which became standard English. But as Northumbrian was more and more drawn into the orbit of Chaucer's and Wycliffe's literary triumph, so the Scottish use became modified by other influences, giving rise to a national language quite clearly identifiable as such, in Henrysoun's time or earlier.

Barbour's poem covers the whole of Bruce's career from the time of his taking up the cause of Scotland against English tyranny to his death, including the Irish campaign. The poem is almost fourteen thousand lines long, so that we give here only a glimpse of it. It is a military handbook, among other things, and some of its guerrilla warfare wisdom is still relevant in our own day. Its characterizations of such real men as Bruce and Douglas, its historical trustworthiness (by no means perfect), its general high literary quality and its occasional moments of poetic excellence are its greatest strength. Barbour may have done much translation of French romances, almost certainly did some, and thus had the technique ready to his hand. But the actual romance translations attributed to him (the *Book of Alexander*, for example) cannot be identified as definitely his. The point is that he is writing not out of some divine originality (there is no such thing in poetry) but out of a tradition which had lasted centuries in France and other European countries, and had produced a mass of work: his originality is in the modifications he made of that tradition by introducing a new, national, and historically true subject-matter, the matter of Scotland, the freedom of nationality.

The *Kingis Quair* is also traditional, but in a very different and less enduring tradition. The cult of *courtly love*, essentially

an adulterous love or worship of a great lady by one or other
of her husband's dependants, after its development by the
troubadours of Provence, found its culminating expression
in the first part of *Le Roman de la Rose* by Guillaume de Loris,
and its self-parody in the second part of the same poem by
Jean de Meun. This allegory of the lover and his rose, already
far-gone in decay by the time of James I, provides the con-
ventional machinery of the *Kingis Quair*. But the thought of
the poem, which has only recently begun to receive due at-
tention, is drawn from another great medieval tradition
deriving from the *Consolation of Philosophy* by Boethius.
James had been educated in captivity in England, and his
sources are more likely to be in the translations of Chaucer
than the French and Latin originals. James indeed, is the
first and last 'Scottish Chaucerian', though the royal prestige
gave rise to a cult of lip-service to Chaucer by later Scottish
poets who owed him little else. The poem is anglicized and
derivative, but in its central story of the development of the
mind of a poet and prisoner-king, the touches of realism in
biographical and natural detail, its original blending of
traditional and empirical material, it is a major poem. Its
author was soon too taken up with governing his barbarous
and anarchic nobles to have much time for writing poetry.

But while the aristocrats dreamed of their adulterous
garden of romantic love, the folk were enjoying a very
different kind of poetry of their own. This is essentially
comic, bawdy, ribald, of the earth earthy, but with a wild
imagination too. Such poems as *King Berdok*, *Colkelbie Sow*,
Kind Kittock and many others are full of extravagant imagin-
ation, comic irreverence, and of a wealth of Scots diction
rarely found in the more courtly poetry. Much of this poetry
is parody of upper-class poetry: *Rauf Colyear* is a parody of
the old alliterative stanza of the Middle English romances
such as *Sir Gawain and the Grene Knight*, for example. This
excellent poem is full of vitality, linguistic and imaginative,
and the stanzas I have selected contain early examples of
that shrewd, pawky humour which is an abiding (too abiding
in many ways) characteristic of Scots poetry. The *Wife of*

Auchtermuchty is a classic of peasant wisdom, and of the humorous treatment of the romantic theme of woman's mastery of the male.

Sir Richard Holland's *Book of the Howlat* is another example of parody of the alliterative romance stanza, but the traditional matter he draws upon is this time the beast-allegory of the French Reynard the Fox. The result is a poem unique in Scots, and perhaps in any language, and the allegory is well sustained through the eleven hundred and more lines of the work.

The 'matter' of Scotland, which began with Barbour's *Bruce*, was lost for the romantic matter of the *Kingis Quair*, and, ignored by the popular poetry for the most part, re-appears in full spate in Blin Hary's *Wallace*, a poem of epic proportions if not epic quality, in heroic couplets. No such historical respectability as can be claimed for Barbour's poem belongs to the *Wallace*: Hary is retelling legends that have long been gathering the moss of oral tradition, and some of them make fairy tales look like true stories. The question of whether Hary ever had the use of his sight is important: if he never had, this might account for some of the impossibilities; but on the other hand, it would make us wonder about certain felicities of visual description. But if one takes the poem as it should be taken, as an extravagant poetic entertainment shot through with very real heroic values and patriotism, it would be a very sophisticated taste indeed that could not find poetic pleasure in it.

The matter of Scotland is lost again in Hary's great contemporary, Robert Henrysoun, a man of universal, certainly of European mind and stature. There is a great deal of social satire and description in Henrysoun's work, but it is incidental to his moral and religious purposes. The medieval European traditions he drew upon were already centuries old – the matter of Troy for his *Cresseid*, the fables of Aesop, the pastorelle for his *Robene and Makyne* – but he brought to them an original and powerful mind and imagination, a serene and balanced integration of personality, which transform his borrowings into something uniquely and greatly his own. I have included here the less well known *Tale of the Sheep and the Dog* precisely because it shows his deep social concern, his legal knowledge, his unflinching eye for the reality behind the appearance, as well as his better-known qualities of spiritual high-mindedness. I have left out the *moralitas* of each tale because, although it is essential for the serious student, in each case it actually narrows the vision to something inferior to that which inheres in Aesop's original tale, and in the poetry itself. For readers of poetry for its own sake, that is for those I hope will read this book, the lily of the tale needs no gilding. *The Testament of Cresseid* is the longest poem in this anthology not because there are not other fine long poems in Scots but because, although long poems cannot be given complete in our short space, it is such a magnificent poem that an exception must be made in its case. It is the finest poem in the Scots language. Readers should note that Cresseid is not condemned for sinning against the Christian morality of marriage, but against the courtly love code of loyalty to the paramour.

Opinions differ about whether Henrysoun or Dunbar is the greater poet: perhaps it is a matter simply of taste rather than ultimate values. But there is no doubt that they are entirely different men and different poets – as unlike as two poets so close in time and place and culture could possibly be. One view has it that Henrysoun is the last expression of the great medieval security of spirit before the Renaissance and the Reformation swept away the very foundations of that security, while Dunbar's tormented spirit is typical of the new age. But this is simply not true: Henrysoun is in some ways more a Renaissance man than Dunbar, Dunbar more a medieval one in some ways than Henrysoun. It is true that Dunbar's work does herald the approaching Reformation and leads on to Lyndsay's great satire of the old order, but his centre of vision is as Catholic as Henrysoun's: he is no intellectual revolutionary, as Lyndsay certainly was, embodying new ideas. The difference between the two men is, in my view, chiefly one of temperament, and of circumstance. Dunbar was embittered by disappointment and abuse, a man who never fulfilled himself, whereas Henrysoun was serenely at peace with himself and with his God, though not with what we call 'society' and he would have called 'the world'.

Their difference as poets is seen in the very forms they use, the European traditions they draw upon. Henrysoun was a natural story-teller, he saw life as a continuous and integrated whole in which every part had its place – whether in that proper place or not. Dunbar is essentially a lyric poet, a poet of mood and variety, his vision more fragmentary, 'now sound, now seik, now dansand merry, now like to dee', and his forms are song-forms rather than narrative ones. His range of lyric form, and of mood and emotion, is immense, and in this he has no rival in his century, and few in any century. He is supremely the 'makar', the fashioner of an artefact rather than the conveyor of a philosophy, a vision, new ideas or values, or any other kind of utterance. For of these two chief ingredients of poetry, utterance and artefact, most poets tend more to one than the other, though all poets must have something of both to be poets at all in more than the courtesy sense. And Dunbar has intensity of utterance, passion, in many of his poems: but – and this is something new in Scottish poetry at this time – it is most intense when most self-centred. Other poets, Barbour, Hary, Henrysoun, for example, are concerned not about themselves but about the nation or humanity or something far beyond mere individuality: they are invisible in their own poems. But Dunbar's chief concern, and I cannot but see in this a spiritual inferiority to Henrysoun, is Dunbar. He is most lyrical when he is most self-concerned, as in *The Petition of the Gray Horse, Auld Dumbar*. Here indeed we may discern a 'modern' as distinct from a medieval or classical trait, for he is the first Scots poet of stature to manifest the personalism which has led poetry to its present nadir; the great art which once was the highest of public virtues becomes a petty private vice. Homer sang of Achilles, Virgil of Aeneas, Dante of Beatrice, Shakespeare of a host of heroes and anti-heroes, Barbour of Bruce, Hary of Wallace: but Dunbar sings mostly

of Dunbar. And when a poet has no better subject for his
work than himself, there is no reason why other people
should care tuppence, and the art declines in social value to
mere doodling.

Fortunately there is much more to Dunbar than just that.
His complaints of the abuses of court life, of the law, the
church, the burghs, are full of real poetry, and in his magnifi-
cent *Tretis of the Twa Mariit Wemen and the Wedo* (which I
can give only a taste of here), he himself is in the proper
poetic role of informer. Indeed, in his best work, there is a
blend of the personal and the social which is admirable and
salutary, for of course the personal and the social are inter-
dependent. This is true even of *The Petition*, a magnificently
sustained metaphor, with its subtle revelation of courtly
values, or distortion of values. And in his religious and
meditative poetry he transcends self altogether, at times, and
achieves great poetry, as the voice of his age, or of Mankind
in all ages. The *Lament for the Makaris, Meditatioun in
Winter*, the great hymn *On the Resurrection of Christ, Rorate
celi desuper*, are all transcendent poems in which the poor
little artist, by his art, becomes the voice of humanity,
expresses a greater soul than his own soul. And if a poet
doesn't do that he builds for himself castles in oblivion.

I have tried to give, in the few pages possible here, some
idea of Dunbar's immense range and variety, from the petty
personalities of his headache to the triumph of the Resur-
rection hymn.

Gawin Douglas's place in the great trio of poets whose life
and work began in the reign of that underrated king James
III (and it is to his reign, not that of his overrated son, that
the great period of Scots poetry really belongs) is unique.
With less inventiveness than either Henrysoun or Dunbar,
he had greater linguistic and scholastic ability, and in his
great translation of Virgil's *Aeneid* he raised the Scots
language to a peak of fullness and resource never equalled
before or since, and from which it has all too rapidly declined.
A glossary of Douglas's poetry would be much more nearly a
Scots dictionary of the language up to that time than glossaries

of all the previous poets put together. This linguistic supremacy of Gawin Douglas needs insisting upon, for it marks not only his greatness as a writer, but the role of translation in a developing language: it was the superiority of Virgil's Latin as a linguistic instrument that forced Douglas to develop a greater canon of Scots than previous 'original' poets had needed. Yet Douglas with all his physical vitality and vigour of mind is rather the supreme example of a scholarly versifier than a poet of genius. On the other hand, his 'original' prologue on winter, the seventh, which is included in this book, is great poetry. No other poet, either Scots or English, has equalled this brilliant evocation of winter, not even the Scot James Thomson, an extract from whose *Winter* is also included here.

Although born in the early years of the reign of James IV, David Lyndsay's work is so much in continuity with that of the great trio born in the previous reign that one thinks of him as making a fourth, and less highly gifted member of that great fellowship. He is very much more the bard than any of them, that is to say, a socially committed poet, and in him it is true to say that the matter of Scotland, bypassed by the greater makars, finds new expression. This time, however, it is not a heroic war of independence the poet is concerned with, but the state of the nation whose independence is now secure, but which is going through an internal crisis in church and state – the crisis which resulted in the Reformation. And whereas the weapons of Barbour and Hary were the facts and deeds of warriors, Lyndsay's are the embattled ideas of the Reformers. In this sense, he is the first 'intellectual' poet in Scottish poetry, meaning by that the first whose chief concern is with ideas. It does not mean, of course, that he himself had as good an intellect as Henrysoun, or Dunbar, or Douglas: he had not. But they were concerned with a whole vision of life, largely drawn from unquestioned ideological assumptions; whereas Lyndsay is a revolutionary thinker, a propagandist of that great social revolution in Europe, from feudalism founded on land to capitalism founded on money, which we call the Reformation. From the

first to the last Lyndsay's poetry is full of Reformation
ideology, and his form is the long poem, narrative or dramatic,
with a few minor pieces of a comic nature. Because of its
bulk it has been impossible to give an adequate idea of his
work here, but versions of the *Thrie Estaitis* and his long
romantic poem *Squyer Meldrum* are at present available to
the general public.

The two chief sources of Middle Scots poetry are the Ban-
natyne and Maitland Manuscripts, and the names of their
compilers, George Bannatyne and Sir Richard Maitland,
are revered by scholars. Among the many good poets in
their anthologies is that great and prolific poet 'Anonymous':
his works are so good that attempts are constantly being made
to filch them for other, less protean poets. If one includes
the ballads (only a small selection of which is included in this
book because a separate volume has already been done for
Penguin by Dr William Beattie) the output of 'Anonymous'
in Scottish poetry is larger than any other one poet, and many
of the others have borrowed extensively from him. Of the
wealth of anonymous poetry in the Middle Scots MSS, it
is possible only to include a few specimens – not nearly enough
to give any idea of their variety and excellence. There are
many beautiful lyrics, of which *O Maistress Mine*, given here,
is but one: and *The Bankis of Helicon* was one of the most
popular songs of its time. It has been attributed to Mont-
gomerie because he used the stanza for his major work
The Cherry and the Slae. Another of these poems given here,
The Bewties of the Fute-ball has a remarkably present-day
ring. *Why Sould Nocht Allane Honorit be?* is not only a
hymn in praise of Scotch whisky, but clearly stems from a
fertility cult far older than Christianity. The same cult
survives today, in disguised form, in the worship of a cult-
god 'Rabbie' Burns, a drunken Dionysus worshipped at many
a Burns supper, but having only the remotest relation to a
great poet who died of hard work, poverty, neglect and illness,
by name Robert Burns.

I have already mentioned Sir Richard Maitland as an
anthologist, but he was a good minor poet in his own right.

He seems only to have begun to write late in life, after his retiral from active public life, but he shows a deep social concern and considerable technical ability, mostly influenced by the satires and complaints of Dunbar. He was troubled by the state of Scotland in his age, as the two poems I have chosen show, and he has a typically Scottish downrightness of utterance combined with formal command. He was writing at the beginning of the worst 147 (roughly) years in Scottish history: from the Reformation of 1560 to the Treaty of Union of 1707.

The king who was the centre of Lyndsay's work, and the object of much of his complaint, was the fifth James. To him, for no very good reason that I can discover, is attributed the anonymous *popular* poem, *Christis Kirk on the Green*. It is true he had the habit of going in disguise among the people, mostly for wenching purposes, and he is the centre of a legend and song of *The Jolly Beggar* (from which Byron derived his *So We'll Go No More A-roving*): but so did other Stewart kings. The king and the peasant were certainly close enough in Scotland for it to be perfectly possible for a king to write such a poem; and it is too sophisticated to have been written by other than an educated man. But anonymous it remains, and is the best of a line of such poems from the earlier *Peblis to the Play* to Robert Garioch's take-off of the Edinburgh Festival, *Embro to the Ploy*, also included in this book. The famous stanza is, or ought to be, known as 'the Peblis'. The rumbustious comedy is the eternal stuff of folk-humour in all countries and all times.

One of the results of the Reformation was the suppression of the great tradition of Scots poetry as we have here sketched its development. An ominous sign of the times was the publication of a book now known as *The Good and Godlie Ballatis*, the contents of which are mostly popular secular songs tortured into spurious religious forms, with God taking the place of the adulterous courtly lover (with the most ludicrous consequences), or worse, the place of the Lady. The book is unconscious comedy, evoking little but laughter and scorn for the solemn boobies who compiled it; but precisely because of the excellence of the art which it abominably degrades, here and there one finds a poem not wholly comic or contemptible. One of these I have included – *Go, Hart, Unto the Lamp of Licht*, a religious parody of a secular love-song.

Of the lesser makars who survived the Reformation, the last of a dying race, nothing at all is known of Alexander Scott except that he wrote some exquisite lyrics in the Petrarcan mode of Italian poetry, helping to spread the Italian influence in Scots. I have included in the small selection from his work a poem which is one of the earliest Scots uses of the stanza Burns was to make world-famous: *On Patience.* Scott was our best lyric poet before Burns, with the possible exception of Montgomerie.

Alexander Montgomerie was also under the influence of the Italian school, and the sonnet *To His Mistress* is an example of an involved love-metaphysics with which we associate the name of Donne, but which, as far as I can trace it, stems from the Italian contemporary of Dante, Guido Cavalcante. The sonnet never quite caught on in Scotland, although the number of them must be nearing four figures: certainly between five hundred and a thousand of them exist, but they remain something of an exotic plant. Montgomerie is the finest of all technicians of verse in Scottish poetry except Dunbar at his best. The beautiful song *The Nicht is Near Gone*, sung to the same tune as *Scots Wha Hae*, is a folk-song re-cobbled by Montgomerie: an early example of the art of song-cobbling which Burns was to make peculiarly and supremely his own.

The finest sonnet in the Scots language is Mark Alexander Boyd's *Venus and Cupid*. The last line is an echo of Ronsard's 'Que l'homme se deçoit/quand plein d'erreur un aveugle il reçoit/pour sa conduite, un enfant pour son maistre.' (Qui voudra voir . . .). For the tradition that Venus was blind, see Cresseid's complaint against Cupid and his mother in *The Testament of Cresseid:* if 'tradition' is not too strong a word.

Scots poetry, which took a severe if not mortal blow from the Reformation, took a further and worse one from the Union

of the Crowns in 1603. This calamity for Scotland, amounting
to treason by the king, and scarcely less for England (there is
some evidence that Shakespeare and his friends dreaded the
accession of this 'satyr to Hyperion'), began the usurpation
of the very language of our poetry by English. It was the
beginning of the end of Scotland as a separate kingdom; of
the House of Stewart; and of Scots poetry in the great
tradition. The court moved south and began to 'knapp
sudron', speak and write English; and in place of the great
poetry of the makars, European and universal, a rash of
anglicizing poets and poetasters appeared. Of these, William
Drummond belongs to the English tradition of poetry, where,
for the purposes of this anthology, I am content to leave him.
Among other 'cavalier' poets Robert Aytoun was a mediocre
versifier and Latinist who wrote an amusing piece *Upone
Tabacco*, which I have included here. James Graham, Marquis
of Montrose, is saved from mediocrity as a poet by the sheer
quality of the man and the heroism of his life and death:
but he is still of little poetic significance.

Scotland, up to the Union of the Crowns, was an integral
part of Europe, a free nation among free nations ('freedom'
of course is a relative term), sharing the common culture; and
in its literature playing Scottish variations on European
themes. The centre of European culture was France, and
Scotland had, via the Auld Alliance, been in particularly
close contact with France for centuries. The story of European
literature is very largely the story of French literature. But
from about the fourteenth century and the rise of English
nationalism, England had pursued a more isolated course, and
was hostile chiefly to the French, on whom, among others,
they made imperialistic wars. The first result of the Union of
the Crowns was to associate Scotland with English foreign
policy, weakening the ties with Europe, reducing Scotland to
a province of England. The story of Scottish literature from
here on is largely a story of provincialization and the struggle
against it. The poetry of the European-educated makar is
swept away and replaced by the poetry of the provincial
petty laird – as amateur as the makars were professional.

One effect of this collapse of literary into folk culture was that folk songs and ballads began to fascinate the literati. These natural children of the intercourse of literature and the folk, insofar as they have been written down, belong chiefly to the sixteenth and seventeenth centuries, though mostly published in later centuries. The tune is half the work, and they are not 'poems' in the literary sense at all, except the 'spurious' ones created by poets – among them, I suspect, *Edward*, by Lord Hailes. There was a confusion of traditions here: oral tradition allows and approves of 'improving', and literary tradition forbids it, because the work is the property of an individual artist. Men like Scott felt themselves to belong to both traditions, and so 'improved' ballads, in the oral way – to the outraged cries of such literati and scholars as Ritson. Both parties have right on their side: but a text should be established as it is received before it is 'improved'. Only a few of these magnificent survivals can be given here, but there are fine collections easily available.

The key figure in the seventeenth century decline is Sir Robert Sempill, laird of Beltrees, and the key poem his *Life and Death of Habbie Simson*. The stanza of this poem, which Alexander Scott used in *On Patience*, was probably invented by the first of the troubadours, Guillaume, Count of Poitou, in the eleventh century: but because of what Scots poetry made of it we call it 'Standard Habbie', after the Sempill poem, or 'the Burns Stanza'. Barbour celebrated Bruce, Hary sang of Wallace, Henrysoun of Troilus and Cresseid, Dunbar lamented the makars and hymned the resurrection of Christ, Douglas re-sang the *Aeneid*, Lyndsay lashed the whole Scottish state and church in his satire: Sempill writes a mock elegy on a wandering piper. I don't want to overstress the contrast, but it is very real: even the humour of the poem is drawn from Sempill's awareness of the triviality of his subject, and worse, of the deepening provinciality of his language. The same stanza was taken up by William Hamilton of Gilbertfield in his *The Last Dying Words of Bonnie Heck*. Here the subject is a greyhound, and these two mock elegies set a fashion well into and beyond the Burns era.

The seventeenth century is a poetic wasteland, few birds being heard to sing, although the jackdaw clacked loudly enough in the pulpit. The great art-poetry has gone completely and only some bits of folk-poetry float down to us from the wreck. Fortunately much of it is very good, and the folk were keeping the traditional culture (the only kind that's 'culture' at all) alive while their 'betters' were busy selling the pass. Some of these are given here: they point forward to the essentially peasant and mock-peasant poetry of the eighteenth century.

The beginning of the partial renaissance of the eighteenth century was an anthology of old poems and songs called the *Choice Collection of Scottish Poems*, by James Watson, published in 1706–11. It was the first sign of thaw since the Reformation and, poor enough as it is, having almost nothing of the great tradition in it, it was a start. It was followed up in 1724 by Allan Ramsay's first *Tea Table Miscellany* and *The Evergreen*. The trickle soon swelled to, if not a major river, at least a good brawling, vivacious stream. Ramsay has been derided by prim-mouthed scholars, and not without some justice: but his editorial failings are nothing compared to the fact that he was the saviour of Scottish poetry for a hundred years and made Fergusson and Burns possible, which none of the reigning professors ever did, being more likely to betray than save. His own poetry is overshadowed by his greater successors, but that he was no mere poetaster I have tried to show in the small selection possible here.

Among the poems now beginning to be printed in the anthologies were a few of the great ones by the makars: but so few they were that they made little impression. The vast wealth of the Bannatyne, Maitland, and other manuscripts was not available to the general public, and to beginning poets. Those who knew of the treasures left by the pre-Reformation kingdom were themselves unable to grasp their significance: they were regarded as rather quaint works 'wrote by the ingenious' of the quaint age before 1603, instead of as masterpieces of a great and European culture. The mind of Scottish poetry had shrunk from the universe to the farmyard, and those who had any inkling at all of their situation were too confused to grasp the reality of it.

Into this poetic wasteland was born the first poet of genius since the Union of the Crowns: James Thomson. He quickly enough assessed the position, in one sense, and not being genius enough to roll up his sleeves and pitch into the mess, he took the road to London where he used his Scottish heritage to write a unique poetry in English. Meantime such minor poets as were left in Scotland, Skirving, Skinner, and their like, got on with the job. Then in 1750 was born another genius, who did not take the road to London: Robert Fergusson. This Edinburgh poet was the first man born after the Reformation to show the ability to carry on the great tradition from such men as Henrysoun, Dunbar, Douglas and Lyndsay. But he too knew little of that tradition, failed to grasp its significance, and starved in the midst of the plenty they had left behind. Instead of these men, he took Allan Ramsay for his model, and certain fashionable English minor poets such as Gray and Shenstone. Yet by the age of twenty-three Fergusson had already published, in periodicals, a body of work exceeding in quality anything since Montgomerie, and in quantity the surviving works of Dunbar. Over a hundred poems, mostly written between the ages of twenty and twenty-three, some thirty of them in Scots, have been preserved. Fergusson has been grossly under-rated as a mere precursor of Burns (as if there were nothing more to Marlowe than fore-running Shakespeare); and his early death in the local bedlam, with the scandal of previously having caught syphilis, ruled him out with the respectable Edinbourgeoisie. We today look on the unfortunate boy genius with less despicably inhuman eyes, and note that here was a man who had it in him to revive the great tradition of Scottish poetry as Burns could not have done. Fergusson was an intellectual, well-educated, at home in Latin and the classics, brilliantly inventive, perceptive, witty, imaginative, of large vocabulary and linguistic range and command, patriotic, and a townsman. He is one of the earliest of a line of urban poets (John Gay was the best English influence on

him) leading up to our own time, through Baudelaire to
Laforgue, Eliot, Auden and others: a very different line from
that of the peasant Burns. If Burns had died at the age
Fergusson died at, we would have almost nothing to guess his
genius by. Fergusson was essentially an elegiac poet, and I
don't mean the mock-elegiac of *Habbie Simson*: he did write
mock elegies, brilliant ones, the best up to his time, in Scots,
but in his best poems he can strike a true elegiac note which
is classical and deep, both in Scots and English. He is the best
poet in Scots after Montgomerie and the most promising in
Scots-English after Thomson. I have here been able to give
only a slight indication of his wealth and power: he was
unquestionably a major poet. The fact that he came down
solidly against the Treaty of Union of 1707 has also con-
tributed to his neglect in 'North Britain', alias Scotshire.

The Treaty of Union, that first and biggest take-over bid
in British history, completed the work begun by the lament-
able James VI, whose death as James I of England was fol-
lowed in a few decades by the political murder of his son by
his English subjects, and in a few decades more by the ex-
pulsion of his grandson and the end of the House of Stewart's
rule. The Kingdom of Scotland, established by Kenneth
MacAlpin in 843, re-established by Robert Bruce from 1306–
1328, seemed at last to have been destroyed, through Scottish
ruling-class greed, by the Auld Enemy. Only the kirk and the
law were left as some remnant of separate Scottish identity.
There was a swelling *trahison des clercs*, treason of the
intellectuals, in the universities, which has gone on ever
since, and still goes on; and all seemed lost. But it was pre-
cisely at this time that some recovery of the lost heritage
began among the poets, and also among certain antiquarians,
leading up to the work not only of Burns but to some extent
of Scott also. Ramsay outlived his junior, Fergusson;
Burns was a precocious fifteen when Fergusson died in his
manic-depressive cell in 1774; Scott at the same age of fifteen
or so met and impressed the mature Burns at an Edinburgh
party. The line is unbroken, if wavering.

Little need be said here of Burns. There is some poetic

justice in the fact that the peasant poet, cut off from the
European Renaissance world of Henrysoun and Dunbar,
ranging no further than his own back-door, should have
become the most universally loved of all poets, not excluding
Shakespeare: but it could only happen once. The same Burns
was told, as every young Scots poet is told, that he had better
learn to write in English or he would get nowhere: he wrote in
Scots and got everywhere, translated into almost every
literary language under the sun, while the anglicizing poe-
tasters around scarcely even hold a corner in a large English
anthology of the age. The same can be said of MacDiarmid.
Burns, like Shakespeare and many great artists, was a
'plagiarist' pillaging everybody and everything for his own
work, quite serenely convinced, if he thought about it at all,
that he had a heaven-sent right to do so, and that he was
merely saving inferior work from the jaws of oblivion. He is
one of the greatest song-collectors of all time, and *the* greatest
song-cobbler of all time, as well as being a great poet. Yet
it is by no means true that he always improved the songs he
thought he was improving: some of them were bawdy,
earthy songs, full of innocent peasant vitality, and Burns
merely sentimentalized and weakened them. I have given
here half a dozen of these *Merry Muses* poems, that the reader
can judge for himself, in the hope that the time has come when
these simple fertility songs no longer need to be apologized
for among intelligent people. If Mrs Grundy finds them too
much for her prim taste, let her charitably skip the few
pages spared these by-blows of the Muse. To my mind they
are infinitely preferable to the sickly rubbish of the senti-
mental Burns imitators.

After Burns, the deluge – of slop and twaddle and couthy
kailyairdy rubbish, with only one or two good poets or good
poems here and there, and of course Walter Scott, who
belongs also to the world outside. The chief thing about Scott
is that he restored the lost subject matter, which I have
called 'the matter of Scotland', to central importance. In
poetry, his spiritual father was the great original, John Bar-
bour: it's a pity Scott didn't also use a form of Barbour's

language. He had a far greater spoken Scots of his own
than any of us have had since. He could have been our
great epic poet, given just that little something extra:
instead, he became our greatest (hélas!) novelist. Edwin
Muir has said that Scott failed to achieve the best that was in
him because Scotland let him down: but it can be argued that
the opposite is true – that he failed Scotland. Scott was
greatly torn by the terrible conflict of his country throughout
its history, but particularly after the Treaty of Union. Against
his own instincts and better judgement (as can be deduced
from novel after novel) he took the expedient line of support-
ing the Union. This, as he was the first major Scottish writer
to do so, greatly endeared him to the Unionist Establish-
ment: but it cost him his integrity as a bard, and a great
bard, therefore carrying great responsibilities, at that.
Opinions of course will vary, even today, on these matters,
and on Scott's personal ambitions, his using his talent to
advance his own social ambitions instead of for the good of
his people. But few will doubt that his gifts – which were
immense – were greater than his actual achievement, for-
midable as that was.

In the space available here it is impossible to give more than
the merest taste of the heroic quality of his vast output of
verse.

I don't propose to discuss all the minor poets after Burns,
and have given only a few of their better works. Carolina
Oliphant, one of so many fine, but never great, women poets
in Scottish literature, had perhaps the purest and best lyric
gift of them all. Tannahill was a good and genuine minor
poet, but the couthy sentimentality is in all his work too. I
have said nothing about Jacobite poetry as a genre, but in
such pieces as the anonymous *Somebody* and Allan Cunning-
ham's *Wee, Wee German Lairdie* (a Jacobite view of George
I), we get a taste of the best of it, its sentiment, its scorn.
I have said elsewhere that the Rising of 1745 was the right
rebellion, that is of the Scots against the Treaty of Union,
lost in the wrong cause, that is to say the Restoration of the
House of Stewart, the deposition of which is the one clear

benefit Scotland has had from England. But interested readers should consult James Hogg's *Jacobite Relics*.

William Tennant's *Anster Fair* is a long poem of unique interest and originality, if no great poetic quality. It is a comedy deriving from Francis Sempill's Song, *Maggie Lauder* (see page 237), but written in an English which tries to capture some of the comic qualities of Scots humorous verse, especially of 'crambo-clink', deliberately comical rhyming, such as Byron's rhyming 'intellectual' and 'hen-pecked you all' (see page 392) in *Don Juan*. And it is perhaps as an anticipator of Byron that Tennant's chief claim to attention rests: he was writing 'Byronic' verse long before Byron did.

Byron himself, son of a Scottish mother and educated during his most impressionable years in Scotland, is included here by right. T. S. Eliot has remarked, in the best essay yet published on Byron, that he is an example of Scottish poetic genius achieving itself as best it may in the medium of English: hence the awkwardness of fitting him into an English literary picture. But if the reader is surprised to find him here, he should remember that if it is possible to include native Scots poets in such English anthologies as the *Oxford Book of English Verse*, as northern English, then it is also possible to include English poets in Scottish anthologies as southern Scottish. By such standards there is no reason why that great South Briton, Shakespeare, should not be included here. However, for many reasons I draw the line at only those border-line cases who are at least as much Scottish as English. Byron certainly is one such. There are few major English poets who can be heard sung in peasant bothies among the more native fare, but Byron's *Lachin Y Gair* is a popular favourite, and those sophisticated critics who sneer at the poem but don't know the tune should hear it sung by a farm-labourer's *tenore robusto*.

Alexander Smith is one of the few poets of the time to take up the poetry of cities, though his junior by four years, James (B.V.) Thomson wrote his *City of Dreadful Night*. I have not included an excerpt from that lengthy, but unsatisfactory poem here, but I have included a condensed version of Smith's *Glasgow*, which is less ambitious and more successful, to my mind. The city has always been problematic to poets, though Baudelaire in this period was writing a great and terrible poetry of the city, making possible the later achievements of Laforgue and Eliot, and even of Auden.

Robert Louis Stevenson, with greater innate gifts, was a less serious poet than either Thomson or his own junior, John Davidson. He was a born entertainer, and it was only in his later years, and particularly his last novel, that the real power of his talent began to come through – too late. But he was aware of the problems that agonized his fellow-Scots writers, if less willing to grapple with them, and he wrote some good Scots poems among the more drawing-room kind. Scotland, before MacDiarmid, has been little blessed with mystical poets, and one regrets that the real vein of mysticism in Stevenson never developed into important art.

John Davidson is one of the most tormented figures even in Scottish poetry, a man of great gifts which never, to my mind, found their proper language and form. There is something almost inevitable about his suicide by wading into the English Channel, rather like his own Runnable Stag, hounded by despair, illness, frustration and bafflement. He must be read in bulk to get some idea of his stature.

Charles Murray gets less attention than he deserves today, but the reason may be that he writes in a local dialect rather than literary Scots. Yet *Dockens afore his Peers*, included here, is a small masterpiece. But this dialectal writing indicates how far Scots had fallen from the days when it could meet Virgil on his own ground.

The position was indeed grim, the efforts to revive the dying tradition seemingly hopeless, when in 1925 appeared a small volume of lyrics called *Sangschaw* by one Hugh MacDiarmid. This was the pen-name of an already well-known Scottish writer, Christopher Murray Grieve, and it was clear at once that a poet of genius had arisen, using Scots with a new power, vitality, subtlety of thought, and grasp of diction and idiom. A year later appeared *A Drunk Man looks at the Thistle*, a poem over 3,000 lines in length and by far the most sustained and philosophical poem yet written in Scots. Scotland was staggered, the poem in David Daiches's phrase 'breaking on a startled and incredulous Scotland with all the shock of a childbirth in church'. The revival of the great tradition of Scottish poetry, dormant since the age of the makars, had begun, and MacDiarmid's dictum 'Not Burns – Dunbar' showed the true line for a Scots revival to take. He did not, himself, follow up all the linguistic and formal implications of his own dictum, as younger poets were to do later, but in scouring Scots verse of sentimentality, couthiness, kailyairdism, all manner of petty-mindedness and false-heartedness; above all in re-intellectualizing it, in raising it to a height and intensity of sheer thinking unequalled anywhere else in Scots, the work of this son of a Langholm postman is one of the wonders of our literature. MacDiarmid's output is vast, in both verse and prose (he is the sort who sleeps once a week) and, because of the publishing difficulties bedevilling a Scots poet, he probably has more work unpublished, as yet, than has issued in print. His influence too is wide and strong; he has been translated into many languages, and of course in the Communist countries he is *the* British poet of the twentieth century. But it was T. S. Eliot, the greatest poetry critic of our time and since Coleridge, who said that MacDiarmid had been a good influence not only on Scottish but on English poetry, precisely because he revitalized Scots. I myself, after losing direction during the last world war, found it again partly by an involuntary upwelling of Scots in me, and partly thanks to Eliot and MacDiarmid. The former directed me to translate Villon into Scots (I had already tinkered with it), thus opening up the great Franco-Scots medieval tradition to me; and the latter's dictum 'Not Burns – Dunbar' encouraged my instinct. My own conversion was, therefore, that of a groping practitioner, for I rarely waste time on sterile academic theories.

MacDiarmid was a catalyst and a fertilizing influence,

even when only negatively, on almost everybody who came
within his orbit. This is true even of Edwin Muir whose book
Scott and Scotland (1936) disappointed MacDiarmid, who had
eagerly awaited it as the great critical work of the Scots
Renaissance. He at once denounced it as a betrayal and ever
after pursued Muir with the enmity one reserves for traitors.
Certainly the book was a bad one and played into the hands
of the Unionist Establishment, but Muir was guilty of nothing
worse than a rather passive attitude to mere power as
'history'. It is really a difference of temperament: to Muir
history was to be submitted to even if immoral and destruc-
tive: to MacDiarmid history is made by men and can be
changed by men if it is evil. To Muir the triumph of English
in Scotland was an established though regrettable fact and
Scots writers must therefore become English imitators,
second-rate though they could not but be: to MacDiarmid
the English Ascendancy was a historical iniquity with no
right but might behind it, and to be overthrown by all good
men and true. The one, Muir, accepted power as authority,
might as right, in this instance: the other was a revolutionary
to whom there is no authority but Justice, however powerless
it might be. Neither man was as inflexibly insistent on his
position as he appeared to be in print: MacDiarmid has
encouraged Anglo-Scots writing, and practised it, and Muir
has encouraged Scots writers, including the present one.

It is typical of the really tragic history of Scotland and its
continual and continuing internecine conflicts that the two
most gifted writers of their age should become irreconcilable
enemies. But each, in his different way, lifted the eyes of
Scottish poetry from its own kailyaird to the great world
outside: each brought back the European and universal
vision of the makars. The Scots poet today inherits not only
his own parish or town, but the whole culture of Europe, the
Renaissance (killed in its infancy in Scotland by the Kirk),
and the sense of being not only a citizen of Scotland but a
citizen of the world. His imagination feeds on all history,
everything that is human comes within his range, limited
only by his own limitations. He is intensely a nationalist and

an internationalist at the same time, for the very good reason
that you cannot be one without the other.

William Jeffrey has never had the recognition that the
quality and quantity of his output suggest are his due: and
I can do him but scant justice here. William Soutar came early
under the influence of MacDiarmid, but circumstances, and
perhaps temperament, kept his imagination, as a rule, nearer
home. His often exquisite lyric poetry is more in the dialectal,
Burnsian tradition than that of the Makars, although his
sympathies as a man were international. The world of a man
paralysed in bed for the last fourteen years of his life is in-
evitably somewhat restricted, and Soutar's achievement in
his circumstances is remarkable indeed.

Kathleen Raine, like Byron, may seem to some people an
unusual poet to find in this setting: but her mother was
Scottish born and bred; she herself comes from part of
'unreclaimed Scotland', Northumberland; Scotland has been
her spiritual home for many years; she has lived in Ross for
part of each year for a long time; and her work is full of atmo-
sphere partly at least drawn from Wester Ross. Her poetry
has close affinities with that of Edwin Muir.

Robert Garioch is an Edinburgh man who has spent most of
his life, like that other Edinburgh man Norman MacCaig,
teaching school: but the quality of his work exceeds its bulk.
MacCaig's work is admired for wrong reasons: for its merely
clever 'metaphysical' wit, which to my mind is not true
imagination but 'conceit'. He can produce a genuinely
philosophical poetry, as in the hedonistic *Golden Calf*, but
his real gift is for an almost mystical poetry of the eye.

The work of Sydney Goodsir Smith in Scots ranks in
achievement second only to MacDiarmid's. Born in New
Zealand of Scottish parents, and ancestry, son of a professor
of Forensic Medicine, Smith's education was as international
as it was good. But it was only after his arrival in Scotland
that his poetry began to take direction, in his early manhood,
and he experienced a conversion (there is no other word for
it) to Scots, after some wandering in the sudron dialect. The
suppressed Scots in him began to find expression, and he

swiftly showed an instinctive grasp of its values truly remarkable in a man who had not been, as most of us are, brought up with a vigorous if basic Scots spoken round about him. The fact that he was already a highly educated man, born as it were with an intellectual silver spoon in his mouth, and already at home in the whole poetry of Europe from the classics of Greece and Rome to the *Surréalistes*, made possible such achievements as the twenty-four elegies of *Under the Eildon Tree*, based on classical models and drawing on classical lore and traditions; and the Sapphoesque lyrics of *So Late into the Night*. His energy and originality also broke new ground with a heroic verse-play, *The Wallace*, which was a popular and financial success at the Edinburgh Festival of 1960. He has also started something of a craze for TV poem-films about Scottish towns and places – a much more dubious line of development. The verse is usually execrable, the film sentimental, though one or two of them have not been too bad, notably MacDiarmid's on his home-town of Langholm, Dumfries: but there are ominous signs of regression to kailyairdism, that slough of couthy slop into which Scottish poetry is ready to plunge at the least opportunity, in the genre. Sentimentality is the soft underbelly of Smith's work, failing it ultimately (so far) of major achievement. He lacks a grasp of certain basic social and spiritual realities, and has been infected by the Edinbourgeois vice of pretending to live in the eighteenth century, all conviviality and snuff-mulls, instead of the Age of Horror, all murderous warfare and man's inhumanity to man. The Burns' clubs with their false bonhomie and jolly-beggarism, and their shrewd, worldly business-men with a ruthless eye to the main chance and worship of the Golden Calf of 'getting-on', are a source of sentimental corruption lethal to any poet. And it is well to remember that sentimentality is masked brutality.

The Gaelic anthology which I hope will be added to this series before long, and by some Gaelic poet, will feature largely two men now living: Sorley MacLean, a major poet by present-day European standards, and George Campbell

Hay. I have here included one of the latter's poems in Scots, but MacLean writes only in Gaelic. I could have put in Scots translations of his work by such poets as Goodsir Smith and Douglas Young, but translations always belong to their translators, not their originals, for better or, more commonly, for worse.

Those Scottish poets who have grown up since the first or second world wars inherit a very different poetic climate from the one in which the young MacDiarmid and Muir grew up. The latter inherited a claustrophobic kailyairdism, a Scots so limited in range and debased in mind that no serious poet could use it at all, a mental climate so moribundly provincial that the universal mind of the great European tradition was as remote from ordinary life as were Asia and atomic physics. They changed all that, and we today take the whole world for our proper hunting-ground, the whole range of human history and experience. Our imaginations know no limitations except those of nature, and though we speak up simply in our own Scots accent, we write about a universe of which Scotland is an integral part: and we see the part in the whole as well as the whole in the part. We take, in MacDiarmid's phrase, 'Auchtermuchty as pairt o' an eternal mood'.

What poetry is largely about is the interplay of the actual and the desirable, of the apparent and the real, with what is and what ought to be. Scottish poetry differs only in degree and intensity from other poetry in this regard. The vision of the Good Society permeates most great poetry, but perhaps more intensely in Scottish poetry than, for instance, in English, under pressure of necessity. The apocalyptic vision of New Jerusalem, of a world in which worth equals value and vice versa, permeates the poetry of Henrysoun and Dunbar, the satire of Lyndsay and the Reformers, the pasquils of the anti-unionists, the work of Fergusson and Burns, the songs of 'red' Clydeside, the work of MacDiarmid, and of the later generations. It is the central stream of Scottish poetry to which others are but backwaters or tributaries.

The post-war scene in Scotland has included a revival of

interest in, and singing of, folk-songs, and what can only be termed pseudo-folk-songs – songs, written in a folk idiom by highly educated poets. I have included here one or two which seem genuine. Among these I would gladly have included stanzas from the great bawdy epic, the *Ball o' Kirriemuir,* if it had come within the scope of the present anthology:

> Five and twenty virgins cam doun frae Aviemore,
> Ane o them got back sae, but she wes double-bore.
> Singin fa'll dae it this time, fa'll dae it noo?
> The ane that did it last time cannae dae it noo.

Unfortunately it will have to be held over for another volume I have in mind. No picture of Scottish poetry in its heights and depths can ignore it, for it is the darling of student and plough-boy alike. It is impossible that all the verses made to the tune will ever be collected, but enough may be to fill a small book.

Finally, a word about texts. We today live in a world in which spelling 'correctly' is taken for granted. It never occurs to most of us that there is no such thing as 'correct' spelling, and that this obsessional neurosis, imposed on us by teachers at school, was originally imposed on teachers, and on all society, by ignorant printers who couldn't spell. They had to have everything reduced to an easy standard that they could learn. Thus tyranny of the press is now so taken for granted that an author sometimes, often, has to fight like a tiger to be allowed to punctuate his work the way it ought to be punctuated instead of mangled into nonsense by some tyrannical and illiterate system used by printers – and he usually loses unless he is prepared to stop publication.

To the great Scottish poets of the pre-Reformation era, and even after that, this nonsense was as unknown as the know-ledge of good and evil to Adam before the Fall. They spelt any old how, were totally inconsistent, spelt how they heard, or thought, or felt, and that only according to mood. You will find the same word spelt several different ways in the same short poem. Moreover, we have no definitely 'author-ized' texts, that is, known to be the author's own. The great MSS are an orthographic wilderness, a printer's nightmare.

For academic purposes, that is, for establishing these texts in print as they really are, all this profusion of word forms must be reproduced with meticulous exactness. That is the business of the textual scholar, and is primary. But once the scholar has established the text, there is no need to set it up as an idol and worship it at the expense of the living god that called it into being – the poem. The poem lives in the text, as God to the religious may live in the Church, but the text is not the poem and the poem is not the text. Therefore, for poetic purposes, once the text in itself has been established, there is no reason why one should not take liberties with the text in order to improve relations between poem and reader. In books for advanced academic students this liberty must be kept to an absolute minimum, but for books, such as this, meant for general readers, and for young and overseas ones far furth of Scotland, there is every reason to take very daring liberties indeed. There has never been, until 1947, any 'standard' Scots at all: but in that year, bowing to the triumphs of standardization, an attempt was made by a committee of practising poets to standardize their orthography for the sake of breaking down barriers between reader and writer. In this anthology I have taken the step of trying to apply this principle of a standard Scots to the great pre-Reformation writers, where possible. This will be anathema to purist academics who set textual idolatry above true worship of the living poem, but this book is not intended for purist academics.

It is impossible to lay down a set body of rules for such work. The most that can be done is to get one's basic principles straight, then play it by ear, for it is a matter of taste, tact, and sensibility, subtle and ever-changing according to unique problems as they arise. What is right for line four of a certain poem may be wrong for line five, and only one's sensitivity can know that.

My first principle has been, in rationalizing these texts, to be faithful to the integrity of the poem. My second, to go as far as possible to meet the uninstructed reader. When the second conflicted with the first, I sacrificed it: for the rest, I have tried to walk the razor's edge between the two. I have not anglicized the Scots, but rather aimed at a standard Scots, usually in terms of the poet's own practice (or his scribe's), but also in terms of modern standard Scots. I have everywhere sacrificed the Middle and Early Scots 'quh' for the modern 'wh', with some misgivings: for Scots 'wh' is not the same as English: 'whale' in Scots is pronounced 'hwale', not 'wale', and the 'quh' form had the virtue of emphasizing the aspiration. But once that is grasped, there should be little difficulty.

THE POEMS

Anonymous

c. 1300

SCOTLAND'S CONDITION AFTER DEATH OF ALEXANDER III IN 1286

Sen Alexander our king wes deid
    That Scotland left in luve and lee,
Away wes sonse of aill and breid,
    Of wine and wax, of gamin and glee.
The gold wes changit all in leid,
    The frute failyeit on everilk tree.
Christ succour Scotland and remeid
    That stad is in perplexitie.

TO THE MAIDENS OF ENGLAND AFTER BANNOCKBURN 1314

(Fabyan's *Chronicles*)

Maydens of Englonde, sore may ye morne
For your lemans ye have loste at Bannockisborne,
    With heve a lowe.
What wenyth the kynge of Englonde
So soone to have wonne Scotlande
    With rumbylowe.

lee peacetime	*stad* in a condition of
sonse abundance	*lemans* sweethearts
gamin entertainment	*wenyth* imagined
remeid remedy	

John Barbour

c. 1320–95

FROM THE BRUCE

—

1. ON FREEDOM

A! Freedom is a noble thing!
Freedom makis man to have liking;
Freedom all solace to man givis:
He livis at ease that freely livis!
A noble hart may have nane ease,
Na ellis nocht that may him please,
Gif freedom failye; for free liking
Is yarnit owre all othir thing.
Na he, that ay has livit free,
May nocht knaw weill the propyrtie,
The anger, na the wretchit dome,
That is couplit to foul thirldome.
But gif he had assayit it,
Then all perquer he suld it wit,
And suld think freedom mare to prize
Than all the gold in warld that is.

liking choice
yarnit yearned for
owre over, above
na nor
ay always

dome fate
thirldome slavery
gif if, given
all perquer . . . he should learn it
    thoroughly

2. BRUCE'S ADDRESS TO HIS
BANNOCKBURN ARMY

(excerpt)

And when it cummis to the ficht,
Ilk man set his hert and micht
To stint our fais mekill pride.
On horse they sall arrayit ride,
And cum on you in weill great hy;
Meet them with spearis hardely
And wreik on them the mekill ill
That they and thairis has done us til,
And are in will yet for til do,
Gif they have micht til cum thare-to.
And, certis, me think weill that we,
For-out abasyng, aucht til be
Worthy, and of great vassalage;
For we have three great avantage.
The first is, that we have the richt,
And for the richt ilk man suld ficht.
The tother is, they are cummin here,
Forlipning in their great power,
To seek us in our awn land,
And has brocht here, richt til our hand
Riches into so great plentee
That the poorest of you sall be
Baith rich and michty therewithal
Gif that we win, as weill may fall.
The third is that we for our livis
And for our childer and our wivis
And for the freedom of our land,

stint quench	*aucht* ought
mekill large, great	*vassalage* prowess
in weill great hy in great haste	*forlipning* trusting utterly
for-out abasyng without cowardice	

Are streinyeit in battale for to stand,
And they for their micht anerly,
And forthat they leit of us lichtly,
And for they wad destroy us all,
Makis them to ficht; bot yet may fall
That they sall rue their barganing.
And, certes, I warn you of æe thing
To happen them, as God forbeid,
Who find faintness in our deed –
Gif so that they win us openly,
They sall have on us no mercy.

streinyeit constrained   *leit* consider
anerly only

James I

1394–1437

—

CANTUS

Worship, ye that loveris bene, this May,
  For of your bliss the kalendis are begonne,
And sing with us, away, winter, away!
    Cum, somer, cum, the swete seasoun and sonne!
    Awake for shame that have your hevinnis wonne,
And amorously lift up your hedis all,
Thank luve that list you to his merci call.

When they this song had sung a litill thrawe,
  They stent a while, and therewith unafraid,
As I beheld and kest mine eyne alawe,
  From beugh to beugh they hippit and they plaid,
  And freshly in their birdis kynd arraid,
Their fetheris new, and fret them in the sonne,
And thankit luve, that had their makis wonne.

This was the plane ditee of their note,
  And therewithall unto myself I thocht,
'What life is this, that makis birdis dote?
  What may this be, how cummyth it of oucht?'

kalendis first day	*hippit* hopped
thrawe time, while	*fret* preened
stent stopped	*makis* mates
alawe downward	*oucht* ought

What nedith it to be so dere yboucht?
It is nothing, trowe I, but feynit chere,
And that men list to counterfeten chere.'

Eft wald I think; 'O Lord, what may this be?
    That luve is of so noble might and kynd,
Luving his folk, and such prosperitee
    Is it of him, as we in bukis fynd?
    May he our hertes setten and unbynd?
Hath he upon our hertis such maistrye?
Or all this is but feynyt fantasye!

For gif he be of so grete excellence,
    That he of every wight hath cure and charge,
What have I gilt to him or doon offens,
    That I am thrall, and birdis gone at large,
    Sen him to serve he might set my corage?
And gif he be nocht so, then may I seyn,
What makis folk to jangill of him in veyn?

Can I nocht elles fynd, but gif that he
    Be Lord, and as a God may live and reigne,
To bynd and lous, and maken thrallis free,
    Than wold I pray his blisfull grace benigne,
    To hable me unto his service digne;
And evermore for to be one of tho
Him trewly for to serve in wele and wo.'

And therwith kest I doun myne eye ageyne,
    Where as I sawe, walking under the tour,
Full secretly new cummyn her to pleyne,
    The fairest or the freshest yong floure

list make shift, employ   *jangill* gossip
eft afterwards   *hable* make fit
setten make fast   *digne* worthy
sen since   *tho* those, them
seyn say   *pleyne* play, amuse

That ever I saw, me thoucht, before that houre,
For which sodayn abate, anon astert,
The blude of all my body to my hert.

And though I stude abaisit tho a lyte,
    No wonder was, forwhy my wittis all
Were so owercom with pleasance and delyte,
    Onely throu latting of myne eyen fall,
    That sudaynly my hert become her thrall
For ever of free will; for of manace
There was no takyn in her swete face.

And in my hede I drew rycht hastily,
    And eftsones I lent it forth ageyne,
And saw her walk, that verray womanly,
    With no wight mo but onely women tweyne.
    Then gan I studye in myself and seyne,
'A! swete, are ye a warldly creature,
Or hevinly thing in likeness of nature?

Or are ye god Cupidis owin princess,
    And cummyn are to louse me out of band?
Or are ye verray nature the goddess,
    That have depaynted with your hevinly hand
    This gardyn full of flouris, as they stand?
What sall I think, allace! What reverence
Sall I minster to your excellence?

Gif ye a goddess be, and that ye like
    To do me payne, I may it nocht astert;
Gif ye be warldly wight, that dooth me sike,

astert leapt	*mo* more, besides
tho a lyte then a little	*louse* loosen
manace menace	*astert* leap aside, avoid
takyn token, sign	*dooth me sike* makes me sigh
eftsones soon after	

Why lest God mak you so, my derrest hert,
  To do a sely prisoner thus smert,
That luvis you all, and wote of nocht but wo?
And therefore, merci, swete! sen it is so.'

lest pleased   *wote* knows
sely innocent

Anonymous

c. 1500

KING BERDOK

Sim of Lintoun, by the ramis horn
When Phebus rang in sing of Capricorn
And the moon wes past the goosis cro,
There fell in France ane jeoperdie forlo,
By the great king of Babylon, Berdok,
That dwelt in simmer intil ane bowkail stock;
And into winter, when the frostis are fell,
He dwelt for cauld intil a cokkil shell.
Kingis usit nocht to weir claithes in thae dayis
But gaed nakit, as mine aucthour sayis.
Weill could he play in clarshocht and on lute
And bend ane aipron bow, and nipshot shoot.
He wes ane stalwart man of hairt and hand.
He wooit the gowk seven year, of Maryland,
Mayiola, and she wes but yearis three,
Ane bonny bird, and had but ane ee.
Nevertheless, king Berdok luvit her weill
For her forefoot wes langer than her heel.
The king Berdok, he fure owre sea and land
To raveis Mayok, the gowk of Maryland,
And nane with him but ane bow and ane bowt.
Syne hapnit him to cum amang the nowt,

rang reigned	*nipshot* backwards
sing sign	*gowk* cuckoo
goosis cro sow's sty	*fure* fared
forlo forlorn, luckless	*bowt* bolt
bowkail cabbage	*nowt* cattle
clarshocht harping	

And, as this Berdok about him coud espy,
He saw Mayok milkand her muderis kye,
And in ane creel upoun his back her kest.
When he come hame, it wes ane houlet nest
Full of skait-birdis; and then this Berdok gret,
And ran again Mayok for to get.
The king of Faery, her fader, then blew out
And socht Berdok all the land about,
And Berdok fled intil a killogy:
There wes no grace but get him, or else dee.
There wes the kingis of Pechtis and Portingaill,
The king of Napilis and Navern, alhail,
With bowis and brandis with sieges they umbeset him –
Sum bade tak, sum slay, sum bade bide till they get him.
They stellit guns to the killogy laich
And proppit them with bullets of raw daich.
Then Jupiter prayit to god Saturn
In likeness of ane tod he wald him turn:
But soon the gracious god Mercurius
Turnit Berdok intil ane bracken buss;
And when they saw the buss wag to and frae,
They trowed it wes ane ghaist, and they to-gae.
Thir fell kingis thus Berdok wald have slane –
All this for luve, luvaris suffers pane.
Boece said, of poetis that wes flour,
'Thoch luve be sweet, oftimes it is full sour'.

muderis kye mother's cows	*stellit* set
houlet owl	*proppit* primed
skait-birdis skuas	*daich* dough
gret wept	*tod* fox
killogy hearth of a kiln	*fell* murderous
umbeset besieged	

FROM RAUF COLYEAR

Soon was the supper dicht and the fire bet,
And they had weshin, I wis, the worthiest was there.
'Tak my wife by the hand in fere withoutin let,
And gang begin the board', said the Colyear.
'That were unseemand, forsooth, and thyself unset',
The King profferit him to gang, and made ane strange fair.
'Now is twice', said the carle, 'me think thou hes forget'.
He let gird at the King withoutin ony mair
And hit him under the ear with his richt hand
    Whill he stakkerit therewithal
    Half the breadth of the hall,
    He faind never of ane fall
        Whill the eard fand.

He stert up stoutly agane, unease micht he stand,
For anger of that outray that he had there tane.
He callit on Gilliane his wife, 'Gae tak him by the hand
And gang agane to the board, where ye suld ere have gane.
Shir, thou are unskilful, and that I sall warrand:
Thou burd to have nurture eneuch, and thou has nane.
Thou has walkit, I wis, in mony wild land:
The mair vertew thou suld have to keep thee frae blame.
Thou suld be courteous of kind, and ane cunnand courtier.
    Thoch that I simple be,
    Do as I bid thee,
    The hous is mine, pardie,
        And all that is here.'

dicht set out
bet stirred up
weshin washed
worthiest best of fare
gang ... board begin the meal
unseemand not seemly
unset not seated

fair deprecatory gesture
let gird struck out
faind stopped
eard earth
outray outrage
burd ought

The King said to himself, 'This is ane ill life,
Yet was I never in my life thusgait leard,
And I have oft times been where gude has been rife
That maist couth of courtasie in this Cristin eard:
Is nane sae gude as leave off, and mak nae mair strife,
For I am stonishit at this strake that has me thus steird.'
In fere fairlie he foundis with the gude wife
Where the Colyear bade, sae braithlie he beird.
When he had done his bidding, as him gude thocht,
    Doun he sat the King near
    And made him glaid and gude cheer,
    And said, 'Ye are welcum here,
        By Him that me bocht.'

When they were servit and set to the supper,
Gill and the gentil King Charle of micht,
Syne on the tother side sat the Colyear.
Thus were they marshallit but mair, and matchit that nicht.
They brocht breid to the board, and brawn of ane bair,
And the worthiest wine went upon hicht.
Thae bairnis, as I ween, they had eneuch there
Within that burelie bigging, burnand full bricht:
Syn enteris their dainties on dais dicht daintillie,
    Within that worthie wane
    Forsooth wantit they nane.
    'With blyth cheer', sayis Gilliane,
        'Shir does glaidlie.'

thusgait in this manner
leard instructed
is nane . . . it's best to leave off
foundis seated himself
braithlie angrily
beird roared
Charle . . . Charlemagne
but mair without more ado
brawn flesh

bair boar
upon hicht passed round
thae those
bairnis worthy persons
burelie well-built
bigging building
dais boards, trays
dicht dressed, set out
wane dwelling

The carle carpit to the King cumlie and clear:
'Shir, the foresters forsooth of this forest,
They have me all at envy for dreid of the deer.
They threep that I thring doun of the fattest!
They say I sall to Paris, there to compeir
Before our cumlie King, in dule to be drest.
Sic manacing they me mak, forsooth, ilk year,
And yet eneuch sall I have for me and ane Guest:
Therefore, sic as thou seeis, spend on and not spare'.
        Thus said gentil Charle the Main
        To the Colyear agane:
        'The King himself has been fain
            Sum time of sic fare'.

FROM COLKELBIE SOW

    Here I give you cais,
    Umwhile a merry man wais
    Callit Colkelbie.
    He had a simple blak sow
    And he sald her but how
    For penneis three, as eftir ye may see.
    And verily, as I hard,
    Thus the money he ward:
    The first penny of the three
    For a girl gave he;
    The secund fell in a furde;
    The third he hid in a hurde.
    Now whilk penny of the three

carle elderly man		*fain* glad	
carpit chatted		*sic* such	
dreid dread		*sald* sold	
threep complain		*hard* heard	
thring strike		*ward* spent, invested	
compeir give account		*furde* ditch	
dule sorrow		*hurde* hoard	

Wes best bestowit, say ye?
The lost penny wes unpleasit;
The girl for the time pleasit;
But the penny that wes hid,
I hold least gude did:
For in old proverb, we sing
Cumis little gude of gathering.
Where wrechit avarice birnis,
Hyding hurdis in to hirnis,
And knawis nevir whom til,
Letting wirshep to go will.
Great laubor is to get gear,
And to conserve it is fear;
And more anger it to lease
Thir three perverst propirteiss . . .

The penny lost in the lak
Wes fundin and uptak,
And he that fand it did buy
With the samyn penny
A little pig for his prow
Off Colkelbeis sow.
A harlot wonnit near by
And sho wald mak at mangery,
And had no substance at all
But this puir pig stall,
To furniss a great feist
Withouttin stuff, but this beast;
And yet sho callit to her cheir
One apostita freir,
A perverst pardonier,

gathering hoarding	*thir* these
birnis burns, rages	*prow* profit
hirnis secret places	*wonnit* dwelt
wirshep worship, proper behaviour	*mangery* feast (Latin *mando*, I chew)
gear worldly goods	*stall* stole

And practand palmair,
A witch, and a wobstare,
A milygant, and a mychare,
A fond fule, fariar,
A cairtar, a cariar,
A libber, and a lyar,
And riddill revar;
A tuttivillus, a tutlar,
And a feinyeit flatterar,
A forfarn falconar,
A malgratious millare,
A berward, a brawlar,
And ane aip leader;
With a cursit custumar,
A tratlar, and tinklar,
And mony uthir in that hour
Of all evill ordour.
First with a fulish flouer,
Ane ald monk, a lechour,
A drunkin drechour,
A double-toungit counsalour,
A trumpour, a truccour,
A hangman, a hasardour,
A tyrant, a tormentour,
A truphane, a tratlour,
A faynit nigremansour,
A japer, a juglour,
A lass that luvis but for lour,

---

wobstare weaver
milygant evildoer (O. French *male-gent*)
mychare thief
libber beast-gelder
riddill revar fortune-teller
tuttivillus fiend
tutlar ?
forfarn worn-out

berward bear-keeper
aip ape
custumar burgh rate-payer
tratlar slanderer
tinklar tinker (*zingaro*)
drechour good-for-nothing
trumpour cheat, trickster
truccour spiv
but for lour casually

And a man merrour,
An evill wyffis mirrour,
In all their semblance sour,
With a noyfull neichtbour,
A lunatik, a sismatyk,
An heretyk, a purspyk,
A lombard, a lolard,
Ane usurar, a bard,
Ane ypocreit in haly kirk,
A burn-grange in the dirk,
A shipman on sea and sand
That takis lyfe and gude on hand
And knawis nowther course nor tide,
But presumpteouss in pride,
Practing nothing expert
In cunning, compass, nor kert.

THE WIFE OF AUCHTERMUCHTY

In Auchtermuchty there dwelt ane man,
   Ane husband, as I hard it tauld,
Wha weell could tipple out a can,
   And naither luvit hunger nor cauld,
Whill anis it fell upoun a day,
   He yokkit his pleuch upoun the plain:
Gif it be trew, as I hard say,
   The day was foull for wind and rain.

mirrour marrer, crippler	*husband* farmer
lombard banker	*hard* heard
burn-grange incendiary	*tauld* told
dirk dark	*pleuch* plough
kert maps	*gif* if, given

He lousit the pleuch at the landis end,
    And drave his oxen hame at e'en;
When he come in, he lukit bend,
    And saw the wife baith dry and clean
And sittand at ane fire, beikand bauld,
    With ane fat soup, as I hard say:
The man being very weet and cauld,
    Between thae twa it was nae play.

Quoth he, where is my horsis corn?
    My ox hes naither hay nor stray.
Dame, ye maun to the pleuch to-morn,
    I sall be hussy, gif I may.
Husband, quoth sho, content am I
    To tak the pleuch by day about,
Sae ye will rule baith knavis and kye,
    And a the hous baith in and out.

But sen that ye will hussyskip ken,
    First ye sall sift, and syne ye sall kned:
And aye as ye gang butt and ben,
    Luke that the bairnis dirt not the bed.
Yeis lay a soft wisp to the kill,
    We have ane dear ferm on our heid;
And aye as ye gang furth and in,
    Keep weell the gaisslings frae the gled.

The wife was up richt late at e'en,
    I pray God gif her ill to-fare,
She kirn'd the kirn and scum'd it clean,
    And left the gudeman but the bledoch bare.

lousit unloosed
ben(d) into the kitchen
beikand getting warm
thae those
hussy housewife
hussyskip housewifery
ken understand, know
kned knead

butt and ben in and out the
    house: parlour and kitchen
bairnis children
kill kiln
gled kite
kirn churn
bledoch buttermilk

Then in the morning up sho gat,
  And on her hairt laid her disjeune.
Sho put as meikle in her lap
  As micht have served them baith, at noon.

Sayis, Jock, will thou be maister of wark,
  And thou sall haud, and I sall kaa;
Ise promise thee ane gude new sark
  Aither of round claith or of smaa.
She lowsit oxen aucht or nine,
  And hint ane gadstaff in her hand;
And the gudeman raise efter syne,
  And saw the wife had done command.

And kaa'd the gaislingis furth to feed
  (There was but sevensome of them aa)
And by there comis the greedy gled
  And lickit up five, left him but twa.
Then out he ran in aa his main,
  How sune he hard the gaislingis cry;
But then, or he come in agane,
  The calvis brak lowse and soukit the kye.

The calvis and kye being met in the lone,
  The man ran with ane rung to redd;
Then by there comis ane ill-willy cou
  And broddit his buttock whill that it bled.
Then hame he ran to ane rock of tow,
  And he sat doun t' essay the spinning;
I trow he lowtit owre near the lowe:
  Quod he, this wark has ill beginning.

disjeune breakfast (Fr. *déjeuner*)	*kye* cows
meikle much	*lone* lane
kaa drive	*rung* cudgel
sark shirt	*redd* restore order
smaa small	*rock of tow* spindle and distaff
hint took up	*lowtit* stooped
aa all	*lowe* flame

Then to the kirn that he did stour,
  And jumlit at it whill he swatt;
When he had jumlit a full lang hour,
  The sorrow crap of butter he gat.
Albeit nae butter he could get,
  Yet he wes cummerit with the kirn,
And syne he het the milk owre het,
  And sorrow a spark of it wald yirn.

Then ben there come ane greedy sou,
  (I trow he cun'd her little thank)
And in she shot her meikle mou,
  And aye sho winkit and sho drank.
He cleikit up ane crukit club,
  And thoucht to hit the sou ane rowt:
The twa gaislingis the gled had left,
  That strake dang baith their harnis out!

He gat his foot upon the spire
  To have gotten the flesh doun to the pat:
He fell backward into the fire,
  And brak his head on the keming stack.
Yet he gat the meikle pat on the fire,
  And gat twa cans, and ran to the spout:
Ere he came it, (what thoucht ye of that?)
  The fire burnt aa the pat-arse out!

Then he bure kindling to the kiln,
  But sho start aa up in ane lowe;
Whatever he hard, whatever he saw,

jumlit shook	*dang* dashed
crap crop	*harnis* brains
cummerit encumbered	*spire* iron projection from wall
het heated, hot	*keming stack* rippling card
yirn curdle	support
cun'd gave	*spout* pump
rowt blow	*bure* bore

That day he had nae will to mowe.
Then he gaed to tak up the bairns,
   Thocht to have fund them fair and clean:
The first that he gat in his armis
   Was aa bedirtin to the een.

The first that he gat in his armis
   It was aa dirt up to the een:
The Deil cut aff their hands, quod he,
   That fild you aa sae fou this strene.
He trailit foull sheetis doun the gait,
   Thocht to have weshed them on ane stane;
The burn wes risen great of spate:
   Away from him the sheets hes tane.

Then up he gat on ane knowe heid,
   On her to cry, on her to shout;
Sho hard him, and she hard him not
   But stoutly steer'd the stottis about.
She drave the day unto the nicht,
   She lowsit the pleuch, and syne come **hame;**
She fand aa wrang that sould been richt –
   I trow the man thoucht richt great shame.

Quoth he, my office I forsaik
   For aa the dayis of my life;
For I wald put ane hous to wreck
   Had I been twenty dayis gudewife.
Quoth sho, weel mot ye bruke your place,
   For trewlie I will neer accep' it;
Quoth he, feind faa the liaris face
   But yet ye may be blyth to get it.

mowe joke	*stottis* oxen
strene urine	*mot* may
knowe knoll	*feind faa* devil take

Then up sho gat ane meikle rung
   And the gudeman made to the door;
Quoth he, Dame, I sall hauld my tongue,
   For, and we fecht, I'll get the waur,
Quoth he, when I forsuke my pleuch,
   I trow I but forsuke my seill;
And I will to my pleuch agane,
   For I and this hous will neer do weill.

waur worse   *seill* happiness

Sir Richard Holland

?1420–?1485

FROM THE BOOK OF THE HOWLAT

—

THE BARD, AND OTHER ENTERTAINERS AT THE FEAST

Sae come the Ruke, with a rerd and rane roch,
A bard out of Ireland, with 'Banachadee'.
Said: 'Gluntow guk dynydrach, hala mischy doch –
Rax her a rug of the roast, or sho shall ryme thee.
Mich macmory ach mach mountir moch loch –
Set her doun, give her a drink, what deil ails thee?
O dermyn, O Donall, O Dochardy droch.
Thir are the Ireland kingis of the Irishery:–
O Knewlyn, O Connochar, O Gregor MacGrane.
    The Shennachy, the Clarsach,
    The Ben shene, the Ballach,
    The Crekery, the Corach,
        Sho kennis them ilkane.'

ruke rook
rerd hubbub
rane roch rough chatter
banachadee blessing of God
gluntow, etc. imitation Gaelic
hala mischy doch I can take drink
rax reach

rug slice
ryme satirize
mich, etc. imitation Gaelic
set her i.e. the bard (Gaelic construction)
O dermyn, etc. (here the bard is showing off his bardry)

Mony lesingis he made, wald let for no man
To speak whill he spoken had, sparit no thingis.
The dean rural, the Raven, reprovit him then,
Bade him his lesingis leave before thae lordingis.
The bard worth brane wod, and bitterly couth ban: –
'How, Corby messenger', quoth he, 'with sorrow now singis!
Thou issuit out of Noae's ark, and to the eard wan,
Taryit as a traitour, and brocht nae tithings.
I sall ryme thee, Raven, baith guts and gall!'
    The dean rural worthit reid,
    Staw for shame off the steid;
    The bard held a great pleid
        In the hie hall.

In come twa flyrand fulis, with a fand-fare,
The Peewit and the gukkit Gowk, and gaed hiddy-giddy:
Rushit baith to the bard and ruggit his hair;
Callit him thrice-thievesneck, to thraw in a widdy.
They fylit him frae the foretop to the fute there.
The bard, smaddit like a smaik smorit in a smiddy,
Ran fast to the dure, and gave a great rair:
Socht water to wesh him there out in an eddy.
The lordis leuch upon loft, and liking they had
    That the bard was so beat.
    The fulis fond in the fleet,
    And mony mowis at meat
        On the flure made.

lesingis lies   *gowk* cuckoo
let stop   *thraw* strangle
thae those   *widdy* halter
worth grew   *smaddit* dirtied
brane wod stark mad   *smaik* rascal, fellow
ban curse   *smorit* begrimed
steid place   *leuch upon loft* laughed aloud
flyrand grimacing   *mowis* clownings

Syn for ane figonal of fruit they strave in the steid.
The Peewit gird to the Gowk, and gave him a fall,
Rave his tail frae his rig, with a rath pleid,
The Gowk gat up agane in the great hall,
Tit the Peewit by the top, owre-tirvit his heid,
Flang him flat in the fire, featheris and all.
He cryid: 'Allace!' with ane rair, 'reven is my reed!
I am ungraciously gorrit, baith guts and gall!'
Yet he lap frae the lowe richt in a line.

> When they had ramels raucht
> They forthocht that they focht,
> Kissit samyn and saucht,
> > And sat doun syne.

gird struck
rig back
rath pleid angry speech
tit clutched
reven torn
reed wind-pipe

lowe flame
richt in a line straight like a shot
ramels blows
raucht exchanged
forthocht regretted
saucht reconciled

Robert Henrysoun

c. 1420–c. 1490

THE ABBEY WALK

Allone as I went up and doun
In ane abbey was fair to see,
Thinkand what consolatioun
Was best in to adversitie,
On case I cast on side mine Ee,
And saw this writtin upoun a wall:
'Of what estait, man, that thou be,
Obey and thank thy God of all.

'Thy kingdome and thy great empire,
Thy royaltie, nor rich array,
Sall nocht endeur at thy desire,
But as the wind will wend away;
Thy gold and all thy gudis gay,
When fortoun list will frae thee fall;
Sen thou sic sampillis sees ilk day,
Obey and thank thy God of all.

'Job wes maist rich in writ we find,
Thobe, maist full of cheritie:
Job walx puir, and Thobe blind,
Baith tempit with adversitie.
Sen blindness wes infirmitie,

on case by chance   *tempit* tempted
sampillis examples

And povertie wes naturall,
Therefore richt patiently baith he and he
Obeyid and thankit God of all.

'Thoch thou be blind, or have ane halt,
Or in thy face deformit ill,
Sae it cum nocht throu thy defalt,
Nae man suld thee reprief by skill.
Blame nocht thy Lord, sae is his will;
Spurn nocht thy fute againis the wall;
But with meek hairt and prayer still
Obey and thank thy God of all.

'God of his justice maun correct,
And of his mercy petie have;
He is ane Juge to nane suspect,
To puneiss sinfull man and save.
Thoch thou be lord attour the lave,
And eftirward made bound and thrall,
Ane puir begger, with skrip and stave,
Obey and thank thy God of all.

'This changing and great variance
Of eardly statis up and doun
Is nocht but casualitie and chance,
As sum men sayis, without reasoun,
But by the great provisioun
Of God above that rule thee sall;
Therefore evir thou mak thee boun
To obey and thank thy God of all.

'In welth be meek, heich nocht thy self;
Be glaid in wilfull povertie;
Thy power and thy warldis pelf

reprief reprove   *boun* ready
attour above   *heich* elevate
lave the others

Is nocht but very vanitie.
Remember him that deeit on tree,
For thy sake taistit the bitter gall,
Wha heichs low hairtis and lowers hie;
Obey and thank thy God of all.'

THE TESTAMENT OF CRESSEID

Ane doolie seasoun to ane carefull dyte
Suld correspond, and be equivalent.
Richt sae it wes when I began to wryte
This tragedie, the weader richt fervent,
When Aries, in middis of the Lent,
Shouris of haill can frae the north discend,
That scantlie frae the cauld I micht defend.

Yet nevertheless within mine orature
I stude, when Titan had his beamis bricht
Withdrawin doun, and sylit under cure
And fair Venus, the bewtie of the nicht,
Upraise, and set unto the west full richt
Hir goldin face in oppositioun
Of God Phebus, direct discending doun.

Throu out the glass hir beamis brast sae fair
That I micht see, on everie side me by,
The Northin wind had purifyit the Air
And shed the mistie cloudis frae the sky;
The frost freesit, the blastis bitterly
Frae Pole Artick come whisling loud and shill,
And causit me remuve againis my will.

hie exalted	*sylit* hidden
doolie doleful	*cure* cover
dyte written story	*brast* burst

For I traisit that Venus, luvis Quene,
To whom sum time I hecht obedience,
My fadit hart of luve sho wald mak green,
And therupon with humbill reverence,
I thocht to pray her hie Magnificence;
But for greit cald as then I lattit was,
And in my Chalmer to the fire can pass.

Thoch luve be het, yet in ane man of age
It kendillis nocht sae soon as in youtheid,
Of whom the blude is flowing in ane rage,
And in the auld the curage doif and deid,
Of whilk the fire outward is best remeid;
To help by Phisik where that nature faillit
I am expert, for baith I have assailit.

I mend the fire and beikit me about,
Then tuik ane drink my spreitis to comfort,
And armit me weill frae the cauld thereout:
To cut the winter nicht and mak it short,
I tuik ane Quair, and left all uther sport,
Writtin by worthie Chaucer glorious,
Of fair Cresseid, and worthie Troylus.

And there I fand, efter that Diomeid
Ressavit had that Lady bricht of hew,
How Troylus near out of wit abraid,
And weepit sore with visage paill of hew;
For whilk wanhope his tearis can renew
Whill Esperus rejoisit him agane,
Thus while in Joy he levit, while in pane.

hecht promised, vowed	*beikit, etc* made myself warm
lattit prevented	*quair* book
het hot	*abraid* started
doif dulled	*wanhope* despair
whilk which	*levit* lived

Of her behest he had great comforting,
Traisting to Troy that sho suld mak retour,
Whilk he desyrit maist of eardly thing
Forwhy sho was his only Paramour;
But when he saw passit baith day and hour
Of her ganecome, then sorrow can oppress
His wofull hart in care and heaviness.

Of his distress me needis nocht rehears,
For worthie Chauceir in the samin buik
In gudelie termis and in Joly verse
Compylit hes his caris, wha will luik,
To brek my sleep ane uther quair I tuik,
In whilk I fand the fatall destenie
Of fair Cresseid, that endit wretchitlie.

Wha wait gif all that Chauceir wrait was trew?
Nor I wait nocht gif this narratioun
Be authoreist, or fenyeit of the new
By sum Poet, throu his Inventioun,
Made to report the Lamentatioun
And wofull end of this lustie Cresseid,
And what distress sho tholit, and what deid.

When Diomeid had all his appetite,
And mair, fulfillit of this fair Ladie,
Upon ane uther he set his haill delyte
And send to her ane lybell of repudie,
And her excludit frae his companie.
Than desolait sho walkit up and doun,
And sum men sayis into the Court commoun.

traisting trusting   *lybell of repudie* bill of divorce
ganecome return   *and sum men sayis* ... i.e. became
wait knows   a courtesan, whore
tholit endured

O fair Creisseid, the flour and A per se
Of Troy and Greece, how was thou fortunait!
To change in filth all thy Feminitie,
And be with fleshlie lust sae maculait,
And go amang the Greekis air and lait
Sae giglotlike, takand thy foull pleasance!
I have pietie thou suld fall sic mischance.

Yet nevertheless what ever men deem or say
In scornfull langage of thy brukkilness,
I sall excuse, als far furth as I may,
Thy womanheid, thy wisdom and fairness;
The whilk Fortoun hes put to sic distress
As her pleasit, and naething throu the guilt
Of thee, throu wickit langage to be spilt.

This fair Lady, in this wyse destitute
Of all comfort and consolatioun,
Richt privilie, but fellowship, on fute
Disguisit, passit far out of the toun
Ane mile or twa, unto ane Mansioun
Beildit full gay, where her father Calchas,
Whilk then amang the Greekis, dwelland was.

When he her saw, the cause he can inquire
Of her cumming; sho said, siching full sore:
'Frae Diomeid had gottin his desyre
He wox wearie, and wald of me no more.'
Quod Calchas, 'dochter, weep thou not therefore;
Peraventure all cummis for the best;
Welcum to me, thou art full dear ane Gest.'

fortunait destined   *giglotlike* wantonly
maculait stained   *brukkilness* frailty
air and lait early and late   *frae* from the time that

This auld Calchas, efter the Law was tho,
Wes keeper of the Tempill as ane Preist,
In whilk Venus and her Son Cupido
Were honourit, and his Chalmer was them neist,
To whilk Cresseid with baill aneuch in breist
Usit to pass, her prayeris for to say.
Whill at the last, upon ane solemn day,

As custom was, the pepill far and near
Before the noon, unto the Tempill went,
With sacrifice, devoit in their maneir:
But still Cresseid, heavie in her intent,
Into the Kirk wald not her self present,
For giving of the pepill ony deming
Of her expulse frae Diomeid the King:

But past into ane secreit Orature
Where sho micht weep her wofull desteny,
Behind her bak sho closit fast the dure,
And on her kneis bair fell doun in hy.
Upon Venus and Cupid angerly
Sho cryit out, and said on this same wyse,
'Allace that ever I made you Sacrifice.

'Ye gave me anis ane devine responsaill
That I suld be the flour of luve in Troy,
Now am I made ane unworthie outwaill,
And all in care translatit is my Joy,
Wha sall me guide? wha sall me now convoy
Sen I frae Diomeid and nobill Troylus
Am clene excludit, as object odious?

tho then
neist next
baill aneuch trouble enough
deming chance to condemn

hy haste
responsaill answer to prayer
outwaill outcast

'O false Cupid, is nane to wyte but thou,
And thy Mother, of luve the blind Goddess.
Ye causit me alwayis understand and trow
The seed of luve was sawin in my face,
And ay grew grene throu your supplie and grace.
But now allace that seed with frost is slane,
And I fra luveris left and all forlane.'

When this was said, doun in ane extasie,
Ravishit in spreit, intill ane dream sho fell,
And by appearance heard, where sho did ly,
Cupid the King ringand ane silver bell,
Whilk men micht hear frae hevin unto hell;
At whais sound before Cupid appearis
The seven Planetis discending frae their Spheiris,

Whilk hes power of all thing generabill
To rule and steer by their great Influence,
Weader and wind, and coursis variabill:
And first of all Saturn gave his sentence,
Whilk gave to Cupid litill reverence,
But, as ane busteous Churl on his maneir,
Come crabitlie with austere luik and cheir.

His face fronsit, his lyre was like the Leid,
His teith chatterit, and cheverit with the Chin,
His ene droopit, how sonkin in his heid,
Out of his nois the meldrop fast can rin,
With lippis blae and cheekis lean and thin;
The iceshoklis that frae his hair doun hang
Was wonder great, and as ane spear als lang.

wyte blame	*lyre* skin
generabill born	*cheverit* shivered
busteous blustery	*how* hollow
crabitlie crabbedly	*meldrop* mucus
fronsit wrinkled	*iceshoklis* icicles

Atouir his belt his lyart lokkis lay
Felterit unfair, owerfret with frostis hoar,
His garmound and his guise full gay of gray,
His witherit weed frae him the wind out wore;
Ane busteous bow within his hand he bore,
Under his girdill ane flash of felloun flanis,
Feaderit with ice, and heidit with hailstanis.

Then Juppiter, richt fair and amiabill,
God of the starnis in the firmament,
And nureis to all thing generabill,
Frae his father Saturn far different,
With burelie face, and browis bricht and brent,
Upon his heid ane garland, wonder gay,
Of flouris fair, as it had been in May.

His voice was clear, as cristall were his ene,
As goldin wire sae glitterand was his hair;
His garmound and his guise full gay of green,
With golden listis gilt on everie gair;
Ane burelie brand about his midill bair;
In his richt hand he had ane groundin spear,
Of his father the wrath frae us to weir.

Nixt efter him come Mars, the God of Ire,
Of strife, debait, and all dissensioun,
To chide and fecht, als feirce as ony fire;
In hard harness, helmound and habirgeoun,
And on his haunch ane roustie fell fachioun;
And in his hand he had ane roustie sword;
Wrything his face with mony angrie word,

atouir above	*starnis* stars
lyart hoary	*nureis* succourer
felterit matted	*burelie* goodly, stalwart
owerfret overlaced	*brent* smooth
weed clothing	*listis* edgings
flash quiver	*gair* pleat
felloun deadly	*habirgeoun* mail-coat
flanis darts, arrows	*fachioun* small sword, dagger

Shakand his sword, before Cupid he come
With reid visage, and grislie glowrand ene;
And at his mouth ane bullar stude of foam
Like to ane bair whetting his tuskis kene,
Richt tuillyeour-like, but temperance in tene;
Ane horn he blew, with mony busteous brag,
Whilk all this warld with weir hes made to wag.

Then fair Phebus, lantern and lamp of licht
Of man and beast, baith frute and flourishing,
Tender nureis, and banisher of nicht,
And of the warld, causing, by his moving
And influence, life in all eardlie thing,
Without comfort of whom, of force to nocht
Must all gae dee that in this warld is wrocht.

As King Royall he rade upon his chair
The whilk Phaeton guidit sum time upricht;
The brichtnes of his face when it was bare
Nane micht behald for peirsing of his sicht.
This goldin cart with firie bemis bricht
Four yokit steedis full different of hew,
But bait or tiring, throu the spheiris drew.

The first was sorr, with mane als reid as rose,
Callit Eoye into the Orient;
The secund steed to name hecht Ethios,
Whitelie and paill, and sum deill ascendent;
The third Peros, richt het and richt fervent;
The fourd was blak, callit Philologie
Whilk rollis Phebus doun into the sea.

bullar mass of bubbles	*but bait* without pause
bair boar	*sorr* sorrel
tuillyeour-like warrior-like	*hecht* called
tene rage	*sum deill* somewhat
weir war	

Venus was there present, that goddess gay,
Her sonnis querrell for to defend and mak
Her awin complaint, cled in ane nice array,
The ane half green, the uther half sabill black;
White hair as gold kemmit and shed abak;
But, in her face seemit great variance,
Whiles perfyte treuth, and whiles inconstance.

Under smiling sho was dissimulait,
Provocative, with blenkis amorous,
And suddanly changit and alterait,
Angrie as ony serpent vennemous
Richt pungitive, with wordis odious.
Thus variant sho was, wha list tak keep,
With ane ee lauch, and with the uther weep:

In taikning that all fleshlie paramour
Whilk Venus hes in rule and governance,
Is sum time sweet, sum time bitter and sour
Richt unstabill, and full of variance,
Mingit with careful joy and false pleasance,
Now het, now cauld, now blyth, now full of wo,
Now green as leaf, now witherit and ago.

With buik in hand then come Mercurius,
Richt eloquent, and full of rethorie,
With polite termis and delicious,
With pen and ink to report all reddie,
Setting sangis and singand merilie:
His hude was reid, heklit atouir his croun,
Like to ane poet of the auld fassoun.

querrell quarrel, case	*in taikning* in token
kemmit combed	*mingit* mingled
tak keep take heed	

Boxis he bair with fine electuairis,
And sugerit syropis for digestioun,
Spycis belangand to the pothecairis,
With mony hailsum sweet confectioun,
Doctour in Phisick cled in ane skarlot goun,
And furrit weill, as sic ane aucht to be,
Honest and gude, and not ane word could lee.

Nixt efter him come Lady Cynthia,
The last of all, and swiftest in her spheir,
Of colour blak, buskit with hornis twa,
And in the nicht sho listis best appear.
Haw as the leid, of colour naething clear;
For all her licht sho borrowis at her brother
Titan, for of her self sho hes nane uther.

Her guise was gray, and full of spottis blak,
And on her breist ane churl paintit full evin,
Beirand ane bunch of thornis on his bak,
Whilk for his thift micht clim na near the hevin.
Thus when they gatherit were, thir Goddes sevin,
Mercurius they chosit with ane assent
To be forespeaker in the parliament.

Wha had been there, and liken for to hear
His facound toung, and termis exquisite,
Of rethorick the practick he micht lear,
In brief sermone ane pregnant sentence wryte:
Before Cupid veiling his cap alyte,
Speiris the cause of that vocatioun,
And he anone shew his intentioun.

bair bore
haw pallid
ane churl, etc. man in the moon,
　put there for theft of thorns,
　according to folk-lore, for-
bidden to rise further in the
　nine planetary spheres of
　heaven (*See* Dante's *Paradiso*)
facound eloquent
speiris inquires

'Lo!' (quod Cupid), 'wha will blaspheme the name
Of his awin God, outher in word or deid,
To all Goddis he dois baith lak and shame,
And suld have bitter panis to his meid.
I say this by yone wretchit Cresseid,
The whilk throu me was sum time flour of luve,
Me and my mother starklie can repruve,

'Saying of her great infelicitie
I was the cause, and my mother Venus,
Ane blind Goddes, her cald, that micht not see,
With sclander and defame injurious;
Thus her leving unclene and lecherous
Sho wald returne on me and my mother,
To whom I shew my grace abone all uther.

'And sen ye are all sevin deificait,
Participant of devyne sapience,
This great injurie done to our hie estait
Me think with pane we suld mak recompence;
Was never to Goddess done sic violence.
Asweill for you, as for myself I say,
Therefore gae help to revenge I you pray.'

Mercurius to Cupid gave answeir
And said: 'Shir King my counsall is that ye
Refer you to the hiest planeit here,
And tak to him the lawest of degree,
The pane of Cresseid for to modifie;
As god Saturn, with him tak Cynthia.'
'I am content' (quod he), 'to tak they twa.'

Then thus proceedit Saturn and the Mone,
When they the mater ripelie had degest,
For the dispite to Cupid sho had done,

lak disparagement   deificait deified, divine
meid reward   modifie determine
starklie strongly, violently

And to Venus oppin and manifest,
In all her life with pane to be opprest,
And torment sair, with seikness incurabill,
And to all lovers be abominabill.

This duleful sentence Saturn tuik on hand,
And passit doun where carefull Cresseid lay,
And on her heid he laid ane frostie wand;
Then lawfullie on this wyse can he say:
'Thy great fairness and all thy bewtie gay,
Thy wantoun blude, and eik thy goldin hair,
Here I exclude frae thee for evermair.

'I change thy mirth into melancholy,
Whilk is the mother of all pensiveness;
Thy moisture and thy heit in cald and dry;
Thyne insolence, thy play and wantoness
To great disease; thy pomp and thy richess
In mortall need; and great penuritie
Thou suffer sall, and as ane beggar dee.'

O cruell Saturn! fraward and angrie,
Hard is thy dome, and too malitious;
On fair Cresseid why hes thou nae mercie,
Whilk was sae sweet, gentill and amorous?
Withdraw thy sentence and be gracious
As thou was never; so shawis thou thy deid,
Ane wraikfull sentence gevin on fair Cresseid.

Then Cynthia, when Saturn past away,
Out of her sait discendit doun belyve,
And read ane bill on Cresseid where sho lay,
Contening this sentence diffinityve:
'Fra heit of bodie I thee now depryve,
And to thy seikness sall be nae recure,
But in dolour thy dayis to indure.

duleful tragic   *wraikfull* vengeful
eik also   *belyve* swiftly

'Thy cristall ene minglit with blude I mak,
Thy voice sae clear, unpleasand hoar and hace,
Thy lustie lyre owerspred with spottis blak,
And lumpis haw appearand in thy face.
Where thou cumis, ilk man sall flee the place.
Thus sall thou go begging frae hous to hous
With cup and clapper like ane Lazarous.'

This doolie dream, this ugly visioun
Brocht to ane end, Cresseid frae it awoke,
And all that court and convocatioun
Vanishit away, then raise sho up and tuik
Ane poleist glass, and her shaddow culd luik:
And when sho saw her face sae deformait
Gif sho in hart was wae aneuch God wait.

Weeping full sair, 'Lo what it is' (quod sho),
'With fraward langage for to muve and steir
Our craibit Goddis, and sae is seen on me!
My blaspheming now have I bocht full dear.
All eardlie joy and mirth I set arreir.
Allace this day, allace this wofull tyde,
When I began with my Goddis for to chyde.'

By this was said ane chyld come frae the hall
To warn Cresseid the supper was reddy,
First knokkit at the dure, and syne culd call:
'Madame your father biddis you cum in hy.
He hes mervell sae lang on grouf ye ly,
And sayis your prayers beer too lang sum deill:
The goddis wait all your intent full weill.'

hoar aged	*wait* knows
hace hoarse	*arreir* behind
lyre skin	*hy* haste
lazarous leper	*grouf* prostrate, grovelling
shaddow reflection	

Quod sho: 'Fair chyld gae to my father dear,
And pray him cum to speak with me anone.'
And sae he did, and said: 'dochter what cheer?'
'Allace' (quod sho), 'Father my mirth is gone.'
'How sae' (quod he); and sho can all expone
As I have tauld, the vengeance and the wraik
For her trespass, Cupid on her culd tak.

He luikit on her ugly lipper face,
The whilk before was white as lillie flour,
Wringand his handis oftimes he said allace
That he had levit to see that wofull hour,
For he knew weill that there was nae succour
To her seikness, and that doublit his pane.
Thus was there care aneuch betuix them twane.

When they togither murnit had full lang,
Quod Cresseid: 'Father, I wald not be kend.
Therefore in secreit wyse ye let me gang
Into yone hospitall at the tounis end.
And thither sum meat for cheritie me send
To leive upon, for all mirth in this eard
Is frae me gane, sic is my wickit weird.'

Then in ane mantill and ane baver hat,
With cup and clapper wonder privily,
He opnit ane secreit yett, and out thereat
Convoyit her, that nae man suld espy,
Into ane village half ane mile thereby,
Deliverit her in at the spittaill hous,
And daylie sent her part of his almous.

expone expound   *spittaill hous* hospital
weird fate   *almous* alms
baver hat one hiding the face

Sum knew her weill, and sum had nae knawledge
Of her because sho was sae deformait,
With bylis blak owerspred in her visage,
And her fair colour fadit and alterait.
Yit they presumit for her hie regrait
And still murning, sho was of nobill kin:
With better will therefore they tuik her in.

The day passit, and Phebus went to rest,
The cloudis blak owerwhelmit all the sky.
God wait gif Cresseid was ane sorrowfull gest,
Seeing that uncouth fare and harbery:
But meat or drink sho dressit her to ly
In ane dark corner of the hous allone.
And on this wyse weeping, sho made her moan:

THE COMPLAINT OF CRESSEID

'O sop of sorrow, sonkin into care:
O cative Cresseid, for now and ever mair,
Gane is thy Joy and all thy mirth in eard,
Of all blythnes now art thou blaiknit bair.
There is nae salve may save thee of thy sair,
Fell is thy fortoun, wickit is thy weird:
Thy bliss is baneist, and thy baill on breird,
Under the earth, God gif I gravin were:
Where nane of Greece nor yit of Troy micht heird.

'Where is thy chalmer wantounlie beseen?
With burely bed and bankouris browderit bene,
Spycis and wine to thy collatioun,
The cuppis all of gold and silver sheen:

bylis boils	*heird* hear it
regrait remorse	*burely* handsome
harbery lodging	*bankouris* trappings
sonkin steeped	*browderit* embroidered
blaiknit blackened	*bene* well
baill on breird woe is burgeoning	

The sweet meatis, servit in plaitis clene,
With saipheron saus of ane gude seasoun:
Thy gay garmentis with mony gudely goun,
Thy pleasand lawn pinnit with goldin prene:
All is areir, thy great royall renoun.

Where is thy garding with thir gressis gay?
And freshe flowris, whilk the Quene Floray
Had paintit pleasandly in everie pane,
Whair thou was wont full merilye in May,
To walk and tak the dew by it was day
And hear the merle and mavis mony ane,
With ladyis fair in carrolling to gane,
And see the Royall Rinkis in their array,
In garmentis gay garnishit on everie grane.

'Thy great triumphand fame and hie honour,
Where thou was callit of eardlye wichtis flour,
All is decayit, thy weird is welterit so.
Thy hie estait is turnit in darkness dour.
This lipper lodge tak for thy burelie bour.
And for thy bed tak now ane bunch of stro;
For waillit wyne, and meatis thou had tho,
Tak mowlit breid, perrie and cedar sour:
But cup and clapper, now is all ago.

'My clear voice, and courtlie carrolling,
Where I was wont with ladyis for to sing,
Is rawk as rook, full hideous hoar and hace;

saipheron saffron
prene pin
merle blackbird
carrolling dancing carols
rinkis notabilities
grane colour
welterit reversed, turned upside
   down

dour bleak
stro straw
waillit choice
tho then
mowlit mouldy
cedar cider
rawk raucous

My pleasand port all utheris precelling,
Of lustiness I was hald maist conding.
Now is deformit the figour of my face,
To luik on it, nae leid now liking hes:
Sowpit in syte, I say with sair siching,
Lodgeit amang the lipper leid: 'Allace!'

'O ladyis fair of Troy and Greece, attend
My miserie, whilk nane may comprehend.
My frivoll fortoun, my infelicitie:'
My great mischief whilk nae man can amend.
Bewar in tyme, approachis near the end,
And in your mind ane mirrour mak of me:
As I am now, peradventure that ye
For all your micht may cum to that same end,
Or ellis waur, gif ony waur may be.

'Nocht is your fairness but ane fading flour,
Nocht is your famous laud and hie honour
But wind inflat in uther mennis earis.
Your rosing reid to rotting sall retour:
Exempill mak of me in your memour,
Whilk of sic thingis wofull witnes beiris,
All welth in eard, away as wind it weiris.
Bewar therefore, approachis near the hour:
Fortoun is fikkill, when sho beginnis and steiris.'

Thus chidand with her drearie desteny,
Weeping, sho woke the nicht frae end to end.
But all in vane; her dule, her carefull cry

precelling excelling   *lipper leid* leper-folk
conding worthy   *waur* worse
leid person(s)   *rosing reid* rosy-complexion
sowpit soaked   *steiris* stirs
syte grief   *dule* grief

Micht not remeid, nor yet her murning mend.
Ane lipper lady raise and til her wend,
And said: 'Why spurnis thou aganis the wall,
To slay thy self, and mend naething at all?

'Sen thy weeping doubillis but thy wo,
I counsall thee mak vertew of ane need.
To lear to clap thy clapper to and fro,
And lear efter the law of lipper leid.
There was nae buit, but furth with them sho yeid,
Frae place to place, whill cauld and hunger sair
Compellit her to be ane rank beggair.

That samin time of Troy the garnisoun,
Whilk had to chiftane worthie Troylus,
Throu jeopardie of weir had strikken doun
Knichtis of Greece in number mervellous,
With great triumph and laud victorious
Agane to Troy richt royallie they raid
The way where Cresseid with the lipper baid.

Seeing that companie, they come all with ane stevin
They gave ane cry and shuik cuppis gude speid.
Said 'worthie lordis for goddis luve of Hevin,
To us lipper part of your almous deed.'
Then to their cry nobill Troylus tuik heed,
Having pietie, near by the place can pass
Where Cresseid sat, not witting what sho was.

Then upon him sho kest up baith her ene,
And with ane blenk it come into his thocht,
That he sumtime her face before had sene,
But sho was in sic plye he knew her nocht;

remeid cure	*weir* war
wend went, made her way	*ane stevin* united clamour
buit alternative, help	*blenk* glance
yeid went	*plye* plight

Yet then her luik into his mind it brocht
The sweet visage and amorous blenking
Of fair Cresseid, sumtime his awin darling.

Nae wonder was, suppose in mind that he
Tuik her figure sae soon, and lo now why?
The idol of ane thing, in case may be
Sae deep imprentit in the fantasy
That it deludis the wittis outwardly,
And sae appearis in form and like estait,
Within the mind as it was figurait.

Ane spark of luve then til his hart culd spring
And kendlit all his bodie in ane fire.
With hait fever ane sweit and trimbling
Him tuik, whill he was reddie to expire.
To beir his sheild, his breist began to tire.
Within ane whyle he changit mony hew,
And nevertheless not ane ane uther knew.

For knichtlie pietie and memoriall
Of fair Cresseid, ane gyrdill can he tak,
Ane purs of gold, and mony gay jowell,
And in the skirt of Cresseid doun can swak;
Then raid away, and not ane word he spak,
Pensive in hart, whill he come to the toun,
And for great care oftsyis almaist fell doun.

The lipper folk to Cresseid then can draw,
To see the equall distributioun
Of the almous, but when the gold they saw,
Ilk ane to uther previlie can roun,

tuik, etc. half-recognized her
idol image
in case perchance
figurait imaged

sweit sweat
can swak flung
oftsyis ofttimes
can roun whispered

And said: 'Yone lord hes mair affectioun,
How ever it be, unto yone lazarous
Than to us all, we knaw by his almous.'

'What lord is yone' (quod sho), 'have ye nae feill,
Hes done to us so great humanitie?'
'Yes' (quod a lipper man), 'I knaw him weill,
Shir Troylus it is, gentill and free:'
When Cresseid understude that it was he,
Stiffer than steell, there stert ane bitter stound
Throuout her hart, and fell doun to the ground.

When sho overcome, with siching sair and sad,
With mony carefull cry and cald 'Ochane!
Now is my breist with stormie stoundis stad,
Wrappit in wo, ane wretch full will of wane.'
Than swoonit sho oft, or sho culd refrane,
And ever in her swooning cryit sho thus:
'O fals Cresseid and trew knicht Troylus!

'Thy luve, thy lawtie, and thy gentilness,
I countit small in my prosperitie,
Sae elevait I was in wantoness,
And clam upon the fickill wheill sae hie:
All faith and luve I promissit to thee,
Was in the self fickill and frivolous:
O fals Cresseid, and trew knicht Troylus!

'For luve, of me thou keept gude continence,
Honest and chaist in conversatioun,
Of all wemen protectour and defence
Thou was, and helpit their opinioun.

feill knowledge   lawtie loyalty
stound pang   wheill wheel of Fortune
stad beset, bested   the self myself
will of wane unstable   opinioun good reputation

My mind in fleshlie foull affectioun
Was inclynit to lustis lecherous:
Fy fals Cresseid, O trew knicht Troylus!

'Lovers bewar and tak gude heed about
Whom that ye luve, for whom ye suffer paine.
I lat you wit, there is richt few thereout
Whom ye may traist to have trew luve agane.
Preif when ye will, your labour is in vain.
Therefore, I reid, ye tak them as ye find,
For they are sad as weddercock in wind,

'Because I knaw the great unstabilness
Brukkill as glass, into my self I say,
Traisting in uther als great unfaithfulness:
Als unconstant, and als untrew of fay.
Thocht sum be trew, I wait richt few are they,
Wha findis treuth, lat him this lady ruse:
Nane but my self as now I will accuse.'

When this was said, with paper sho sat doun,
And on this maneir made her Testament.
'Here I beteiche my corps and carioun
With wormis and with taidis to be rent.
My cup and clapper and myne ornament,
And all my gold the lipper folk sall have
When I am deid, to burie me in grave.

'This royal ring, set with this rubie reid,
Whilk Troylus in drowrie to me send,
To him agane I leiv it when I am deid,
To mak my carefull deid unto him kend:

thereout living	*fay* faith
preif test	*ruse* value, praise
reid counsel, advise	*taidis* toads
sad serious	*drowrie* troth
brukkill brittle	*kend* known

Thus I conclude shortlie and mak ane end,
My spreit I leiv to Diane where sho dwellis,
To walk with her in waste woodis and wellis.

'O Diomeid, thou hes baith brooch and belt
Whilk Troylus gave me in takning
Of his trew luve' – and with that word sho swelt.
And soon ane lipper man tuik off the ring,
Syne buryit her withoutin tarying.
To Troylus furthwith the ring he bair,
And of Cresseid the deith he can declair.

When he had hard her great infirmitie,
Her legacie and lamentatioun,
And how sho endit in sic povertie,
He swelt for woe, and fell doun in ane swoon.
For great sorrow his hart to burst wes boun.
Siching full sadlie, said: 'I can no more!
Sho wes untrew, and woe is me therefore!'

Sum said he made ane tomb of merble gray,
And wrait her name and superscriptioun,
And laid it on her grave, wherethat she lay,
In goldin letteris, conteining this reasoun:
'Lo, fair ladyis, Cresseid of Troyis toun,
Sumtime countit the flour of womanheid,
Under this stane, late lipper, lyis deid.'

Now, worthie wemen, in this ballet short
Made for your worship and instuctioun,
Of cheritie, I monish and exhort –
Ming not your luve with false deceptioun.
Bear in your mind this short conclusioun
Of fair Cresseid, as I have said before.
Sen sho is deid, I speak of her no more.

wellis marshes   *swelt* fainted
swelt expired   *boun* ready

ROBENE AND MAKYNE

Robene sat on gude green hill,
Keepand a flock of fee:
Mirry Makyne said him til,
'Robene, thou rew on me;
I have thee luvit loud and still
Thir yearis two or three;
My dule in dern but gif thou dill,
Doutless but dreid I dee.'

Robene answert, 'by the Rude,
Naething of luve I knaw,
But keepis my sheep undir yone wude,
Lo whair thay raik on raw:
What hes marrit thee in thy mude,
Makyne, to me thou shaw;
Or what is luve, or to be lude?
Fane wald I lear that law.'

'At luvis lair gif thou will lear,
Tak there ane a b c:
Be heynd, courtass, and fair of feir,
Wyse, hardy and free;
So that no danger do thee deir,
What dule in dern thou dree;
Press thee with pane at all poweir,
Be patient and previe.'

fee sheep	*marrit* marred
rew have pity	*lude* loved
loud, etc. openly and secretly	*lair* lore
dule, etc. my hidden woe unless you share	*heynd* gentle
	feir manner
doutless, etc. I shall certainly die	*deir* frighten
raik on raw range in row	*dree* endure

Robene answerit her agane,
'I wait not what is luve;
But I have mervell incertane
What makis thee this wanruve:
The weader is fair, and I am fane,
My sheep gois haill above;
And we wald play us in this plane,
They wald us baith reprove.'

'Robene, tak tent unto my tale,
And wirk all as I reid,
And thou sall have my hairt all haill,
Eik and my madinheid.
Sen god sendis bute for baill,
And for murning remeid,
In dern with thee, but gif I daill,
Doutless I am but deid.'

'Makyne, to morne this ilka tide,
And ye will meet me here,
Peraventure my sheep may gang beside,
Whill we have liggit full near;
But maugre have I and I byde
Frae they begin to steer;
What lyis on hairt I will not hyde,
Makyne, then mak gude cheer.'

wait know	*daill* deal, dally
wanruve uneasy	*ilka tide* same time
fane glad	*liggit* lain
and if (an)	*maugre* ill-will (Fr. *malgré*)
reid advise	*byde* remain, linger
eik and and also	*frae* from the time that
bute for baill cure for grief	*steer* stir
dern secret	

'Robene, thou reivis me roif and rest;
I luve but thee allone.'
'Makyne, adew, the sun gois west,
The day is near hand gone.'
'Robene, in dule I am so drest,
That luve wilbe my bane.'
'Ga luve, Makyne, where evir thou list,
For lemman I bid nane.'

'Robene, I stand in sic a style;
I sich, and that full sair.'
'Makyne, I have been here this while;
At hame god gif I wair.'
'My huny, Robene, talk ane while,
Gif thou will do nae mair.'
'Makyne, sum uthir man begyle,
For hamewart I will fair.'

Robene on his wayis went,
Als licht as leaf of tree;
Makyne murnit in her intent,
And trowd him nevir to see.
Robene braid attour the bent;
Then Makyne cryit on hie,
'Now may thou sing, for I am shent!
What alis luve at me?'

Makyne went hame withoutin fail,
Full weary eftir couth weep:
Then Robene in a fulfair dail
Assemblit all his sheep.
By that sum pairt of Makynis ail

reivis robs
roif peace
drest smothered
bane death, doom
style state

sich sigh
wair were
braid, etc. strode across the moor
hie high, aloud
eftir, etc. like to weep

Outthrou his hairt couth creep;
He followit her fast, there til assail,
And til her tuke gude keep.

'Abide, abide, thou fair Makyne,
A word for ony thing;
For all my luve it sall be thine,
Withoutin depairting.
All hail thy hairt for til have mine
Is all my coveting;
My sheep to-morn whill houris nine
Will need of no keeping.'

'Robene, thou hes hard sung and say
In gestis and stories auld,
The man that will nocht when he may,
Sall have nocht when he wald.
I pray to Jesu every day
Mot eik their caris cauld
That first pressis with thee to play,
By firth, forest, or fauld.'

'Makyne, the nicht is soft and dry,
The weader is warm and fair,
And the green wood richt near us by
To walk attour all where;
There may nae janglour us espy,
That is to luve contrair;
Therein, Makyne, baith ye and I
Unseen we may repair.'

'Robene, that warld is all away
And quite brocht til ane end,
And nevir agane thereto, perfay,

gestis romances   *fauld* pasture
mot eik may compound   *janglour* slanderer
firth field   *perfay* by faith

Sall it be as thou wend;
For of my pane thou made it play,
And all in vane I spend;
As thou hes done, sae sall I say,
Murn on, I think to mend.'

'Makyne, the hope of all my heill,
My hairt on thee is set,
And evirmair to thee be leal,
Whill I may leve but let;
Nevir to feill, as utheris feill,
What grace that evir I get.'
'Robene, with thee I will nocht deal;
Adew, for thus we met.'

Makyne went hame blyth anewch,
Attour the holtis hair;
Robene murnit, and Makyne lewch,
Sho sang, he sichit sair;
And so left him, baith woe and wreuch,
In dolour and in care,
Keepand his hird under a heuch,
Amangis the holtis hair.

THE TALE OF THE SHEEP AND THE DOG

Esope ane tale puttis in memorie
How that ane dog, because that he wes puir,
Callit ane sheep to the consistorie,
Ane certane breid frae him for to recure.

wend desire	*attour, etc.* over the grey hills
heill well-being	*lewch* laughed
leal loyal	*heuch* cliff
but let without hindrance	*puir* poor
feill fail	*breid* loaf of bread
anewch enough	*recure* recover

Ane fraudfull wolf was juge that time, and bure
Authoritie and jurisdictioun,
And on the sheep send furth ane strait summoun.

For by the use and course and commoun style,
On this maner made his citatioun:
'I, Maister Wolf, partless of fraud and gyle,
Under the panis of Hie Suspensioun,
Of Great Cursing and Interdictioun,
Shir Sheep, I charge thee for to compeir,
And answer to ane dog before me here.'

Shir Corbie Ravin wes made apparitour,
Wha pykit had full mony sheepis ee;
The charge hes tane and on the letteris bure;
Summonit the sheep before the wolf, that he
Peremptourlie, within twa dayis or three,
Compeir under the panis in this bill,
'To hear what perrie dog will say thee til.'

This summondis made before witness anew
The ravin – as to his office weill effeird;
Indorsat hes the writ, and on he flew;
The selie sheep durst lay nae mouth on eard
Till he before the awfull juge appeird,
The 'our of cause whilk that the juge usit than,
When Hesperus to shaw his face began.

The fox wes clerk and noter in the cause;
The gled, the graip, at the bar couth stand;
As advocatis expert into the lawis
The doggis plea togither tuke on hand,

bure bore	*effeird* fitted
partless free	*selie* innocent
compeir, compair stand trial	*than* then
apparitour court-clerk	*gled* kite
tane taken	*graip* vulture
perrie hairy	

Whilk were confidderit straitlie in ane band
Aganis the sheep to procure the sentence;
Thoch it wes false they had nae conscience.

The clerk callit the sheep, and he wes there;
The advocatis on this wyse couth propone:
'Ane certane breid worth fyve shilling or mair
Thou aw the dog, of whilk the term is gone.'
Off his awin heid, but advocate, allone,
The sheep avysitlie gave answer in the case:
'Here I decline the juge, the time, the place.

'This is my cause, in motive and effect:
The law sayis it is richt perrillous
Til enter in plea before ane juge suspect;
And ye, Shir Wolf, hes been richt odious
To me, for with your tuskis ravenous
Hes slane full mony kinnismen of mine:
Therefore juge as suspect I you decline.

'And shortlie, of this court ye memberis all,
Baith assessouris, clerk and advocate,
To me and mine are enemies mortall,
And ay hes been, as mony shepherd wate;
The place is fer, the time is feriate;
Wherefor nae juge suld sit in consistory
Sae lait at evin; I you accuse forthy.'

When that the juge in this wise wes accusit,
He bad the parteis chuse with ane assent
Twa arbeteris, as in the law is usit,
For to declair and give arbitriment

propone expound   *fer* far
aw owe   *feriate* legal vacation
wate knows   *forthy* therefore

Whither the sheep suld answer in jugement
Before the wolf; and so they did but weir,
Of whom the namis efterwart ye sall hear.

The bear, the brock, the mater tuke on hand,
For to decide gif this exceptioun
Wes of nae strenth nor lawfully micht stand;
And thereupon as jugis they sat doun
And held ane lang while disputatioun,
Seikand full mony decreitis of the law,
And glossis als, the veritie to knaw.

Of civil law volumis full mony they revolve,
The codies and digestis new and auld;
(Contra and pro, strait) argumentis they resolve,
Sum objecting, and sum can hauld;
For prayer or price trow ye that they wald fauld?
But hauld the gloss and text of the decreis
As trew jugis; I beshrew them ay that lee's.

Shortlie to mak ane end of this debait:
The arbiters then swearand plane,
The sentence gave and process fulminait:
The sheep suld pass before the wolf agane
And end his plea. Then wes he naething fane,
For frae their sentence couth he not appeal.
On clerkis I dout gif this sentence wes leill.

The sheep agane before the wolf derenyeit,
But advocate, abasitlie couth stand.
Up rais the dog and on the sheep thus plenyeit:
'Ane sum I payit have before-the-hand
For certaine breid.' Thereto ane borrow he fand

but weir without argument	*fulminait* issued
brock badger	*on clerkis, etc.* the learned can
sum, etc. objecting to some,	estimate this decision
upholding others	*borrow* pledge
fauld give up	*fand* found

That wrangouslie the sheep did hald the breid –
Whilk he denyit; and there began the pleid.

And when the sheep this strife had contestait,
The justice in the cause furth can proceed;
Lowrence the actis and process wrait,
And thus the plea unto the end they speed.
This cursit court, corruptit all for meid,
Aganis gude faith, law, and eik conscience,
For this false dog pronuncit the sentence.

And it til put to executioun
The wolf chargit the sheep, without delay,
Under the panis of interdictioun,
The sum of silver or the breid to pay.
Of this sentence, allace, what sall I say,
Whilk damnit hes the selie innocent
And justifyit the wrangous jugement?

The sheep dreidand mair the executioun,
Obeyand to the sentence, he couth tak
His way unto ane merchant of the toun,
And sauld the wool that he bure on his back,
Syne bocht the breid and to the dog couth mak
Reddie payment, as it commandit was;
Naikit and bare syne to the field couth pass.

THE TALE OF THE UPONLANDIS MOUSE
AND THE BURGESS MOUSE

Aesope mine authour makis mentioun
Of twa mice, and they were sisteris dear,
Of wham the eldest dwelt in ane borough-toun,

pleid discussion	*couth tak* took
meid gain	*couth mak* made
eik also	*syne* then
dreidand dreading	*couth pass* passed

The uther wonnit uponland weill near,
Solitar, while under busk, while under breir,
Whilis in the corn, and uther mennis skaith,
As outlawis dois and livis on their waith.

This rural mouse into the winter-tide
Had hunger, cauld, and tholit great distress;
The uther mouse that in the burgh can bide,
Was gild-brother and made ane free burgess –
Toll-free als, but custom mair or less,
And freedom had to gae wherever sho list,
Amang the cheese in ark, and meal in kist.

Ane time when sho wes full and unfutesair,
Sho tuke in mind her sister uponland,
And langit for to hear of her weilfair,
To see what life sho had under the wand:
Barefute, allone, with pikestaff in her hand,
As puir pilgrim sho passit out of toun,
To seek her sister baith owre dale and doun.

Furth mony wilsum wayis can sho walk;
Throu moss and muir, throu bankis, busk and breir,
Sho ran cryand whill sho come to a balk:
'Cum furth to me, my awin sister dear;
Cry peep anis!' With that the mouse culd hear,
And knew her voice, as kinnisman will do,
By very kind; and furth sho come her to.

wonnit dwelt	*kist* chest
uponland in the countryside	*wand* rod
busk bush	*wilsum* bewildering, wild
skaith harm	*balk* field
waith cunning, hunting-skill	*anis* once
tholit suffered	*kind* family-likeness
but custom untaxed	

The hartlie joy God give ye had seen
Beis kith when that thir sisteris met!
And great kindness wes shawin them between,
For whilis they leuch, and whilis for joy they gret,
Whilis kissit sweet, whilis in armis plet;
And thus they fure whill soberit wes their mude,
Syne fute for fute unto the chalmer yude.

As I hard say, it wes ane sober wane,
Of fog and fern full febilie wes made –
Ane sillie sheill under ane steidfast stane,
Of whilk the entress wes not hie nor braid;
And in the samin they went but mair abaid,
Without fyre or candill birnand bricht,
For commonly sic pykeris luvis not licht.

When they were lugit thus, thir sely mice,
The youngest sister into her butterie glide,
And brocht furth nuttis and candill insteid of spice;
Gif this wes gude fare, I dout on them beside.
The burgess-mouse prompit furth in pride,
And said: 'Sister, is this your daily fude?'
'Why not?' quod sho. 'Is not this meat richt gude?'

'Na, by my saul, I think it but ane scorn.'
'Madame,' quod sho, 'ye be the mair to blame;
My mother said, sister, when we were born,
That I and ye lay baith within ane wame:
I keep the rate and custom of my dame,
And of my living into povertie,
For landis have we nane in propertie.'

hartlie cordial
beis kith was shown
gret wept
fure fared
yude went
fog foliage
sheill shelter

abaid abiding, delay
pykeris pilferers
sely, selie harmless
I dout, etc. I leave to others to
    judge
wame womb, abdomen
rate standard

'My fair sister,' quod sho, 'have me excusit –
This rude diet and I can not accord;
To tender meat my stomak is ay usit,
For whilis I fare als weill as ony lord;
Thir witherit peas and nuttis, or they be bored,
Will brek my teeth, and mak my wame full sklender,
Whilk wes before usit to meatis tender.'

'Weil, weil, sister,' quod the rural mouse,
'Give it please you, sic thing as ye see here,
Baith meat and drink, harberie and house,
Sall be your awin, will ye remain all year;
Ye sall it have with blyth and merry cheer –
And that suld mak the messis that are rude,
Amang freindis, richt tender and wonder gude.

'What plesure is in the feastis delicate,
The whilks are given with ane gloumand brou?
Ane gentill hart is better recreate
With blyth curage, than seethe to him ane cou;
Ane modicum is mair for til allou,
Sae that gude will be carver at the dais,
Than thrawin vult and mony spicit mess.'

For all her merry exhortatioun,
This burgess-mouse had littil will to sing;
But heavilie sho kest her browis doun
For all the dainties that sho culd her bring.
Yet at the last sho said, half in hething:
'Sister, this victual and your royal feast
May weill suffice unto ane rural beast.

or before   *vult* visage
harberie lodging   *hething* scorn
thrawin twisted, disapproving

'Let be this hole, and cum into my place;
I sall to you shaw by experience
My Gude Friday is better nor your Pase;
My dish-lickings is worth your hail expense.
I have housis aneuch of great defence;
Of cat nor fall-trap I have nae dreid.'
'I grant,' quod sho; and on togither they yeid.

In stubbil array throu gress and corn,
And under buskis privilie couth they creep –
The eldest wes the guide and went before,
The younger to her wayis tuke gude keep;
On nicht they ran, and on the day can sleep,
Whill in the morning, or the laverok sang,
They fand the toun, and in blythlie couth gang.

Not far frae thince unto ane worthie wane,
This burgess brocht them soon where they suld be;
Without 'God speed!' their herberie wes tane,
Into ane spence with vittel great plentie;
Baith cheese and butter upon their skelfis hie,
And flesh and fish aneuch, baith fresh and salt,
And seckis full of meal and eik of malt.

Eftir when they disposit were to dine,
Withoutin grace they wesh and went to meat,
With all coursis that cukis culd devine –
Mutton and beef, strikin in tailyeis great;
Ane lordis fare thus couth they counterfeit –
Except ane thing – they drank the watter clear
Insteid of wine: but yet they made gude cheer.

Pase Easter feast   *spence* larder
aneuch enough   *skelfis* shelves
yeid went   *hie* high
keep heed   *wesh* washed
laverok lark   *tailyeis* slices
wane dwelling

With blyth upcast and merrie countenance,
The eldest sister speirit at her guest
Gif that sho by reason fand difference
Betwix that chalmer and her sarie nest.
'Yea, dame,' quod sho, 'how lang will this lest?'
'For evermair, I wait, and langer to.'
'Gif it be sae, ye are at ease,' quod sho.

Til eik their cheer ane subcharge furth sho brocht –
Ane plait of grottis, and ane dish full of meal;
Thraf-caikkis als, I trow, sho spairit nocht
Aboundantlie about her for to deal;
And mane full fine sho brocht insteid of geill,
And ane white candill out of ane coffer stall,
Insteid of spice to gust their mouth withal.

Thus made they merry whill they micht nae mair,
And 'Hail, Yule! Hail!' cryit upon hie.
Yet efter joy oftimes cummis care,
And troubil efter great prosperitie:
Thus as they sat in all their jollitie,
The spencer come with keyis in his hand,
Openit the dure, and them at denner fand.

They taryit not to wesh, as I suppose,
But on to-gae, wha that micht foremost win.
The burgess has ane hole, and in sho goes;
Her sister had nae hole to hide her in:
To see that silly mouse it was great sin,
Sae desolate and will of ane gude reid;
For very dreid sho fell in swoon near deid.

upcast raillery
wait know
eik add to
subcharge second course
grottis husked oats
thraf-caikkis wheaten cakes
mane fine bread

geill jelly
stall stolen
spencer butler
win attain
and will, etc. at a loss for good counsel

But as God wald, it fell ane happie case;
The spencer had nae leisure for to bide,
Nowther to seek nor search, to scare nor chase;
But on he went, and left the dure ope wide.
The bauld burgess his passing weill hes spied;
Out of her hole sho come, and cryit on hie:
'How fare ye, sister? Cry peep, wherever ye be!'

This rural mouse lay flatling on the ground,
And for the deith sho wes full sair dreidand,
For til her hart straik mony woeful stound;
As in ane fever sho trimblit fute and hand.
And when her sister in sic plye her fand,
For very petie sho began to greit,
Syne comfort her with wordis humble and sweet.

'Why lie ye thus? Rise, my sister dear!
Cum to your meat; this peril is owerpast.'
The other answerit her with heavie cheer:
'I may not eat, sae sair I am aghast!
I had leifer thir forty dayis fast
With water-kail, and to gnaw beans or peas,
Than all your feast in this dreid and disease'.

With fair treatie yet sho gart her uprise,
And to the board they went and togither sat;
And scantlie had they drunkin ance or twice,
When in come Gib Hunter, our jollie cat,
And bade 'God speed!' The burgess up with that,
And to the hole sho went as fire on flint:
Baudrons the other by the back hes hint.

dure door	*water-kail* cabbage-water
plye plight	*gart* made, caused
greit weep	*hint* seized
leifer rather	

Frae fute to fute he kest her to and frae,
Whilis up, whilis doun, als cant as ony kid;
Whilis wald he let her rin under the strae,
Whilis wald he wink, and play with her buk-heid.
Thus to the selie mouse great pain he did,
Whill at the last, throu fortune and gude hap,
Betwix ane board, and the wall, she crap.

And up in haste behind ane parraling
Sho clam sae hie that Gilbert micht not get her –
Syne by the cluke there craftilie can hing,
Till he wes gane; her cheer wes all the better.
Syne doun sho lap when there wes nane to let her,
And to the burgess-mouse loud can sho cry:
'Fareweill, sister, thy feast here I defy!

'Thy mangerie is mingit all with care.
Thy goose is gude, thy gansell sour as gall.
The subcharge of they service is but sair.
Sae sall thou find here-efterwart nae fall.
I thank yon curtain and yon perpall wall
Of my defence nou frae yon cruel beast.
Almichty God keep me frae sic ane feast!

'Were I into the kith that I come frae,
For weill nor woe suld I never cum again'.
With that sho tuke her leave and furth can gae,
Whilis throu the corn, and whilis throu the plain.
When sho wes furth and free, sho wes full fain,
And merrilie markit into the muir.
I can not tell how weill therefter sho fure.

cant playful	*mangerie* feasting
strae straw	*mingit* mingled
buk-heid hide-and-seek	*gansell* sauce
crap crept	*perpall* partition
parraling partition	*kith* home
cluke claw	*markit* marched, rode
let prevent	

But I hard say sho passit to her den
Als warm as wool, suppose it was not great;
Full beinly stuffit, baith butt and ben,
Of beanis and nuttis, peas, rye, and wheat.
Whenever sho list, sho had aneuch to eat
In quiet and ease, withoutin ony dreid:
But to her sisteris feast nae mair sho yeid.

beinly comfortably   *ben* kitchen
butt parlour

Blin Hary the Minstrel

fl. c. 1460–90

FROM THE WALLACE, *c.* 1460

—

WALLACE'S LAMENT FOR GRAHAM

When they him fand, and gude Wallace him saw,
He lichtit doun, and hint him frae them aw
In armis up; behaldand his paill face,
He kissit him, and cryit full oft, 'allace!
My best brother in warld that evir I had!
My aefald freind when I was hardest stad!'
My hope, my heill, thou was in maist honour!
My faith, my help, strenthiast in stour!
In thee was wit, freedom, and hardiness;
In thee was truth, manheid, and nobilness;
In thee was rewll, in thee was governans;
In thee was vertu withoutin varians;
In thee lawtie, in thee was great largeness;
In thee gentrice, in thee was stedfastness.
Thou was great cause of winning of Scotland,
Thoch I began, and tuke the weir on hand.
I vow to God, that has the warld in wauld,
Thy dead sall be to Southeroun full dear sauld.
Martyr thou art for Scotlandis richt and me;
I sall thee venge, or ellis tharefore to dee.'

lichtit lighted	*rewll* discipline
hint took hold of	*lawtie* loyalty
aw all	*largeness* generosity
aefald truest-hearted	*wauld* control
stad bested, oppressed	*sauld* sold

DESCRIPTION OF WALLACE

Wallace stature of greatness, and of hicht,
Was judgit thus, by discretioun of richt,
That saw him baith dissembill and in weid:
Nine quarters large he was in lenth indeed;
Third part lenth in shouders braid was he,
Richt seemly, strang, and lusty for to see,
His limbis great, with stalwart pace and sound,
His browis hard, his armes great and round.
His handis, made richt like til a palmer,
Of manlike make, with nailis great and clear.
Proportionate lang and fair was his visage;
Richt sad of speech, and able in curage;
Braid breist and heich, with sturdy crag and great;
His lippis round, his nose was square and tret;
Bowand broun hairit, on browis and breis licht,
Clear asper eyn, like diamondis bricht.
Under the chin, on the left side, was seen
By hurt, a wain; his colour was sanguine.
Woundis he had in mony divers place,
But fair and weill keepit was his face.
Of riches, he keepit no proper thing;
Gave as he won, like Alexander the king.
In time of peace, meek as a maid was he;
Where weir approchit the richt Hector was he.
To Scottis men a great credence he gave;
But knawin enemies they could him not dissaive.

dissembill undressed	*bowand* lank
in weid dressed	*breis* eyebrows
quarters quarter-ells	*asper* keen
palmer palm-tree	*wain* scar
sad serious	*weir* war
crag neck	*dissaive* deceive
tret large, shapely	

Anonymous

? early 16th Century

―――――――

THE BALLAD OF KIND KITTOCK

My Guddame wes a gay wife, but she wes richt gend.
   She dwelt furth far into France, upon Falkland Fell.
They callit her Kind Kittock, whasae her weill kend.
   She wes, like a caldron cruke, clear under kell.
They threepit that she deeit of thirst, and made a gude end.
   Eftir her dead, she dreidit nocht in hevin for to dwell.
And sae to hevin the hieway, dreidless, she wend;
   Yet she wanderit and gaed by to ane elrich well.
     She met there, as I ween,
       Ane ask ridand on a snaill,
       And cryit, 'Owretaen fellow, haill!'
       And raid ane inch behind the tail,
     Till it wes near even.

Sae she had hap to be horsit to her herbry
   At ane ailhouse near hevin, it nichtit them there.
She deeit of thirst in this warld, that gert her be so dry;
   She never ate, but drank owre meisure and mair.
She sleepit whill the morn at noon, and raise early,
   And to the yettis of hevin fast can the wife fare,

guddame grandmother	*wend* made her way
gend comic	*ask* newt
whasae whoever	*herbry* lodging
kend knew	*gert* caused
she wes, etc. she was beautiful under hat as a pot-hook	*owre* over
	whill until
threepit related	*yettis* gates

And by Sanct Peter, in at the yett she stole priviely:
   God lukit and saw her lattin in, and lewch his hert sair.
     And there, yeiris sevin,
       She livit a gude life,
       And wes our Ladyis hen wife,
       And held Sanct Peter at strife
     Aye while she wes in hevin.

She lukit out on a day and thocht richt lang
   To see the ailhouse beside, intil ane ill hour;
And out of hevin the hie gait cocht the wife gang
   For to get her a fresh drink – the ail of hevin wes sour.
She come again to hevinis yett, when the bell rang:
   Sanct Peter hat her with a club, whill a great clour
Raise in her heid, because the wife gaed wrang.
     Then to the ailhouse again she ran, the pitchers to pour,
     And for to brew and to bake.
       Freindis, I pray you hertfully,
       Gif ye be thirsty or dry,
       Drink with my Guddame, as ye gae by,
     Anys for my sake.

lewch laughed   *clour* stabbing pain
hie gait high road   *anys* once
cocht gang went

William Dunbar

?1460–?1520

MEDITATIOUN IN WINTER

In to thir dirk and drublie dayis,
Whone sabill all the hevin arrayis,
   With mistie vapouris, cloudis, and skyis,
   Nature all curage me denyis
Of sangis, ballattis, and of plays.

Whone that the nicht dois lenthin houris
With wind, with haill, and havy shouris,
   My dule spreit dois lurk for shore,
   My hart for languor dois forlore
For lack of simmer with his flouris.

I wak, I turn, sleep may I nocht.
I vexit am with havy thocht.
   This warld all owre I cast about,
   And ay the mair I am in dout,
The mair that I remeid have socht.

I am assayit on everie side.
Despair sayis ay, 'In time provide
   And get sum thing whairon to leif,
   Or with grit trouble and mischeif
Thou sall in to this court abide'.

dirk dark   *shore* apprehension
drublie dank, dismal   *forlore* weaken
dule depressed   *remeid* salvation, remedy
spreit spirit   *leif* live

Then Patience sayis, 'Be not aghast:
Haud Hope and Truth within thee fast,
   And let Fortoun work furth hir rage,
   Whome that no rasoun may assuage,
While that hir glass be run and past'.

And Prudence in my ear sayis ay,
'Why wad thou haud that will away?
   Or crave that thou may have no space,
   Thou tending to ane other place,
A journey going everie day?'

And then sayis Age, 'My freind, cum neir,
And be not strange, I thee requeir:
   Cum, brodir, by the hand me tak,
   Remember thow hes count to mak
Of all thy time thou spendit heir'.

Syne Deid casts ope his yettis wide,
Saying, 'Thir open sall thee abide:
     Albeit that thou wer neer sae stout,
     Under this lyntall sall thou lout,
Thair is nane other way beside'.

For fear of this all day I droop:
No gowd in kist, nor wine in coop,
     No ladeis bewtie, nor luvis bliss
     May let me to remember this,
How glaid that e'er I dine or soop.

yettis gates   *lout* stoop

Yet, whone the nicht beginnis to short,
It dois my spreit sum pairt confort,
     Of thocht oppressit with the shouris.
     Cum, lustie simmer! with thy flouris,
That I may leif in sum disport.

THE DANCE OF THE
SEVIN DEIDLY SYNNIS

Of Februar the fiftene nicht,
Full lang before the dayis licht,
     I lay in til a trance;
And then I saw baith hevin and hell:
Me thocht, amangis the feindis fell,
     Mahoun gart cry ane dance
Of shrewis that were nevir shrevin,
Aganis the feist of Fasternis evin
     To mak thair observance;
He bad gallandis gae graith a gyis,
And kast up gamountis in the skyis,
     That last came out of France.

'Lat see,' quod he, 'Now wha beginnis;'
With that the foull Sevin Deidly Synnis
     Begowth to leip at anis.
And first of all in dance wes Pryde,
With hair wyld bak and bonet on syde,
     Like to mak wastie wanis;

And round about him, as a wheill,
Hang all in rumpillis to the heill
     His kethat for the nanis:

Mahoun Mahomet, i.e. the devil   *at anis* at once
Fasternis evin Eve of Lent   *waistie wanis* desolate houses
graith a gyis prepare a play   *kethat* cloak
gamountis gambols, dances   *nanis* nonce

Mony proud trumpour with him trippit,
Throu skaldand fyre ay as thay skippit
  They gyrnd with hiddous granis.

Heilie harlottis on hawtane wyis
Come in with mony sindrie gyis,
  But yet leuch nevir Mahoun,
Whill preistis come in with bair shavin nekkis,
Then all the feindis leuch and made gekkis,
  Blak Belly and Bawsy Broun.

Than Yre come in with sturt and stryfe;
His hand wes ay upoun his knyfe,
  He brandeist like a bear:
Bostaris, braggaris, and barganeris,
Eftir him passit in to pairis,
  All bodin in fear of weir;
In jakkis, and strippis and bonettis of steill,
Their leggis were chainyeit to the heill,
  Frawart wes their affeir:
Sum upoun udir with brandis beft,
Sum jaggit uthiris to the heft,
  With knivis that sherp coud sheir.

Nixt in the dance followit Invy,
Fild full of feid and fellony,
  Hid malyce and dispyte;
For privie hatrent that tratour trimlit.
Him followit mony freik dissimlit,
  With fenyeit wirdis whyte;

trumpour deceiver	*jakkis* jackets
gyrnd grimaced	*affeir* bearing
granis groans	*beft* struck
hawtane proud	*feid* feud
gyis disguises	*hatrent* hatred
gekkis mocking faces	*freik* men
weir war	

And flattereris in to menis facis;
And bakbitaris in secret places,
    To lee that had delyte;
And rounaris of false lesingis;
Allace! that courtis of noble kingis
    Of them can nevir be quyte.

Nixt him in dance come Cuvatyce,
Rute of all evill and grund of vyce,
    That nevir coud be content;
Catyvis, wrechis, and ockeraris,
Hud-pykis, hurdaris, and gadderaris,
    All with that warlo went:
Out of their throtis they shot on udder
Hett moltin gold, me thocht a fudder,
    As fyreflawcht maist fervent;
Ay as they tomit them of shot,
Feindis fild them new up to the throt
    With gold of allkin prent.

Syne Sweirness, at the secound bidding,
Come like a sow out of a midding,
    Full slepy wes his grunyie:
Mony sweir bumbard belly huddron,
Mony slute daw and slepy duddroun,
    Him servit ay with sounyie;
He drew them furth in til a chainyie,
And Belliall, with a brydill renyie,
    Evir lasht them on the lunyie:

rounaris	whisperers	*sweirness*	sloth
lesingis	lies, slanders	*grunyie*	muzzle
ockeráris	userers	*sweir*	lazy
hud-pykis	misers	*bumbard belly*	huge-bellied
hurdaris	hoarders	*huddron*	drone
warlo	wizard	*slute daw*	sluttish slattern
a fudder	a great amount	*duddroun*	sloven
fyreflawcht	lightning	*sounyie*	care
tomit	emptied	*lunyie*	loin
allkin	various		

In dance they were so slaw of feit,
They gaif them in the fyre a heit,
   And made them quicker of counyie.

Then Lichery, that lathly corse,
Come bearand like a bagit horse,
   And Ydilness did him lead;
There wes with him ane ugly sort,
And mony stynkand foull tramort,
   That had in syn bene deid.
When they were entrit in the dance,
They were full strange of countenance,
   Like turkas birnand reid;
All led they uthir by the tersis,
Suppois they fylit with their ersis,
   It mycht be nae remeid.

Then the foull monstir Glutteny,
Of wame unsasiable and gredy,
   To dance he did him dress:
Him followit mony foull drunckart,
With can and coppel, cup and quart,
   In surffet and excess;
Full mony a waistless wallydrag,
With wamis unweildable, did furth wag,
   In creish that did incress:
'Drink!' ay they cryit, with mony a gaip,
The feindis gave them het leid to laip,
   Thair livery wes na less.

counyie step	*wallydrag* weakling
bagit male and randy	*creish* fat
tramort corpse	*het leid* hot lead
turkas pincers	*laip* lap
tersis penises	*livery* allowance
wame belly	

Nae menstrallis playit to them but dout,
For gleemen there were haldin out,
   By day and eik by nicht;
Except a menstrall that slew a man,
Sae til his heretage he wan,
   And entirt by breif of richt.

TO A LADYE

Sweet rose of vertew and of gentilness,
Delytsum lillie of everie lustyness,
   Richest in bontie and in bewtie cleir,
   And everie vertew that is (held most) deir,
Except onlie that ye ar mercyless.

In to your garth this day I did persew,
Thair saw I flouris that freshè wer of hew:
   Baith white and reid most lusty wer to seen,
   And halesum herbis upon stalkis green:
Yet leif nor flour find could I nane of rew.

I dout that Merch, with his cauld blastis keen,
Hes slain this gentill herb that I of mene,
   Whois peteous deith dois to my hart sic pane
   That I wad mak to plant his rute again,
So confortand his leavis unto me been.

FROM THE TRETIS OF THE TWA MARIIT WEMEN AND THE WEDO

Apon the Midsummer even, mirriest of nichtis,
I muvit furth allane, near as midnicht wes past,
Besyde ane gudelie green garth, full of gay flouris,

eik also	*rew* rue (mercy)
garth garden	

Hedgeit, of ane huge hicht, with hawthorne trees;
Whereon ane bird, on ane branche, so birst out her notis
That never ane blythfuller bird was on the beuch hard:
What throu the sugarat sound of her sang glaid,
And throu the savour sanative of the sweet flouris,
I drew in dern to the dyke to dirkin efter mirthis;
The dew donkit the daill and dynnit the foulis.

   I hard, under ane holyn hevinlie green hewit,
Ane hie speech, at my hand, with hautand wordis;
With that in haist to the hedge so hard I inthrang
That I was heildit with hawthorn and with heynd leveis:
Throu pikis of the plet thorne I presandlie luikit,
Gif ony persoun wald approche within that pleasand garding.

   I saw three gay ladeis sit in ane green arbeir,
All grathit in to garlandis of fresh gudelie flouris;
So glitterit as the gold were their glorius gilt tressis,
Whill all the gressis did gleme of the glaid hewis;
Kemmit was their clear hair, and curiouslie shed
Attour their shulderis doun shyre, shyning full bricht;
With curches, cassin there abone, of kirsp clear and thin:
Their mantillis green were as the gress that grew in May
                                                    season,
Fetrit with their whyte fingeris about their fair sydis:
Off ferliful fyne favour were their faceis meek,
All full of flurist fairheid, as flouris in June;
Whyte, seemlie, and soft, as the sweet lillies
New upspred upon spray, as new spynist rose;
Arrayit royallie about with mony rich vardour,
That nature full nobillie annamalit with flouris

sanative healthful	*attour* above
in dern secretly	*shyre* fell
dirkin eavesdrop	*curches* kerchiefs
hard heard	*kirsp* lawn
inthrang pressed in	*fetrit* adjusted
heildit hidden, covered	*ferliful* wonderful
heynd protecting	*new spynist* new-burgeoned
grathit attired	*vardour* verdure
curiouslie carefully	

Off alkin hewis under hevin, that ony heynd knew,
Fragrant, all full of fresh odour fynest of smell.
Ane cumlie tabil coverit wes before tha clear ladeis,
With royall cuppis apon rawis full of rych wynis.
And of thir fair wlonkes, twa weddit war with lordis,
Ane wes ane wedow, I wis, wantoun of laitis.
And, as thay talk at the tabill of many taill sindry,
Thay wauchtit at the wicht wyne and waris out wourdis;
And syne thay spak more spedilie, and sparit no matiris.

Bewrie, said the Wedo, ye weddit wemen yung,
What mirth ye fand in maryage, sen ye were menis wyvis;
Reveill gif ye rewit that rakless conditioun?
Or gif that ever ye luvit leyd upone life mair
Nor them that ye your faith hes festinit for ever?
Or gif ye think, had ye choice, that ye wald choose better?
Think ye it nocht ane blest band that bindis so fast,
That none undo it a deill may but the deith ane?

FIRST WIFE'S COMPLAINT

Then spak ane lusty belive with lustie effeiris:
It, that ye call the blest band that bindis so fast,
Is bare of bliss, and bailfull, and great barrat wirkis.
Ye speir, had I free choice, gif I wald choose better?
Chainyeis ay are to eschew; and changeis are sweet:
Sic cursit chance til eschew, had I my choice anis,
Out of the chainyeis of ane churl I chaip suld for evir.

heynd person
clear peerless
wlonkes beauties
laitis behaviour
wauchtit quaffed
waris out expended
bewrie confess
rakless carefree

leyd man
that none, etc. that none can at
    all undo except by death
belive presently
effeiris gestures
barrat trouble, strife
speir ask
chaip escape

God gif matrimony were made to mell for ane year!
It were but merrens to be mair, but gif our myndis pleasit:
It is agane the law of luve, of kynd, and of nature,
Togither hairtis to strain, that stryveis with uther:
Birdis hes ane better law na bernis by meikill,
That ilk year, with new joy, joyis ane maik,
And fangis them ane fresh fere, unfulyeit, and constant,
And lettis their fulyeit feris flie where they please . . .

   I have ane wallidrag, ane worm, ane auld wobat carle,
A wastit wolroun, nae worth but wordis to clatter;
Ane bumbart, ane drone bee, ane bag full of flewme,
Ane skabbit skarth, ane scorpioun, ane scutard behind;
To see him scart his awin skin great scunner I think.
When kissis me that carybald, then kindillis all my sorrow;
As birs of ane brym bair, his berd is als stif,
But soft and soupill as the silk is his sary lume;
He may weill to the sin assent, but saikless is his deedis.
With goreis his twa grim ene are gladderrit all about,
And gorgeit like twa guttaris that were with glar stoppit;
But when that glowrand ghaist grippis me about,
Then think I hiddowus Mahoun hes me in armes;
There may nae sanyne me save frae that auld Sathane;
For, thoch I croce me all clean, frae the croun doun,
He will my corse all beclip, and clap me to his breist.

mell be conjoined	*skarth* cormorant
merrens plaguey	*scutard* beshitten
bernis humans	*scart* scratch
meikill much	*scunner* revulsion, nausea
maik mate	*carybald* cannibal
fangis takes	*birs* hairs
fere companion	*brym* fierce
unfulyeit unspoiled	*bair* boar
wallidrag weakling	*lume* penis, tool
wobat exhausted	*saikless* innocent
carle old man	*goreis* encrusted pus
wolroun boar	*gladderrit* caked
clatter discuss	*glar* mud
bumbart braggart	*sanyne* signing with the cross

When shaivine is that ald shalk with a sharp rasour,
He shovis on me his shevill mouth and shedis my lippis;
And with his hard hurcheon skin sae heklis he my cheekis,
That as a gleamand gleyd glowis my chaftis;
I shrink for the sharp stound, but shout dar I noucht,
For shore of that auld shrew, shame him betide!
The luve blenkis of that bogill, frae his bleard ene,
As Beelzebub had on me blent, abasit my spreit;
And when the smy on me smirkis with his smake smolet,
He fepillis like a farcy aver that flyrit on a gillot.
   When that the sound of his saw sinkis in my earis,
Then ay renewis my noy, or he be near cumand:
When I hear nemmyt his name, then mak I nine crocis,
To keep me frae the cummerans of that carll mangit,
That full of eldning is and anger and all evill thewis.
I dar noucht luke to my luve for that lean gib,
He is sae full of jelusy and engyne fals;
Ever imagining in mind materis of ill,
Compassand and castand casis a thousand
How he sall tak me, with a trawe, at tryst of ane othir:
I dar noucht keek to the knaip that the cup fillis,
For eldning of that ald shrew that ever on evill thinkis;
For he is wastit and worn frae Venus werkis,
And may noucht beat worth a bean in hed of my mystirs.

ald shalk old churl
shevill twisted
hurcheon hedgehog
heklis prickles, scores
gleyd ember
chaftis cheeks
shore fear
bogill ghost
blent glanced
smy wretch
smake smolet ?randy ogling
fepillis fidgets
farcy diseased old horse

flyrit leered
gillot young mare
saw speech
noy annoyance
cummerans embrace
carll mangit mangy dotard
eldning jealousy
gib tom-cat
engyne imagination
trawe trick
knaip youth
mystirs desires

He trowis that young folk I yearn yeild, for he gane is,
But I may yuke all this year, or his yerd help.
   Ay when that caribald carl wald climb on my wame,
Then am I dangerus and dain and dour of my will;
Yet let I never that larbar my leggis gae between,
To fyle my flesh, na fumyll me, without a fee great;
And thoch his penie puirly me payis in bed,
His purse pays richly in recompense efter:
For, or he climb on my corse, that carybald forlane,
I have conditioun of a curch of kersp allther finest,
A goun of engranyt claith, richt gaily furrit,
A ring with a royall stane, or other rich jewel,
Or rest of his rousty raid, thoch he were rede wod:
For all the buddis of Johne Blunt, when he abone climis,
Me think the baid dear abocht, sae bawch are his werkis;
And thus I sell him solace, thoch I it sour think:
Frae sic a syre, God you save, my sweet sisteris dear!

   When that the seemly had said her sentence to end,
Then all they leuch apon loft with latis full mery,
And raucht the cup round about full of rich wynis,
And ralyeit lang, or they wald rest, with riotus speech.

for he, etc. because he is past sex
yuke itch with desire
or before
yerd penis
dain disdainful
dour unyielding
larbar impotent man
forlane forlorn
rousty raid spiritless ride

rede wod stark mad with anger
buddis bribes
Johne Blunt proverbial briber
baid bribe
bawch feeble
seemly charmer
leuch laughed
apon loft aloud
raucht reached

THE PETITION OF THE GRAY HORSE,
AULD DUMBAR

Now liveries cummis with largess loud,
Why sould not palfrayis then be proud,
When gillettis will be shomed and shroud,
That ridden ar baith with lord and lawd?
   Shir, lat it nevir in toun be tald
   That I sould be ane Yulis yald!

When I was young and into ply
And wald cast gammaldis to the sky,
I had been bocht in realmes by,
Had I consentit to be sauld.
   Shir, lat it nevir in toun be tald
   That I sould be ane Yulis yald!

With gentil horse when I wald knip,
Then is there laid on me ane whip;
To coalheavers then maun I skip,
That scabbit ar, hes cruik and cald.
   Shir, lat it nevir in toun be tald
   That I sould be ane Yulis yald!

Thoch in the stall I be not clappit
As coursouris that in silk been trappit,
With ane new hous I wald be happit
Againis this Christinmas for the cald.
   Shir, lat it nevir in toun be tald
   That I sould be ane Yulis yald!

liveries allowances
gillettis young mares
shomed combed
shroud dressed
lawd commoner
tald told
Yulis yald Yule's jade, an old
  horse put to grass

ply good condition
gammaldis gambols
sauld sold
knip nibble
maun must
cald catarrhal cold
thoch though
happit covered

Suppose I were ane ald yaid aver
Shot furth owre cleuch to squash the claver,
And had the strenthis of all Strathnaver,
I wald at Yule be housit and stalled.
   Shir, lat it nevir in toun be tald
   That I sould be ane Yulis yald!

I am ane ald horse, as ye knaw,
That ever in dule dois drudge and draw;
Great court horse puttis me frae the staw
To fang the fog by firth and fald.
   Shir, lat it nevir in toun be tald
   That I sould be ane Yulis yald!

I have run lang furth in the field
On pastures that ar plain and peeled;
I micht be now taen in for eild,
My bekis ar spruning, heich and bald.
   Shir, lat it nevir in toun be tald
   That I sould be ane Yulis yald!

My mane is turnit into white,
And thereof ye have all the wite!
When uther horse had bran to bite,
I had but gress, gripe gif I wald.
   Shir, lat it nevir in toun be tald
   That I sould be ane Yulis yald!

yaid aver useless old horse
owre over
cleuch rocky moorland
claver clover
dule misery
staw stall
fang take
fog greenery
firth woodland
fald field
taen taken
eild age
my bekis, etc. my incisors are
   projecting from the gums
wite blame
gripe, etc. complain however I
   might

I was never dautit in to stabel;
My life hes been so miserabel
My hide to offer I am abel
For ill-showd strae that I reive wald.
   Shir, lat it nevir in toun be tald
   That I sould be ane Yulis yald!

And yet, suppose my thrift be thin,
Gif that I die your aucht within,
Lat nevir the soutteris have my skin,
With uglie gummis to be gnawin.
   Shir, lat it nevir in toun be tald
   That I sould be ane Yulis yald!

The court hes done my curage cule
And made me ane fore-ridden mule;
Yet, to wear trapperis at the Yule,
I wald be spurrit at averie spald.
   Shir, lat it nevir in toun be tald
   That I sould be ane Yulis yald!

RESPONTIO REGIS

Eftir our writingis, thesaurer,
Tak in this gray horse, Auld Dumbar,
Whilk in my aucht with service trew
In lyart changeit is in hew;
Gar house him now agains this Yule,
And busk him like ane bishopis mule,
For with my hand I have indost
To pay whatever his trappouris cost.

dautit petted	by shoemakers to soften
ill-showd dirty	the leather
strae straw	*spald* joint
reive steal	*thesaurer* treasurer
aucht possession	*lyart* grizzled
soutteris shoemakers	*gar* cause
with uglie, etc. i.e. to be chewed	*indost* endorsed

REMONSTRANCE TO THE KING

Shir, ye have mony servitouris
And officiaris of divers curis;
Kirkmen, courtmen, and craftismen fine;
Doctouris in jure, amd medicine;
Divinouris, rethors, and philosophouris,
Astrologis, artists, and oratouris;
Men of airms, and vailyeand knichtis,
And mony uther gudelie wichtis;
Musicianis, menstrals, and mirrie singaris:
Chevalouris, cawandars, and flingaris;
Cunyouris, carvours, and carpentaris,
Beildaris of barks and ballingaris;
Masounis lyand upon the land,
And shipwrichtis hewand upon the strand;
Glazing wrichtis, goldsmiths, and lapidaris,
Printouris, paintours, and potingaris;
And all of their craft cunning,
And all at anis lawboring;
Whilk pleaisand are and honorable,
And to your heiness profitable,
And richt convenient for to be
With your hie regal majestie;
Deserving of your grace most ding
Baith thank, rewarde, and cherissing.
    And thoch that I, amang the lave,
Unworthy be ane place to have,
Or in their nummer to be tald,
Als lang in mynd my wark sall hald,
Als haill in everie circumstance,
In forme, in mater, and substance,

But wearing, or consumptioun,
Roust, canker, or corruptioun,
As ony of their werkis all,
Suppois that my rewarde be small.
  But ye sae gracious are and meek,
That on your hieness followis eik
Ane uther sort, more miserabil,
Thoch they be nocht sae profitable:
Feinyeouris, fleichours, and flatteraris;
Cryaris, craikars, and clatteraris;
Soukaris, groukars, gledars, gunnaris;
Monsiouris of France, gude clarat-cunnaris;
Innopportoun askars of Ireland kynd;
And meat reivars, like out of mynd;
Scaffaris, and scamlers in the neuk,
And hall huntars of draik and deuk;
Thrimlaris and thrustars, as they were wude,
Kokenis, and kennis na man of gude;
Shulderaris, and shovers, that hes no shame,
And to no cunning that can claim;
And ken none uther craft nor curis,
But to mak thrang, Shir, in your duris,
And rush in where they counsale hear,
And will at nae man nurture lear:
In quintiscence, eik, enginouris joly,
That far can multiplie in folie;
Fantastik fulis, baith false and greedy,
Of toung untrue, and hand ill-deedie:
Few daur, of all this last additioun,
Cum in tolbooth without remissioun.

eik also
fleichours fawners
craikars braggarts
clatteraris slanderers
soukaris suckers
clarat-cunnaris knowers of claret
reivars robbers, rustlers
scaffaris beggars

scamlers spongers
thrimlaris jostle
kokenis rogues
shulderaris shoulderers
ken none uther know no other
thrang throng
duris doors
lear learn

And thouch this nobil cunning sort,
Whom of before I did report,
Rewardit be, it were but reasoun,
Thereat suld no man mak encheasoun:
But when the uther fulis nice,
That feistit at Cokelbeis grice,
Are all rewardit, and nocht I,
Then on this false world I cry, Fy!
My hart near burstis then for tein,
Whilk may nocht suffer nor sustene
So great abusioun for to see,
Dailie in court before mine Ee!

And yit more penance wald I have,
Had I rewarde amang the lave,
It wald me sumthing satisfie,
And lease off my malancolie,
And gar me mony falt owersee,
That now is braid before mine Ee:
My mynd so far is set to flyte,
That of nocht else I can endyte;
For either maun my hart to break,
Or with my pen I maun me wreak;
And sen the tane must needis be,
In to malancolie to dee,
Or let the venom ishy all out,
Be war, anon, for it will spout,
Gif that the treackill cum nocht tyte
To swage the swalme of my dispyte!

encheasoun complaint	*wreak* avenge
grice sow (reference poem *Colkelbie Sow*)	*ishy* issue
	treackill medicine
tein wrath	*tyte* quickly
flyte satirically scold	*swage* assuage
endyte write	*swalme* swelling

TO THE QUEEN, ABOUT HER
WARDROBE-MASTER, JAMES DOG

The Wardraper of Venus' bouer,
To give a doublet he is als dour,
As it were of ane fute-side frog:
    Madame, ye have a dangerous Dog!

When that I shaw to him your markis,
He turnis to me again and barkis,
As he were worriand ane hog:
    Madame, ye have a dangerous Dog!

When that I speak til him freindlike,
He barkis like ane midden tyke
Were chasand cattle throu a bog:
    Madame, ye have a dangerous Dog!

He is ane mastiff, mekil of micht,
To keep your wardrape ower nicht
Frae the great Sowtan Gog-ma-gog:
    Madame, ye have a dangerous Dog!

He is ower muckle to be your messan;
Madame, I reid ye get a less ane –
His gang garris all your chalmeris shog:
    Madame, ye have a dangerous Dog!

dour unyielding   *reid* advise
frog cloak   *gang* tread
tyke cur   *garris* causes
ower over   *shog* shake
messan lap-dog

OF THE SAME JAMES,
WHEN HE HAD PLEASIT HIM

O gracious Princess, guid and fair,
Do weill to James your Wardraper;
Whase faythfull bruder maist freind I am:
    He is nae Dog; he is a Lam.

Thoch I in ballet did with him bourde,
In malice spack I nevir ane woord,
But all, my Dame, to do your gam:
    He is nae Dog; he is a Lam.

Your hieness can nocht gett ane meeter
To keep your wardrope, nor discreeter
To rule your robes and dress the same:
    He is nae Dog; he is a Lam.

The Wife that he had in his innis,
That with the tongs wald break his shinnis,
I wald sho drownit war in a dam:
    He is nae Dog; he is a Lam.

The wife that wald him kuckald mak,
I wald sho wer, baith side and back,
Weill batterit with ane barrow tram:
    He is nae Dog; he is a Lam.

He hes sae weill done me obey
In till all thing, therefore I pray
That nevir dolour mak him dram:
    He is nae Dog; he is a Lam.

bourde joke   *tram* shaft
do your gam amuse you   *dram* miserable
innis quarters

LAMENT FOR THE MAKARIS
(when he wes seik)

I that in heill wes and gladness
Am trublit now with gret seikness,
And feblit with infermitie:
   Timor mortis conturbat me.

Our plesance here is all vain glory,
This fause warld is but transitory;
The flesh is brukle, the Fiend is slee:
   Timor mortis conturbat me.

The state of man dois change and vary,
Now sound, now seik, now blyth, now sary,
Now dansand merry, now like to dee:
   Timor mortis conturbat me.

No state in eard here standis sickir;
As with the wynd wavis the wicker,
Wavis this warldis vanitee:
   Timor mortis conturbat me.

On to the dead gois all Estatis,
Princes, Prelates, and Potestatis,
Baith rich and pur of all degree:
   Timor mortis conturbat me.

He takis the knichtis in to field,
Anarmit under helm and shield;
Victor he is at all mellie:
   Timor mortis conturbat me.

Timor, etc. the dread of death
   agitates me
brukle frail

slee subtle
sickir certain

That strang unmerciful tyrand
Takis, on the motheris breist sowkand,
The bab full of benignitie:
    Timor mortis conturbat me.

He takis the campion in the stour,
The capitane closit in the tour,
The lady in bour full of bewtie:
    Timor mortis conturbat me.

He sparis no lord for his puissence,
Nae clerk for his intelligence;
His awfull strak may no man·flee:
    Timor mortis conturbat me.

Art-magicians, and astrologers,
Rhetors, logicians, and theologers,
Them helpis no conclusions slee:
    Timor mortis conturbat me.

In medicine the most practicians,
Lechis, surgeons, and physicians,
Them self frae dead may not supplie:
    Timor mortis conturbat me.

I see that makaris amang the laif
Playis here their pageant, syne gois to graif:
Sparit is nocht their facultie:
    Timor mortis conturbat me.

He hes done peteously devour
The noble Chaucer, of makaris flour,
The Monk of Bury, and Gower, all three:
    Timor mortis conturbat me.

      stour dust of battle

The gude Sir Hew of Eglintoun
And eik Heryot and Wyntoun,
He hes tane out of this cuntrie:
   Timor mortis conturbat me.

That scorpion fell hes done infeck
Maister Johne Clerk and James Affleck,
Frae ballat making and tragidie:
   Timor mortis conturbat me.

Holland and Barbour he hes bereavit;
Allace, that he nocht with us leavit
Shir Mungo Lockert of the Lea!
   Timor mortis conturbat me.

Clerk of Tranent eik he hes tane,
That made th' Aventers of Gawane;
Shir Gilbert Hay endit hes he:
   Timor mortis conturbat me.

He hes Blind Hary and Sandy Traill
Slain with his showr of moral haill,
Whilk Patrick Johnestoun micht nocht flee:
   Timor mortis conturbat me.

He hes reft Merser his endite,
That did in luve so lively write –
So short, so quick, of sentence hie:
   Timor mortis conturbat me.

He hes tane Roull of Aberdeen,
And gentill Roull of Corstorphine;
Two better fellows did no man see:
   Timor mortis conturbat me.

eik also   *endite* writings

In Dunfermline he hes done roun
With Maister Robert Henrysoun;
Shir Johne the Ross embrast hes he:
   Timor mortis conturbat me.

And he hes now tane, last of aw,
Gud gentill Stobo and Quintyne Shaw,
Of wham all wichtis hes petee:
   Timor mortis conturbat me.

Gude Maister Walter Kennedy
In point of deid lyis verily,
Gret reuth it wer that so suld be:
   Timor mortis conturbat me.

Sen he hes all my brether tane,
He will nocht let me live alane;
On forse I man his nixt prey be:
   Timor mortis conturbat me.

Sen for the deid remeid is none,
Best is that we for deid dispone,
Eftir our deid that live may we:
   Timor mortis conturbat me.

ON HIS HEID-AKE

My heid did yak yester nicht,
This day to mak that I nae micht,
  So sair the magryme dois me menyie,
  Peirsing my brow as ony ganyie,
That scant I look may on the licht.

done roun with silenced	*mak* compose verse
dispone prepare	*menyie* afflict
yak ache	*ganyie* dart

And now, shir, latelie, aftir mess,
To dyt thocht I begowth to dress,
   The sentence lay full ill till find,
   Unsleepit in my heid behind,
Dullit in duleness and distress.

Full oft at morrow I uprise,
When that my curage sleeping lyis,
   For mirth, for menstralsie and play,
   For din nor dancing nor deray,
It will nocht wakin me no wise.

ON THE RESURRECTION OF CHRIST

Done is a battell on the dragon black,
Our campioun Christ confoundit hes his force;
The yettis of hell ar broken with a crack,
The sign triumphall rasit is of the croce,
The devillis trimmils with hiddous voce,
The saulis ar borrowit and to the bliss can go,
Christ with his blude our ransonis dois indoce:
Surrexit Dominus de sepulcro.

Dungin is the deidly dragon Lucifer,
The crewall serpent with the mortall stang;
The auld keen tegir with his teeth on char,
Whilk in a wait hes lain for us so lang,
Thinking to grip us in his clawis strang;
The mercifull Lord wald nocht that it wer so,
He made him for to failye of that fang:
Surrexit Dominus de sepulcro.

thocht though	*stang* sting, bite
duleness misery	*tegir* tiger
deray disorder	*on char* ajar
yettis gates	*wait* ambush
indoce endorse	*fang* seizure, plunder
dungin struck down	

He for our sake that sufferit to be slane,
And like a lamb in sacrifice wes dicht,
Is like a lion risen up agane,
And as a gyane raxit him on hicht;
Sprungin is Aurora, radius and bricht,
On loft is gone the glorious Apollo,
The blissfull day depairtit from the nicht:
Surrexit Dominus de sepulcro.

The great victour agane is risen on hicht,
That for our querrell to the death wes woundit;
The sone that wox all pale now shinis bricht,
And dirkness clearit, our faith is now refoundit;
The knell of mercy frae the hevin is soundit,
The Cristin ar deliverit of their woe,
The Jewis and their error ar confoundit:
Surrexit Dominus de sepulcro.

The foe is chasit, the battell is done cease,
The prison broken, the jailouris fleeit and fleemit;
The weir is gone, confermit is the peace,
The fetteris lowsit and the dungeon teemit,
The ransoun made, the prisoneris redeemit;
The field is won, owrcummin is the foe,
Dispulyeit of the treisure that he yeemit:
Surrexit Dominus de sepulcro.

gyane giant		*weir* war	
raxit upreached		*teemit* emptied	
sone sun		*dispulyeit* despoiled	
wox grew		*yeemit* desired to hold	
fleemit banished			

ANE BALLAT OF OUR LADY

Hail, stern supern! Hail, in etern,
  In Godis sicht to shine!
Lucern in dern for to discern
  By glory and grace divine;
Hodiern, modern, sempitern,
  Angelical regine!
Our tern infern for to dispern
  Help, roialest rosine.
      Ave Maria, gracia plena!
Hail, fresh flouer feminine!
Yern us, govern, virgin matern,
  Of ruth baith root and rine.

Hail, ying, bening, fresh flourishing!
  Hail, Alphais habitacle!
Thy ding offspring made us to sing
  Before his tabernacle.
All thing maling we douné thring,
  By sicht of his signacle;
Whilk king us bring unto his ring
  Fro deathis dirk umbracle.
      Ave Maria, gracia plena!
Hail, mother and maid but macle!
Bricht sing, glading our languishing,
  By micht of thy miracle.

stern star
supern superlative, supreme
lucern brightly lit
in dern in darkness
hodiern daily
regine queen (*regina*)
our tern, etc. our term in hell to
  dispel
yern love

rine rind, substance
habitacle dwelling
ding worthy
maling malign
thring hurl down
signacle sign of the cross
umbracle shade
macle spot (*macula*)
sing sign

Hail, bricht by sicht in hevin on hicht!
   Hail, day stern orientale!
Our licht most richt, in clude of nicht,
   Our dirkness for to scale.
Hail, wicht in ficht, putter to flicht
   Of feindis in battale!
Hail, plicht but sicht! Hail, mekle of micht!
   Hail, glorious Virgin, hail!
     Ave Maria, gracia plena!
   Hail, gentil nichtingale!
Way stricht, clear dicht, to wilsome wicht,
   That irk been in travale.

Hail, queen serene! Hail, most amene!
   Hail, hevinlie hie empryce!
Hail, shene unseen with carnal een!
   Hail, rose of paradyce!
Hail, clean, bedeen, aye til contein!
   Hail, fair fresh flour delyce!
Hail, green daiseen! Hail, fro the spleen,
   Of Jesu genetrice!
     Ave Maria, gracia plena!
   Thou bare the prince of price,
Our tein to mein, and gae between
   As hummil oratrice.

Hail, more decore than of before,
   And sweeter by sic sevin,
Our glore forlore for to restore,
   Sen thou art queen of hevin!
Mcmore of sore, stern in Aurore,

plicht sheet-anchor	*daiseen* daisy (day's eye)
mekle much	*spleen* heart of compassion
irk harassed, exhausted	*bare* bore
amene pleasing	*tein* sinfulness
shene beauty	*mein* cure
bedeen entirely	*sic sevin* sevenfold

Lovit with angelis stevin.
Implore, adore, thou indeflore,
  To mak our oddis even.
    Ave Maria, gracia plena!
With lovingis loud elevin:
Whill store and hore my youth devore,
  Thy name I sall aye nevin.

Emprice of price, imperatrice,
  Bricht polisht precious stane;
Victrice of vice, hie genetrice
  Of Jesu, lord soverain,
Our wice pavice frae enemise,
  Agains the feindis train.
Oratrice, mediatrice, salvatrice,
  To God great suffragane!
    Ave Maria, gracia plena!
Hail, stern meridiane!
Spice, flour delice of paradice,
  That bare the glorious grain.

Imperial wall, place palestrall,
  Of peerless pulcritude;
Triumphal hall, hie throne regall
  Of Godis celsitude.
Hospitall roiall, the lord of all
  Thy closet did include;
Bricht ball crystall, rose virginall,
  Fulfillit of angel fude.
    Ave Maria, gracia plena!
Thy birth has with his blude
Frae fall mortall, originall,
  Us ransomed on the rude.

lovit lauded	*nevin* call upon
stevin shouting	*pavice* shield
elevin 'elevated	*pulcritude* beauty
whill until	*celsitude* excellence
store trouble	*birth* child
hore age	

OF THE NATIVITIE OF CHRIST

Rorate celi desuper!
Hevins distil your balmy shouris,
For now is risen the bricht day ster
Fro the rose Mary, flour of flouris.
The clear Son, whom no cloud devouris,
Surminting Phebus in the est
Is cumin of his hevinly touris;
Et nobis puer natus est.

Archangelis, angelis, and dompnationis,
Thronis, potestatis, and marteris seir,
And all ye hevinly operationis,
Ster, planet, firmament, and spheir,
Fire, eard, air, and water clear,
To him give loving, most and lest,
That come in to so meek maneir;
Et nobis puer natus est.

Sinnaris, be glaid, and penance do,
And thank your Makar hertfully;
For he that ye micht nocht cum to,
To you is cummin full humbly,
Your saulis with his blude to buy,
And lowse you of the feindis arrest –
And only of his awin mercy;
Pro nobis puer natus est.

All clergy do to him incline
And bow unto that bairn bening,
And do your observance divine

Rorate, *etc.* second line   *et nobis, etc.* and unto us a child is born
   paraphrases first   *lest* least
ster star   *bening* benign

To him that is of kingis King:
Incense his altar, read and sing
In haly kirk, with mind degest,
Him honouring attour all thing,
Qui nobis puer natus est.

Celestial fowlis in the air,
Sing with your notis upon hicht;
In firthis and in forestis fair
Be mirthful now, at all your micht,
For passit is your duley nicht;
Aurora hes the cloudis pierst,
The Son is risen with glaidsum licht,
Et nobis puer natus est.

Now spring up, flouris, frae the rute;
Revert you upwart naturally
In honour of the blissit frute
That raise up fro the rose Mary:
Lay out your leavis lustely,
Fro deid tak Life now at the lest
In worship of that Prince worthy,
Qui nobis puer natus est.

Sing, hevin imperial, most of hicht,
Regions of air, make armony!
All fish in flude, and fowl of flicht,
Be mirthful and make melody!
All, *Gloria in excelsis* cry –
Hevin, eard, sea, man, bird, and best –
He that is crownit abone the sky
Pro nobis puer natus est.

degest composed, serene   *firthis* woodlands, moors
attour above   *duley* woeful

Gawin Douglas

c. 1475–1522

FROM THE ENEADOS (AENEID)

—

FIRST PROLOGUE, 105–26

First I protest, beaushirs, by your leif,
Be weill advisit my werk or ye reprief;
Considdir it warlie, read oftair than anis;
Weill at ane blenk slee poetry nocht tane is.
And yet, forsuith, I set my busy pain
As that I culd, to mak it braid and plain,
Kepand nae sudroun, but our awin langage,
And speakis as I learit when I was page . . .
Nor yet sae clean all sudroun I refuse,
But sum word I pronunce as nichtbour dois;
Like as in Latin been Greek termes sum,
So me behuvit whilom, or than be dum,
Sum bastard Latin, French, or Inglis oiss,
Whar scant were Scottis I had nae uther choiss.
Nocht for our toung is in the selfin scant
But for that I the foutht of langage want,
Whereas the colour of his propertie
To keep the sentence thereto constrenit me,

leif leave	*sudroun* southern English
or before	*learit* learned
reprief reprove	*or* rather
warlie carefully	*oiss* use
blenk glance	*whar* where
slee subtle	*for* because
tane taken, understood	*foutht* plenitude
braid broad, open	*sentence* meaning

Or than to mak my sang, short sum time,
Mair compendious, or to likelie my ryme.
Therefore, guid freindis, for ane jimp or a bourd,
I pray you note me nocht at every wourd.

SEVENTH PROLOGUE

(excerpt) 1–148

As bricht Phebus, sheyn soverane hevinnis ee,
The opposit held of his chymmys hie,
Clear shynand bemys, and goldyn simmeris hew,
In laton cullour altering haill of new,
Kything no sing of heat by his visage,
So near approchit he his wintir stage;
Reddy he was to enter the third morn
In cloudy skyis under Capricorn;
All thoch he be the hart and lamp of hevin,
Forefeblit wolx his lemand gilty levyn,
Throu the declining of his large round spheir.
The frosty regioun ringis of the year,
The time and season bittir, cald and paill,
The short days that clerkis clepe brumaill,
When brim blastis of the northern airt
Owrwhelmit had Neptunus in his cairt,
And all to-shaik the levis of the treis,
The rageand storm owrweltrand wally seas.
Riveris ran reid on spait with watir broune,
And burnis hurlis all their bankis doune,
And landbrist rumland rudely with sik beir,

likelie, etc. to get true rhyme	*lemand* glowing
jimp shortcoming	*gilty levyn* guided light
bourd folly	*ringis* reigns
sheyn splendid	*brumaill* wintry, misty
chymmys chief dwelling	*brim* fierce
laton brass	*wally* swelling
kything revealing	*landbrist* surf
sing sign	*rumland* rumbling

So loud ne rumyst wild lyoun or bear;
Fludis monstreis, sik as meirswyne or whalis,
Fro the tempest law in the deip devalis,
Mars occident, retrograde in his spheir,
Provocand stryfe, regnyt as lord that year;
Rainy Oryon with his stormy face
Bewavit oft the shipman by his race;
Frawart Saturn, chill of complexioun,
Throu whais aspect darth and infectioun
Been causit oft, and mortal pestilens,
Went progressive the grees of his ascens;
Ane lusty Hebe, Juno's douchtir gay,
Stude spulyeit of her office and array.
The soil ysowpit into watir wak,
The firmament owrcast with rokis blak,
The grond fadyt, and fawch wolx all the feildis,
Montane toppis slekit with snaw owrheildis;
On raggit rolkis of hard harsk whyn stane
With frosyn frontis cauld clinty clewis shane.
Bewtie was lost, and barrand shew the landis,
With frostis hair owrfret the feildis standis.
Seir bittir bubbis and the showris snell
Semyt on the sward a similitude of hell,
Reducing to our mynd, in every sted,
Gousty shaddois of eild and grisly ded.
Thik drumly skuggis dirknit so the hevyn,

rumyst rumbled	*clewis* ravines, cliffs
meirswyne porpoises	*shane* glinted
devalis dive down	*hair* hoary
bewavit stirred up	*seir* one after another
darth dearth	*bubbis* squalls
grees degrees	*snell* biting
ysowpit soaked	*sted* steading
wak weak	*gousty* dreary
rokis clouds	*drumly* dirty
fawch tawny	*skuggis* shadows
owrheildis covered over	*dirknit* darken
clinty stony	

Dym skyis oft furth warpit fearfull levyn,
Flaggis of fire, and mony felloun flaw,
Sharp soppys of sleet and of the snypand snaw.
The dooly dichis were all donk and wet,
The law vallie flodderit all with spait,
The plane streetis, and every hie way
Full of floshis, dubbis, mire and clay.
Laggerit leyis wallowit farnis shew,
Brown muris kythit their wisnit mossy hew,
Bank, brae and boddum blanchit wolx and bare.
For gurl weadir growit beastis hair.
The wynd made waif the red weed on the dyke,
Bedowyn in donkis deep was every sike.
Owr craggis and the front of rochis seir
Hang gret ice-shochlis lang as ony spear.
The grond stud barrant, witherit, dosk or gray,
Herbis, flouris and gersis wallowit away.
Woddis, forrestis, with nakit bewis blowt,
Stude strippit of their weed in every howt.
So bustuusly Boreas his bugill blew,
The deer full dern doun in the dalis drew;
Small birdis, flokkand throu thik ronis thrang,
In chirming and with cheping changit their sang,

warpit threw out	*kythit* revealed
levyn lightning	*gurl* stormy
felloun lethal	*bedowyn* drenched
flaw blast	*sike* stream
soppys flurries	*seir* several
snypand biting	*ice-shochlis* icicles
dooly dismal	*dosk* dark
donk dank	*gersis* grasses
floshis bogs	*blowt* bare
dubbis puddles	*howt* wood
laggerit bemired	*full dern* furtively
leyis hollows	*ronis* thickets
wallowit half-drowned	*thrang* throng
farnis ferns	

Sekand hidlis and hirnis them to hide
Frae fearfull thuddis of the tempestuus tyde;
The watir linnis rowtis, and every lynd
Whislit and brayt of the swouchand wynd.
Puir lauboraris and bissy husband men
Went wet and weary draglit in the fen.
The silly sheep and their litil herd-gromys
Lurkis under lee of bankis, woddis and bromys;
And other dantit grettar beastiall,
Within their stabillis sesyt into stall,
Sik as mulis, horssis, oxin and ky,
Fed tuskyt baris and fat swine in sty,
Sustenyt were by mannys governance
On hervist and on simmeris purvyance.
Wide whar with forse so Eolus showtis shill
In this congealit season sharp and chill,
The callour ayr, penetrative and pure,
Dazing the blude in every creature,
Made seek warm stovis and bein fyris hote,
In doubill garmont cled and wily-coat,
With michty drink and meatis comfortive,
Agane the stern winter forto strive.
Repatyrrit weil, and by the chimney bekit,
At even be time down a bed I me strekit,
Warpit my hed, kest on clathis thrinfald,
Fortil expel the peralous persand cauld;
I crosit me, syne bownit forto sleep,
Whar, lemand throu the glass, I did tak kepe

hidlis and hirnis hiding-places	*shill* shrill
rowtis roar(s)	*callour* fresh
lynd linden-tree	*bein* comfortable
swouchand whistling	*repatyrrit* fed
gromys grooms (shepherds)	*bekit* warmed-up
bromys whin bushes	*warpit* wrapped
dantit tamed	*persand* piercing
sesyt tethered	*bownit* prepared
baris boars	*lemand* gleaming
wide whar everywhere	

Latonya, the lang irksom nicht,
Her subtil blenkis shed and watry licht,
Full hie up whirlit in her regioun
Till Phebus richt in oppositioun
Into the Crab her proper mansioun draw,
Haldand the hicht all thoch the sun went law.
Hornit Hebowd, whilk we clepe the nicht owl,
Within her cavern hard I shout and yowl,
Laithly of form, with crukit camscho beak,
Ugsum to hear was her elrich screek;
The wild geese claking eik by nichtis tide
Atour the citie fleand heard I glide.
On slummer I slid full sad, and sleepit sound
Whil the orient upwart can rebound.
Phebus crownit bird, the nichtis orlager,
Clapping his wingis thrice had crawin clear;
Approaching near the greking of the day,
Within my bed I walkinit whar I lay;
So fast declinis Cynthia the moone
And kayis cecklis on the ruif aboone;
Palamedes birdis crowping in the sky,
Fleand on randon, chapin like ane Y,
And as a trumpet rang thar voicis soun,
Whois cryis been prognosticatioun
Of windy blastis and ventositeis;
Fast by my chalmer, in heich wisnit trees,
The sorr gled whistlis lowd with mony a pew:
Whar by the day was dawin weil I knew,
Bad beat the fyre and the candill alyght,

Crab i.e. Cancer of the Zodiac
clepe name
camscho hooked
orlager time-keeper, domestic
  cock
greking dawn
kayis jackdaws
Palamedes birdis cranes
crowping cawing
fleand flying
randon formation
ventositeis gale-gusts
sorr sorrel
gled kite
bad beat the fyre had the
  fire stoked up

Syne blissit me, and in my weidis dyght,
A shot windo onshet a litill on char,
Persavit the morning blae, wan and har,
With clowdy gum and rack owrwhelmit the air,
The sulyie stythely, hasart, rouch and hair,
Branchis bratling, and blacknit shew the braes
With hirstis harsk of waggand windill straes,
The dew droppis congelit on stibbil and rynd,
And sharp hailstanis mortfundit of kynd
Hoppand on the thack and on the causay by.
The shot I closit, and drew inwart in hy,
Chiverand for cauld, the season was so snell,
Shupe with het flame to fleam the freezing fell.
And, as I bownit me to the fyre me by,
Baith up and down the hous I did aspy,
And seand Virgil on a Lettron stand,
To write onone I hint a pen in hand,
Fortil perform the poet grave and sad,
Wham sae far furth or then begun I had,
And wox ennoyt sum deil in my hart
Thar restit oncompleitit sae great a part . . .

shot windo openable window	*harsk* harsh
onshet unshut, opened	*windill straes* dry straws of grass
on char ajar	*rynd* frost
blae blue-white	*mortfundit* benumbed
har hoary with frost	*causay* causeway, street
gum fog	*hy* haste
rack cloud, mist	*snell* biting
sulyie soil	*fleam* drive out
stythely frozen-stiffly	*fell* lethal
hasart grey	*bownit* hurried
bratling rattling	*lettron* lectern
blacknit blackened	*hint* seized
braes hills	*fortil* in order to
hirstis hillsides	*sum deil* very

FROM BOOK 1
(Cap. III, 1–51)

Hou that Ene was with the tempest shaik
And hou Neptune his navy salvit fra wraik.

Belive Eneas membris shuke for cald,
And murnand baith his handis up did hald
Towart the sternis, with petuus voice thus gan say:
'O sevin timis hou happy and blissit wer they
Under hie wallis of Troy, by dint of swerd,
Deit in ther faderis sicht, bytand the erd!
O thou of Grekis maist forcy, Diomed,
Why micht I not on feldis of Troy have deit
And by thy richt hand yaldin forth my sprete
Wher that the valiant-Hectour losit the swete
On Achillis speir, and grisly Sarpedon,
And ondir flude Symois mony one
With sheld and helm stalwart bodeis lyis warpit?'
And all in vane thus while Eneas carpit,
A blastrand bub out from the north brayng
Gan owr the forship in the baksail ding,
And to the sternis up the flude gan cast.
The aris, hechis and the takillis brast,
The shippis stevin frawart her went gan wryth,
And turnit her braid side to the wallis swyth.
Heich as a hill the jaw of watir brak

belive presently	*carpit* complained
cald cold	*blastrand bub* blasting gust
murnand mourning	*ding* strike
hald hold	*aris* oars
sternis stars	*hechis* hatches
bytand biting	*takillis* rigging
erd earth	*stevin* prow
forcy stalwart	*frawart* waywardly
yaldin yielded	*went* course
sprete spirit	*wallis* waves
swete life	*swyth* swiftly
warpit wrapped, cast down	*jaw* leaping wave

And in ane heap cam on them with a swak.
Sum hesit hoverand on the wallis hicht,
And sum the swowchand sea so law gart licht
Them semit the erd openit amid the flude –
The stour up bullerit sand as it wer wode.
The south wynd, Nothus, three shippis drave away
Amang blynd cragis, whilk huge rockis they say,
Amid the sea, Italianis 'Altaris' callis;
And other three Eurus from the deep wallis
Cachit amang the shald bankis of sand –
Dolorus to see them chop on grond and stand
Like as a wall with sand warpit about.
Ane other, in wham sailit the Lycianis stout,
Whilum fellowis to King Pandor in weir,
And Orontes, Eneas fellow dear,
Before his eyn from the south wynd
Ane hidduus sea shippit at her stern behynd,
Smate furth the skipper clepit Lewcaspis,
His head doun warpit, and the ship with this
Thryce ther the flude whirlit about round,
The swokand swelth sank under the sea and dround.
On the huge deep wheen sailors did appear;
The Trojanis armour, takillis and other gear
Flet on the wallis; and the strang barge tho
Bair Ilioneus, and she that bair also

swak crash	*wode* mad
hesit hoisted	*shald* shoaled
hoverand hovering	*chop* smash against
swowchand sucking	*smate* smote
gart caused	*swokand* sucking
licht alight	*swelth* whirlpool
semit seemed	*wheen* few
stour turbulence	*flet* floated
bullerit boiled, churned	*bair* bore

Forcy Achates, and she that bair Abas,
And she wherin ancient Alethes was,
The storm owrset, raif rovis and side semis –
They all lekit, the salt watir stremis
Fast bullerand in at every rift and bore.

raif tore　　　　　　　　*lekit* leaked
rovis templates　　　　*bullerand* boiling, bubbling
semis seams

Sir David Lyndsay

?1490–1555

FROM THE DREME

—

OF THE REALME OF SCOTLAND

When that I had oversene this Regioun,
The whilk, of nature, is both gude and fair,
I did propone ane litill questioun,
Beseikand her the same for to declare:
What is the cause our boundis bene so bare?
Quod I: or what dois muve our Miserie?
Or whereof dois proceid our povertie?

For, throu the support of your hie prudence,
Of Scotland I persave the properties,
And, als, considderis, by experience,
Of this countrie the great commodities.
First, the aboundance of fishis in our seas,
And fructual mountanis for our beastiale;
And, for our cornis, mony lusty vale;

The rich Riveris, pleasand and profitabill;
The lustie lochis, with fish of sindry kindis;
Hunting, hawking, for nobillis convenabill;
Forrestis full of Dae, Rae, Hartis, and Hyndis;

propone propose
her i.e. Scotland personified

dae doe
rae roe

The fresh fountainis, whose holesum cristal strandis
Refreshis so the fair fluriste green meadis:
So laik we no thing that to nature needis.

Of every mettell we have the rich Minis,
Baith gold, silver, and stonis precious.
How beit we want the spices and the winis,
Or uther strange fructis delicious,
We have als gude, and more needfull for us.
Meat, drink, fire, claithis, there micht be gart abound,
Whilkis als is nocht in all the mapamound;

More fairer people, nor of greater ingyne,
Nor of more strength great deedis til indure.
Wherefore, I pray you that ye wald define
The principal cause wherefor we are so puir;
For I marvell greatlie, I you assure,
Considderand the people and the ground,
That riches suld nocht in this realm redound.

My Son, sho said, by my discretioun,
I sall mak answeir, as I understand;
I say to thee, under confessioun,
The fault is nocht, I dar weill tak on hand,
Nother in to the people nor the land.
As for the land, it lakis nae uther thing
But labour and the pepillis governing.

Then wherein lyis our inprosperitie?
Quod I. I pray you hartfullie, Madame,
Ye wald declare to me the veritie;
Or who sall bear, of our barrat, the blame?

laik lack   *ingyne* ability
gart caused to   *puir* poor
mapamound charted world   *barrat* trouble

For, by my treuth, to see I think great shame
So pleasand people, and so fair ane land,
And so few verteous deedis tane on hand.

Quod sho: I sall, efter my jugement,
Declare sum causis, in to generall,
And, in to termes short, shaw mine intent,
And, syne, transcend more in to speciall.
So, this is mine conclusioun finall:
Wanting of Justice, Policie, and Peace,
Are cause of this unhappiness, allace,

It is deficill riches til incress,
Where policie makith no residence,
And policie may never have entress,
But where that Justice dois diligence
To puneis where there may be found offence.
Justice may nocht have dominatioun,
But where Peace makis habitatioun.

THE COMPLAINT OF THE COMOUN WEILL
OF SCOTLAND

And, thus as we were talking to and fro,
We saw a boustius bern cum ower the bent,
But horse, on fute, als fast as he micht go,
Whose raiment wes all raggit, revin and rent,
With visage lean, as he had fastit lent:
And fordwart fast his wayis he did advance,
With ane richt malancolious countenance.

tane taken   bern man
deficill difficult   but without
boustius robust   revin torn

With scrip on hip, and pikestaff in his hand,
As he had purposit to pass frae hame.
Quod I, Gude man, I wald fain understand,
Give that ye pleasit, to wit what were your name?
Quod, he, My son, of that I think great shame;
But, sen thou wald of my name have ane feill,
Forsooth, they call me Jhone the Comoun Weill.

Shir Comoun Weill, who hes you so disguisit?
Quod I: or what makis you so miserabill?
I have marvell to see you so supprisit,
The whilk that I have seen so honorabill,
To all the warld ye have been profitabill,
And weill honorit in everilk Natioun:
How happinis, now, your tribulatioun?

Allace, quod he, thou seis how it dois stand
With me, and how I am disherissit
Of all my grace, and mon pass of Scotland,
And go, afore whare I was cherissit.
Remain I here, I am but perissit.
For there is few to me that takis tent;
That garris me go so raggit, revin, and rent.

My tender friendis are all put to the flicht;
For Policey is fled agane in France.
My sister, Justice, almaist hath tint her sicht,
That sho can nocht hald evinly the balance.
Plane wrang is plane capitane of Ordinance,
The whilk debarris Lawtie and Reasoun,
And small remeid is found for opin treasoun.

feill information
mon must

tent care
tint lost

In to the south, allace, I was near slane;
Ower all the land I culd find no releif;
Almost betwix the Mers and Lowmabane
I culd nocht knaw ane leill man be ane theif.
To shaw their reif, thift, murthour, and mischeif,
And vicious workis, it wald infect the air:
And als, langsum to me for til declare.

In to the Hieland I culd find no remeid,
But suddantlie I wes put to exile.
Thae sweir swyngeoris they tuke of me no heed,
Nor amang them let me remain ane while.
Als, in the outer Ylis, and in Argyle,
Unthrift, sweirness, falset, povertie, and strife
Pat Policey in danger of her life.

In the Law land I come to seek refuge,
And purposit there to mak my residence.
But Singular Profit gart me soon disluge,
And did me great injuris and offence,
And said to me: swyth, harlot, hy thee hence;
And in this countrie see thou tak no curis,
So lang as my auctoritie induris.

And now I may mak no langer debate;
Nor I wate nocht whome to I suld me mene;
For I have socht throu all the Spirituall state,
Whilkis tuke nae compt for to hear me complene.
Their officiaris, they held me at disdane;
For Symonie, he rewlis up all that route;
And Covatyce, that carle, gart bar me out.

leill loyal		*swyth* quickly	
reif theft		*hy* hie	
langsum tiresome		*curis* cares, duties	
thae those		*mene* complain	
sweir lazy		*route* gang	
swyngeoris parasites		*carle* old rascal	
falset falsehood		*gart* caused	

Pride hath chasit from them Humilitie;
Devotioun is fled unto the freris;
Sensual Pleasour hes banist Chastitie;
Lordis of Religioun, they go like Seculeris,
Taking more compt in telling their denneris
Nor they do of their constitutioun,
Thus are they blindit by ambitioun.

Our gentyl men are all degenerate;
Liberalitie and Lawtie, both, are loste;
And Cowardyce with Lordis is laureate;
And knichtlie curage turnit in brag and boste;
The Civil weir misguidis everilk host.
There is nocht ellis but ilk man for him self,
That garris me go, thus banist like ane elf.

Therefore, adew; I may no langer tary.
Fair weill, quod I, and with sanct Jhone to borrow.
But, wit ye weill, my hart was wounder sary,
When Comoun Weill so sopit was in sorrow.
Yet, efter the nicht cumis the glaid morrow;
Wherefore, I pray you, shaw me, in certane,
When that ye purpose for to cum agane.

That questioun, it sall be soon decidit,
Quod he; there sall nae Scot have comforting
Of me, til that I see the countrie guidit
By wysedome of ane gude auld prudent kyng,
Whilk sall delyte him maist, abone all thing,
To put Justice til executioun,
And on strang tratouris mak puneisioun.

nor than   *sary* sorry
weir war   *sopit* drenched
with sanct Jhone, etc. may St
   John be surety for you

Als yet, to thee I say ane uther thing:
I see, richt weill, that proverb is full trew,
Wo to the realm that hes ower young ane king.
With that, he turnit his bak, and said adew.
Ower firth and fell richt fast frae me he flew,
Whose departing to me was displeasand.
With that, Remembrance tuke me by the hand,

And soon, me thocht, sho brocht me to the roche,
And to the cove where I began to sleep,
With that, one ship did speedily approche,
Full pleasandlie sailing apone the deep,
And syne did slak her sailis, and gan to creep
Towart the land, anent where that I lay:
But, wit ye weill, I gat ane felloun fray.

All her Cannounis sho let crak off at onis.
Doun shuke the streamaris from the topcastell;
They sparit nocht the pouder, nor the stonis;
They shot their boltis, and doun their ankeris fell;
The Marinaris, they did so youte and yell,
That haistilie I stert out of my dreme,
Half in ane fray, and speedilie past hame,

And lichtlie dynit, with lustand appetyte,
Syne efter, past in til ane Oritore,
And tuke my pen, and there began to write
All the visioun that I have shawin afore.
Shir, of my dreme as now thou gettis no more,
But I beseik God for to send thee grace
To rewle thy realm in unitie and peace.

anent nearby   *fray* fright
felloun deadly

Sir Richard Maitland

1496–1586

ON THE NEW YEIR 1560

In this new yeir I see but weir,
Nae cause to sing;
In this new yeir I see but weir,
Nae cause there is to sing.

I cannot sing for the vexatioun
Of Frenchmen, and the Congregatioun,
That hes made trouble in the natioun,
And mony bare bigging.
    In this new yeir . . .

I have nae will to sing or danse
For fear of England and of France.
God send them sorrow and mischance
In cause of their cuming.
    In this new yeir . . .

We are sae rulit, rich and puir,
That we wait not where to be suire,
The bordour as the Borrow muir,
Where sum perchance will hing.
    In this new yeir . . .

weir war   *puir* poor
Congregatioun Reformation lords   *wait* know
bigging building   *hing* hang

And yet I think it best that we
Pluck up our hairt, and mirrie be:
For thoch we wald lie doun and dee,
It will us help nae thing.
   In this new yeir . . .

Let us pray God to staunch this weir,
That we may live withoutin feir
In mirriness, while we are heir:
And hevin at our ending.
   In this new yeir . . .

SATIRE ON THE AGE

Where is the blythnes that hes been
Baith in burgh and landwart seen
Amang lordis and ladeis sheen;
Dansing, singing, game and play?
But weill I wait nocht what they mean:
All merriness is worn away.

For nou I hear nae word of Yule
In kirk, on causay, nor in skuil.
Lordis let their kitchings cule
And drawis them to the Abbay:
And scant hes ane to keep their mule.
All houshalding is worn away.

I saw no gysars all this year,
But kirkmen cled as men of weir;
That nevir cummis in the queir;

landwart countryside   *causay* street
sheen beautiful   *gysars* mummers
wait know   *queir* choir

Like ruffians' is their array:
To preach and teach, that will not lear.
The kirk gudis they waste away.

Kirkmen, afore, were gude of life;
Preachit, teachit, and staunchit strife.
They fearit nother sword nor knife
For luve of God, the suith to say.
All honorit thame, baith man and wife;
Devotioun wes nocht away.

Our faders wice were and discreet;
They had baith honour, men and meat.
With luve they did their tennents treat;
And had aneuch in press to lay.
They wantit nother malt nor wheat,
And merriness was nocht away.

And we hald nother Yule nor Pace,
But seek our meat from place to place,
And we have nother luck nor grace,
We gar our landis doubil pay:
Our tennents cry 'alace, alace,
That ruth and petie is away!'

Now we have mair, it is weill kend,
Nor our forbearis had to spend;
But far less at the yearis end,
And never hes ane merrie day.
God will nae riches to us send
Sae lang as honour is away.

lear learn   *Pace* Easter
wice sensible   *gar* cause
press cupboard

We waste far mair now, lik vain fulis,
We and our page, to turse our mulis,
Nor they did then, that held great Yulis,
Of meat and drink, said never nay.
They had lang formes where we have stulis,
And merriness wes nocht away.

Of our wanthrift sum witis playis,
And sum their wantoun vane arrayis;
Sum the wite on their wifis layis
That in the court wald gang sae gay,
And care nocht wha the merchand payis,
Whil pairt of land be put away.

The kirkmen keepis nae professioun;
The temporal men commits oppressioun,
Puttand the puir from their possessioun –
Nae kynd of fear of God have they.
They cummar baith the court and sessioun
And chasis charitie away.

When ane of them sustenis wrang,
We cry for justice' heid, and hang;
But when our neichbours we owr-gang
We lawbour justice to delay.
Affectioun blindis us sae lang
All equitie is put away.

To mak actis we have sum feil:
God wait gif that we keep them weill!
We cum to bar with jack of steel

turse harness, trappings	*cummar* encumber
stulis stools	*owr-gang* commit a crime against
wanthrift squandering	*feil* inclination
witis blames	*jack* jacket
whil until	

As we wald boast the juge and 'fray:
Of sic justice I have nae skeil,
Where rule and order is away.

Our lawis are lichtleit for abusioun;
Sumtyme is clokit with colusioun,
Whik causis of blude great effusioun,
For nae man sparis now to slay.
What bringis cuntries to confusioun
But where that justice is away?

Wha is to wite, wha can shaw us?
Wha but our nobils, that suld knaw us
And til honorabil deedis draw us?
Let never comoun weil decay,
Or els sum mischief will befaw us,
And nobilness we put away.

Put our awn laws to executioun;
Upon trespasses mak punitioun;
To crewel folk seek nae remissioun;
For peace and justice let us pray,
In dreid sum strange new institutioun
Cum, and our custom put away.

Amend your livis, ane and all,
Else bewar of ane suddane fall:
And pray to God that made us all
To send us joy that lestis ay,
And let us nocht to sin be thrall
But put all vice and wrang away.

as we, etc. as if we would intimi-   *befaw* befall
    date the judge   *lestis* endures
lichtleit scorned

Anonymous

?16th Century

CHRISTIS KIRK ON THE GREEN

Was never in Scotland hard nor seen
Sic dancing nor deray,
Nother in Falkland on the green,
Nor Peblis to the play,
As was of wooeris as I ween
At Christis kirk on ane day.
There oome our Kittie woshon cloan
In her new kirtill of gray,
Full gay,
At Christis kirk on the green.

To dance the damisallis them dicht,
And lassis licht of laittis;
Their gluvis were of the raffell richt;
Their shoon were of the straitis:
Their kirtillis were of the lincum licht
Weill prest with mony plaitis.
They were so nice when men them nicht
They squeild like ony gaitis,
Full loud
At Christis kirk on the green.

deray festivity
nother neither
Falkland, etc. name of a lost
  poem of this genre
Peblis, etc. name of well-known
  poem in this genre
weshen washed
dicht prepared

laittis behaviour
raffell roe-skin
of the straitis from the straits of
  Morocco (leather)
lincum lincoln-green
nicht neared
gaitis goats

Of all thir maidinis mild as meed,
Was nane sae gymp as Gillie;
As ony rose her rude was reid,
Her lyre was like the lillie;
But yallow yallow was her heid,
And she of luve so sillie,
Thoch all her kin suld have been deid,
She wald have but sweet Willie,
Allane,
At Christis kirk on the green.

She scornit Jok and scrippit at him,
And morgeound him with mokkis;
He wald have luvit her; she wald nocht lat him,
For all his yallow lokkis;
He cherist her; she bad gae chat him,
She comptit him nocht twa clokkis;
Sae shamefullie ane short goun sat him,
His lymmis was like twa rokkis,
She said
At Christis kirk on the green.

Steven come steppand in with stendis,
No renk micht him arrest;
Platfut he bobbit up with bendis,
For Mald he made request;
He lap whill he lay on his lendis,
But risand he was prest '
Whill he hostit at baith the endis

gymp neat, slender	*stendis* strides
rude complexion	*renk* man
lyre skin	*Platfut* name of clown and dance
scrippit scoffed	he did (Flatfoot)
morgeound grimaced at	*bendis* leaps
chat him hang himself	*lendis* loins
clokkis clock-beetles	*hostit* coughed
rokkis spindles	

In honour of the feast
That day
At Christis kirk on the green.

Tom Lutar was their menstral meet;
O Lord, gif he could lance!
He playit so shill and sang so sweet
Whill Towsie tuik ane trance;
All auld licht futtis he did forleit
And counterfutit France;
He him avysit as man discreet
And up the morreis dance
She tuik
At Christis kirk on the green.

Then Robene Roy begouth to revell,
And Dowie to him druggit;
'Lat be!' quod Johke, and callit him gavell,
And by the tail him tuggit;
He turnit and cleikit to the cavell,
But Lord then gif they luggit!
They partit their play then with ane nevell
Men wait gif hair was ruggit
Between them
At Christis kirk on the green.

lance spring	*gavell* rogue
shill shrill	*cleikit to* hooked onto
whill until	*cavell* lout
forleit forsake	*luggit* wrestled
counterfutit, etc. imitated	*nevell* exchange of blows
French dances	*ruggit* tugged
druggit dragged	

Ane bend ane bow, sic sturt couth steir him;
Great scaith were to have scard him;
He choosit ane flain as did affeir him;
The tother said dirdum dardum;
Throu baith the cheekis he thocht to cheir him,
Or throu the chaftis have chard him;
But by ane mile it come nocht near him
I can nocht say what mard him
There
At Christis kirk on the green.

With that ane freind of his cryit, fy!
And up ane arrow drew,
He forgeit it so fiercely
The bow in flenders flew;
Sae was the will of God, trow I;
For had the tree been trew,
Men said that kend his archerie
That he had slane aneu(ch)
That day
At Christis kirk on the green.

Ane haistie hensour callit Harie,
Whilk wes ane archer heind,
Tit up ane takill but ony tary
That turment so him teind;
I wait nocht whither his hand cud varie,
Or gif the man was his freind,

sturt anger	*chaftis* jaws
couth steir roused	*chard* pierced
scaith harm	*forgeit* strung
scard scared	*flenders* splinters
flain arrow	*hensour* youth
affeir suit	*heind* trained
dirdum, etc. angry nonsense-	*tit* snatched
words	*teind* angered
cheir pierce	

But he chapit throu the michtis of Marie
As man that nae evill meind
That time
At Christis kirk on the green.

Then Lowrie as ane lyoun lap,
And soon ane flain culd fedder;
He hecht to pierse him at the pap,
Thereon to wed ane wedder;
He hit him on the wambe ane wap,
And it bust like ane bledder;
But lo! as fortoun was and hap,
His doublat was of ledder
And sauft him
At Christis kirk on the green.

The baff so boustuousle abasit him,
To the eard he dushit doun;
The tother for dreid he pressit him
And fled out of the toun;
The wivis come furth and up they paisit him,
And fand life in the loun;
And with three routis they raisit him
And coverit him of swoun
Agane
At Christis kirk on the green.

Ane yaip young man that stude him neist
Lousit off ane shot with ire;
He ettlit the bern evin in the breist,

chapit escaped	*paisit him* set him on his feet
hecht promised, declared	*loun* fellow
wed bet	*routis* shouts
wedder sheep	*coverit* recovered
wambe belly	*yaip* eager, keen
wap blow	*lousit* loosed
baff blow, buffet	*ettlit* aimed at
dushit dashed	*bern* man

The bout flew owre the byre;
Ane cryit that he had slane ane preist
Ane mile beyond ane mire;
Than bow and bag frae him he caist,
And fled als feirse as fire,
Of flint
At Christis kirk on the green.

With forkis and flailis they leit great flappis,
And flang togither with friggis
With bougaris of barnis they birst blew cappis,
Whill they of bernis made briggis;
The rerd raise rudelie with the rappis,
When rungis was laid on riggis;
The wivis come furth with cryis and clappis
'Lo where my liking liggis,'
Quod she
At Christis kirk on the green.

They girnit and leit gird with granis;
Ilk gossop uther grevit;
Sum straikit stingis, sum gadderit stanis,
Sum fled and evil eschevit;
The menstral wan within ane wanis;
That day full weill he previt,
For he come hame with unburst banis,
Where fechtaris were mischevit
For ever
At Christis kirk on the green.

bout bolt	*riggis* backbones
byre cowshed	*liking* sweetheart
friggis stalwarts	*liggis* lies
bougaris rafters	*girnit* bewailed
blew cappis blue bonnets	*leit gird* struck out
briggis bridges	*granis* groans, complaints
rerd din	*stingis* poles
rungis cudgels	*wanis* house

Heich Huchoun with ane hissill ryse
To red can throu them rummill;
He mudlit them doun like ony myse;
He wes nae baty bummill.
Thoch he was wicht, he was nocht wyse,
With sic jatouris to geummill.
For frae his thoum they dang ane sklyse
Whill he cryit 'barlaw fummill
Ouris!'
At Christis kirk on the green.

When that he saw his blude so reid,
To flee micht no man lat him;
He wend it had been for ald feid,
The far sairer it sat him;
He gart his feit defend his heid;
He thocht they cryit 'have at him',
Whill he was past out of all pleid –
He suld be swift that gat him
Throu speed
At Christis kirk on the green.

The toun soutar in breif was boudin;
His wife hang in his waist;
His body was in blude all browdin;
He granit like ony gaist;

hissill ryse hazel-wand	*wend* thought
red put in order	*feid* feud
rummill rumble, drive	*sairer* sorer
mudlit struck	*sat* beset
baty bummill immature weakling	*gart* made
wicht powerful	*pleid* dispute
jatouris tattlers	*soutar* shoemaker
geummill jumble, meddle	*breif* rage
sklyse slice	*boudin* burdened
barlaw fummill Ouris 'parley, enough!'	*browdin* daubed
	gaist ghost
lat prevent	

Her glitterand hairis that were full goldin,
So hard in luve him laist
That for her sake he wes unyoldin
Sevin mile when he wes chaist
And mair
At Christis kirk on the green.

The millar was of manlie mak;
To meet him was nae mowis;
There durst nae ten cum him to tak,
So nobbit he their nowis.
The bushment haill about him brak
And bickert him with bowis,
Syne tratourlie behind his bak
Ane hewit him on the howis
Behind
At Christis kirk on the green.

Twa that was herdismen of the herd
Ran upon uther like rammis;
Thir forsy freikis richt uneffeird
Beat on the barrow trammis;
But where their gobbis were baith ungird,
They gat upon the gammis,
Whill bludie barkit was their berd,
As they had worreit lambis
Most like
At Christis kirk on the green.

The wivis cast up ane hiduous yell,
When all the youngkeris yokkit;
Als feirse as ony fire-flauchtis fell,

laist held	*freikis* stalwarts
unyoldin unyielded	*gobbis* mouths
mowis joke	*ungird* open
nowis heads	*gammis* gums
bushment ambush	*barkit* clotted
bickert assailed	*yokkit* wrestled
howis houghs	*fire-flauchtis* lightning

Freikis to the feild they flokit;
Thae cavellis with clubbis culd uther quell,
Whill blude at breistis out bokkit;
So rudelie rang the Commoun bell
Whill all the steepil rokkit
For rerde
At Christis kirk on the green.

When they had beirit like batit bullis,
And brane-wode brunt in balis,
They wox als mait as ony mulis,
That maggit were with malis;
For faintnes thae forfochin fulis
Fell doun like flauchter falis;
Fresh men come hame and halit the dulis,
And dang them doun in dalis
Bedeen
At Christis kirk on the green.

When all wes done, Dick with an axe
Come furth to fell ane futher;
Quod he, 'Where are yon hangit smaikis
Richt now that hurt my brother?'
His wife bad him gang hame gude glaikis
And sae did Meg his mother,
He turnit and gave them baith their paikis,
For he durst strike nae uther,
Men said
At Christis kirk on the green.

thae those	*forfochin* exhausted
cavellis louts	*flauchter falis* slices of turf
bokkit vomited	*halit the dulis* pulled up the goal-
beirit bellowed	posts: won match
brane-wode brunt ?brushwood	*dalis* heaps
burnt	*futher* great many
balis ?bonfires	*smaikis* wretches
mait tired	*gude glaikis* deluded
maggit burdened	*paikis* thrashing
malis loads	

Anonymous

mid-16th Century

O MAISTRESS MINE

O Maistress mine, til you I me commend!
All hail, my hairt sen that ye have in cure:
For, but your grace, my life is near the end.
Now lat me nocht in danger me endure.
Of lifelike luve suppose I be sure,
Whae wat nae god may me sum succour send?
Then, for your luve, why wald ye I forfure?
O Maistress mine, til you I me commend!

The winter nicht ane hour I may nocht sleep
For thocht of you, but tumland to and fro,
Me think ye are into my armis, sweet,
And when I waaken, ye are so far me fro.
Allace, allace, then waakenis my woe,
Then wary I the time that I you kend:
Were nocht gude hope, my hairt wald burst in two.
O Maistress mine, till you I me commend!

Sen ye are ane that hes my hairt alhail,
Without feinying I may it nocht ganestand.
Ye are the bontie bliss of all my bale;
Baith life and deth standis in to your hand.
Sen that I am sair bundin in your band
That nicht or day I wait nocht where to wend,
Let me anis say that I your freindship fand.
O Maistress mine, til you I me commend!

cure care   *forfure* perished
whae wat who knows   *wary* curse

THE BEWTIES OF THE FUTE-BALL

Brissit brawnis and brokin banis,
Stride, discord and waistie wanis;
Crukit in eild, syne halt withal –
Thir are the bewties of the fute-ball.

FROM THE BANKIS OF HELICON

Declair, ye bankis of Helicon,
Pernassus hillis and daillis ilkon,
    And fontaine Caballein,
Gif onye of your Muses all,
Or Nymphes may be peregall
    Unto my ladye shein;
Or of the ladyis that did lave
    Their bodyis by your brim,
So seimlie war or sa suave,
    So bewtifull or trim.
        Contempill, exempill,
Tak by hir proper port
    Gif onye, so bonye
Amang yow did resort.

No, no, forsuith, wes never none
That with this perfyte paragon
    In beawtie micht compair.
The Muses wald have gevin the grie

brissit burst
brawnis muscles
banis bones
waistie wanis broken homes
syne then

thir these
ilkon each one
peregall equal
shein beautiful
contempill contemplate

To hir, as to the *A per se*
  And peirless perle preclair,
Thinking with admiratioun
  Hir persone so perfyte,
Nature in hir creatioun
  To forme hir tuik delyte.
    Confess then, express then,
    Your Nymphes and all thair trace,
      For bewtie, of dewtie
    Sould yeild, and give hir place.

WHY SOULD NOCHT ALLANE HONORIT BE?

When he wes yung, and cled in grene,
Havand his hair about his ene,
Baith men and wemen did him mene,
When he grew on yon hillis hie; –
Why sould nocht Allane honorit be?

His foster faider fure of the toun,
To visit Allane he maid him boun;
He saw him lyand, allace! in swoun,
For falt of help, and like to dee; –
Why sould nocht Allane honorit be?

They saw his heid begin to ryve;
Syne for ane nurse they send belyve,
Wha brocht with hir fyfty and fyve
Of men of war full prevely; –
Why sould nocht Allane honorit be?

preclair illustrious   *boun* ready
mene esteem   *ryve* burst open
fure fared   *belyve* quickly

They rushit furth like hellis rukis,
And every ane of them had hukis;
They cawcht him shortly in their clukis,
Syne band him in ane creddill of tree; –
Why sould nocht Allane honorit be?

They brocht him inwart in the land,
Syne every freind made him his band,
Whill they micht owdir gang or stand,
Nevir ane fute fra him to flee;
Why sould nocht Allane honorit be?

The greatest cowart in this land,
Frae he with Allane entir in band,
Thocht he may nowdir gang nor stand,
Yit forty sall nocht gar him flee; –
Why sould nocht Allane honorit be?

Shir Allanis helmet is ane cop,
With ane sege feddir in his top:
Frae hand til hand so dois he hop,
Whill sum may nowdir speak nor see; –
Why sould nocht Allane honorit be?

In Yule, when ilk man singis his carrell,
Gude Allane lyis in to ane barrell
When he is there, he dowtis no parrell
To cum on him by land or sea, –
Why sould nocht Allane honorit be?

clukis claws   *cop* cup
credill of tree wooden stack   *feddir* feather
frae from the time that   *whill* until
thocht though   *parrell* peril
gar make

Yit wes there nevir sa gay a gallane,
Frae he meet with our maistir Shir Allane,
But gif he hald him by the hallane,
Bakwart on the floor fallis he; –
Why sould nocht Allane honorit be?

My maistir Allane grew so stark,
Whill he made mony cunning clerk,
Upoun their fais he settis his mark,
A blude reid nose beside their ee; –
Why sould nocht Allane honorit be?

My maistir Allane I may sair curse,
He levis no mony in my purse;
At his command I mon deburse
More nor the twa-pairt of my fee; –
Why sould nocht Allane honorit be?

And last, of Allane to conclude;
He is bening, courtas and gude,
And servis us of our daily fude,
And that with liberalitie; –
Why sould nocht Allane honorit be?

FROM THE GUDE AND GODLIE BALLATIS

—

GO, HART, UNTO THE LAMP OF LICHT

Go, hart, unto the lamp of licht.
    Go, hart, do service and honour,
Go, hart, and serve Him day and nicht:
    Go, hart, unto thy Saviour.

gif unless	*fee* ploughman's wages
hallane partition	*bening* benign
stark strong	

Go, hart, to thy onlie remeid
  Descending from the hevinlie tour,
Thee to deliver from pain and deid;
  Go, hart, unto thy Saviour.

Go, hart, but dissimulatioun,
  To Christ that tuke our wild nature
For thee to suffer passioun;
  Go, hart, unto thy Saviour.

Go, hart, richt humill and meek,
  Go, hart, as leil and trew servitour
To Him that heil is for all seick;
  Go, hart, unto thy Saviour.

Go, hart, with trew and hail intent
  To Christ, thy help and haill succour;
Thee to redeem, He was all rent;
  Go, hart, unto thy Saviour.

To Christ, that raise from deith to live,
  Go, hart, unto my latter hour;
Whase great mercy can nane descrive;
  Go, hart, unto thy Saviour.

but without	*heil* healing
leil loyal	*descrive* describe

Alexander Scott

c. 1520–c. 1590

TO LUVE UNLUVIT

To luve unluvit it is ane pane;
For she that is my soverane
   Sum wantoun man so hie hes set her
That I can get no luve agane,
   But breakis my hairt, and nocht the better.

When that I went with that sweet may
To dance, to sing, to sport and play,
   And oft times in my armis plet her,
I do now mourne both nicht and day,
   And breakis my hairt, and nocht the better.

Where I wes wont to see her go
Richt trimly passand to and fro,
   With cumly smilis when that I met her;
And now I live in pane and woe
   And breakis my hairt, and nocht the better.

Whatten ane glaikit fule am I
To slay myself with melancholy,
   Sen weill I ken I may nocht get her!
Or what sould be the cause, and why,
   To break my hairt, and nocht the better?

hie high
may maid

plet embrace
glaikit idiotic

My hairt, sen thou may nocht her please,
Adieu, as gude luve cumis as gaes;
  Go choose ane uther and forget her.
God give him dolour and disease
  That breakis his hairt, and nocht the better.

Quod Scott when his wife left him.

A RONDEL OF LUVE

~ Lo! what it is to luve,
  Learn ye, that list to pruve,
By me, I say, that no wayis may
  The grund of grief remuve,
But still decay, both nicht and day:
  Lo! what it is to luve.

Luve is ane fervent fire,
  Kendillit without desire;
Short pleasure, lang displeisure,
  Repentence is the hire;
Ane puir treisure without meisure:
  Luve is ane fervent fire.

To luve and to be wice,
  To rage with gude advice,
Now thus, now than, so gois the game,
  Incertane is the dice:
There is no man, I say, that can
  Both luve and to be wice.

puir poor   *than* that way
wice sensible

Flee alwayis from the snair;
Learn at me to be ware;
It is ane pane and doubil trane
Of endless woe and care;
For to refrane that danger plane,
Flee alwayis from the snair.

WHA IS PERFYTE

Wha is perfyte
To put in wryte
The inwart murning and mischance,
Or to indyte
The great delyte
Of lustie luvis observance,
But he that may certane
Patiently suffer pane,
To win his soverane
In recompance.

Albeit I knaw
Of luvis law
The pleisure and the panis smarte,
Yet I stand aw
For to furthshaw
The quiet secretis of my harte;
For it may fortoun raith
To do her body skaith,
Whilk wait that of them baith
I am expert.

trane trap   *raith* anger
indyte write   *skaith* harm
aw all   *wait* knows

She wait my woe
That is ago –
She wait my weilfare and remeid –
She wait also
I luve no mo
But her – the weill of womanheid;
She wait withoutin fail
I am her luver laill;
She hes my harte alhaill
Till I be deid.

That bird of bliss
In bewty is
In eard the only *A per se*,
Whais mouth to kiss
Is worth, I wiss,
The warld full of gold to me;
Is nocht in eard I cure
But please my lady pure,
Syne be her serviture
Unto I dee.

She is my luve;
At her behuve
My harte is subject, bound and thrall;
For she dois muve
My harte abuve
To see her proper persoun small.
Sen she is wrocht at will
That natur may fulfill,
Glaidly I give her til
Body and all.

mo more   *alhaill* entirely
laill loyal

There is nocht wie
Can estimie
My sorrow and my sichings sair;
For I am so
Done faithfullie
In favouris with my lady fair,
That baith our hartes are ane,
Luknit in luvis chain
And everilk grief is gane
For ever mair.

ON PACIENS IN LUVE

That evir I luvit, allace therefore!
This to be pynit with painis sore,
Thirlit throu every vein and bore
Without offens;
Christ send remeid, I say no more
But paciens.

Grisel wes nevir so pacient
As I am for my lady gent,
For in my mind I so imprent
Her excellens
That of my deid I am content
With paciens.

How long sall I this life inlead
That for her sake to suffer deid,
But comfort of her gudely heid
Or yet presens?
I say no more – Christ send remeid
With paciens.

luknit locked	*Grisel* i.e. Chaucer's *Patient Griselda*
pynit afflicted	*gent* noble
thirlit jarred	*deid* death

On paciens I mon perforce
Sen that I go from weill to worse,
Exorting Christ to send remorse
        Of consciens
Sa crewally hes keild my corse
        But paciens.

Paciens owercumis all
And is ane vertew principall:
Sen I am bund to live in thrall
        With insolens
I mon sustene what so befall
        With paciens.

But paciens, I you assure,
Nane may the painis of luve endure,
Nor yet into that luvely bour
        Mak residens,
Without they preive baith sweet and sour
        With paciens.

Luve is made of sic ane kind
That by nae force it may be synd,
But ony be of hummil mind
        With permanens
To thole, suppois the hairt be pynd,
        With paciens.

keild killed   *synd* washed away
preive prove   *thole* endure

Alexander Montgomerie

?1545–?1610

TO HIS MISTRESS

So sweet a kiss yestreen frae thee I reft,
In bowing doun thy body on the bed,
That even my life within thy lips I left.
Sensyne from thee my spirits wald never shed.
To follow thee it from my body fled
And left my corpse als cold as ony key.
But when the danger of my death I dread,
To seek my spreit I sent my hairt to thee;
But it was so enamoured with thine ee,
With thee it mindit likewise to remain.
So thou hes keepit captive all the three,
More glaid to bide than to return again.
    Except thy breath their places had suppleit,
    Even in thine armes, there doutless had I deit.

THE SOLSEQUIUM

    Lyk as the dum
    Solsequium,
    With care owercum,
And sorrow, when the sun goes out of sicht,
    Hings doun his head,
    And droups as dead,
    And will not spread,

sensyne since then   *solsequium* sunflower

But locks his leavis throu langour of the nicht,
    Till folish Phaeton rise,
      With whip in hand,
    To clear the cristall skyis,
      And licht the land:
    Birds in their bour
    Looks for that hour,
And to their prince ane glaid good-morrow givis;
    Frae then, that flour
    List not to lour,
But laughis on Phoebus lousing out his leivis:

    So fairis with me,
    Except I be
    Where I may see
My lamp of licht, my Lady and my Love.
    Frae sho depairts,
    Ten thousand dairts,
    In syndrie airts,
Thirlis throu my hevy hart, but rest or rove;
    My countenance declairs
      My inward grief;
    Good hope almaist dispairs
      To find relief.
    I die – I dwine –
    Play does me pyn–
I loth on eviry thing I look – alace!
    Till Titan mine
    Upon me shine,
That I revive throu favour of her face.

    Frae she appear
    Into her spheir,
    Begins to clear

lour frown	*thirlis* jars, pierces
lousing loosing	*rove* repose
airts points of the compass	*dwine* dwindle, shrink

The dawing of my long desyrit day,
   Then Curage cryis
   On Hope to rise
   Frae he espyis
My noysome nicht of absence worn away.
   No wo, when I awalk,
     May me impesh;
   But, on my staitly stalk
     I florish fresh.
   I spring – I sprout –
   My leavis ly out –
My colour changes in ane hartsum hew.
   No more I lout,
   But stands up stout,
As glad of her, for whom I only grew.

   O happie day!
   Go not away.
   Apollo! stay
Thy chair from going doun into the west:
   Of me thou mak
   Thy zodiak,
   That I may tak
My pleasur, to behold whom I love best.
   Thy presence me restores
     To life from death;
   Thy absence also shores
     To cut my breath.
   I wish, in vane,
   Thee to remane,
Sen primum mobile sayis alwayis nay;
   At leist thy wane
   Turn soon agane.
Fareweill, with patience perforce, till day.

awalk awake   *shores* threatens
impesh prevent, impede   *wane* chariot
lout bow down

THE NICHT IS NEAR GONE

Hay! now the day dawis;
The jolie cok crawis;
Now shroudis the shawis,
    Throu Natur anone.
The thissell-cok cryis
On lovers wha lyis.
Now skaillis the skyis:
    The nicht is near gone.

The feildis overflowis
With gowans that growis
Where lilies like low is,
    Als red as the rone.
The turtill that trew is,
With notes that renewis,
Her pairtie persewis:
    The nicht is near gone.

Now hairtis with hyndis,
Conforme to their kyndis,
Hie tursis their tyndis,
    On grund where they grone.
Now hurchonis, with haris,
Ay passis in pairis;
Whilk duly declaris
    The nicht is near gone.

The season excellis
Thrugh sweetnes that smellis;
Now Cupid compellis

shawis groves	*hie* high
thissell-cok missel-thrush	*tursis* bears aloft
skaillis clears of darkness	*tyndis* antler-tines
low flame	*hurchonis* hedgehogs
rone rowan	

Our hairtis eachone
On Venus wha waikis,
To muse on our maikis,
Syne sing, for their saikis: –
    The nicht is near gone.

All curageous knichtis
Aganis the day dichtis
The breist plate that bright is,
    To feght with their fone.
The stoned steed stampis
Throu curage, and crampis,
Syne on the land lampis:
    The nicht is near gone.

The freikis on feildis
That wight wapins weildis
With shining bricht shieldis
    As Titan in trone:
Stiff spearis in reistis,
Over cursoris creistis,
Are brok on their breistis:
    The nicht is near gone.

So hard are their hittis,
Some sweyis, some sittis,
And some perforce flittis
    On grund whill they grone.
Syne groomis that gay is,
On blonkis that brayis,
With swordis assayis:
    The nicht is near gone.

maikis mates		*freikis* warriors
fone foes		*wight* strong
stoned steed stallion		*wapins* weapons
crampis prances		*trone* armour
lampis gallops		*blonkis* white horses

Mark Alexander Boyd

1563–1601

VENUS AND CUPID

Frae bank to bank, frae wood to wood I rin
Owrhailit with my feeble fantasie,
Like til a leaf that fallis from a tree,
Or til a reed owrblawin with the wind.
Twa gods guides me: the ane of them is blin,
Yea, and a bairn brocht up in vanitie;
The nixt a wife ingenerit of the sea
And lichter nor a dauphin with her fin.

Unhappie is the man for evermair
That tills the sand and sawis in the air;
But twice unhappier is he, I lairn,
That feedis in his hairt a mad desire,
And follows on a woman throu the fire,
Led by a blin, and teachit by a bairn.

owrhailit overwhelmed   *dauphin* dolphin
ingenerit born of

Sir Robert Aytoun

1569–1638

UPONE TABACCO

Forsaken of all comforts but these two,
My faggott and my Pipe, I sitt and Muse
On all my crosses, and almost accuse
The heavens for dealing with me as they do.
Then hope steps in and with a smyling brow
Such chearfull expectations doth infuse
As makes me think ere long I cannot chuse
But be some Grandie, whatsoever I'm now.
But having spent my pipe, I then perceive
That hopes and dreams are Couzens, both deceive.
Then make I this conclusion in my mind,
Its all one thing, both tends unto one Scope
To live upon Tabacco and on hope,
The one's but smoake, the other is but wind.

couzens deceivers

Ballads

SIR PATRICK SPENS

The king sits in Dunfermling toune,
    Drinking the blude-reid wine:
'O whar will I get guid sailor,
    To sail this schip of mine?'

Up and spak an eldern knicht,
    Sat at the kings richt kne:
'Sir Patrick Spens is the best sailor
    That sails upon the se.'

The king has written a braid letter,
    And signd it wi his hand,
And sent it to Sir Patrick Spens,
    Was walking on the sand.

The first line that Sir Patrick red,
    A loud lauch lauched he;
The next line that Sir Patrick red,
    The teir blinded his ee.

'O wha is this has don this deid,
    This ill deid don to me,
To send me out this time o' the yeir,
    To sail upon the se!

'Mak haste, mak haste, my mirry men all,
    Our guid schip sails the morne:'
'O say na sae, my master deir,
    For I feir a deadlie storme.

'Late late yestereen I saw the new moone,
   Wi the auld moone in hir arme,
And I feir, I feir, my deir master,
   That we will cum to harme.'

O our Scots nobles wer richt laith
   To weet their cork-heild schoone;
Bot lang owre a' the play were playd,
   Thair hats they swam aboone.

O lang, lang may their ladies sit,
   Wi their fans into their hand,
Or eir they se Sir Patrick Spens
   Cum sailing to the land.

O lang, lang may the ladies stand,
   Wi thair gold kems in their hair,
Waiting for thair ain deir lords,
   For they'll se thame na mair.

Haf owre, haf owre to Aberdour,
   It's fiftie fadom deip,
And thair lies guid Sir Patrick Spens,
   Wi the Scots lords at his feit.

THE TWA CORBIES

As I was walking all alane,
I heard twa corbies making a mane;
The tane unto the t'other say,
'Where sall we gang and dine to-day?'

kems combs	*tane* one
mane moan, complaint	*gang* go

'In behint yon auld fail dyke,
I wot there lies a new slain knight;
And naebody kens that he lies there,
But his hawk, his hound, and lady fair.

'His hound is to the hunting gane,
His hawk to fetch the wild-fowl hame,
His lady's ta'en another mate,
So we may mak our dinner sweet.

'Ye'll sit on his white hause-bane,
And I'll pike out his bonny blue een;
Wi ae lock o his gowden hair
We'll theek our nest when it grows bare.

'Mony a one for him makes mane,
But nane sall ken where he is gane;
Oer his white banes, when they are bare,
The wind sall blaw for evermair.'

THE DOUGLAS TRAGEDY

'Rise up, rise up, now, Lord Douglas,' she says,
     'And put on your armour so bright;
Let it never be said that a daughter of thine
     Was married to a lord under night.

'Rise up, rise up, my seven bold sons,
     And put on your armour so bright,
And take better care of your youngest sister,
     For your eldest's awa the last night.'

fail dyke wall of turf   *theek* thatch
hause-bane neck-bone

He's mounted her on a milk-white steed,
   And himself on a dapple grey,
With a bugelet horn hung down by his side,
   And lightly they rode away.

Lord William lookit o'er his left shoulder,
   To see what he could see,
And there he spy'd her seven brethren bold,
   Come riding over the lee.

'Light down, light down, Lady Marg'ret,' he said,
   'And hold my steed in your hand,
Until that against your seven brethren bold,
   And your father, I mak a stand.'

She held his steed in her milk-white hand,
   And never shed one tear,
Until that she saw her seven brethren fa',
   And her father hard fighting, who lov'd her so dear.

'O hold your hand, Lord William!' she said,
   'For your strokes they are wond'rous sair;
True lovers I can get many a ane,
   But a father I can never get mair.'

O she's ta'en out her handkerchief,
   It was o' the holland sae fine,
And aye she dighted her father's bloody wounds,
   That were redder than the wine.

'O chuse, O chuse, Lady Marg'ret,' he said,
   'O whether will ye gang or bide?'
'I'll gang, I'll gang, Lord William,' she said,
   'For ye have left me no other guide.'

sair sore   *dighted* wiped
mair more

He's lifted her on a milk-white steed,
  And himself on a dapple grey,
With a bugelet horn hung down by his side,
  And slowly they baith rade away.

O they rade on, and on they rade,
  And a' by the light of the moon,
Until they came to yon wan water,
  And there they lighted down.

They lighted down to tak a drink
  Of the spring that ran sae clear;
And down the stream ran his gude heart's blood,
  And sair she gan to fear.

'Hold up, hold up, Lord William,' she says,
  'For I fear that you are slain!'
'Tis naething but the shadow of my scarlet cloak,
  That shines in the water sae plain.'

O they rade on, and on they rade,
  And a' by the light of the moon,
Until they cam to his mother's ha' door,
  And there they lighted down.

'Get up, get up, lady mother,' he says,
  'Get up, and let me in! –
Get up, get up, lady mother,' he says,
  'For this night my fair lady I've win.

'O mak my bed, lady mother,' he says,
  'O mak it braid and deep!
And lay Lady Marg'ret close at my back,
  And the sounder I will sleep.'

braid broad

Lord William was dead lang ere midnight,
    Lady Marg'ret lang ere day –
And all true lovers that go thegither,
    May they have mair luck than they!

Lord William was buried in St Marie's kirk,
    Lady Margaret in Marie's quire;
Out o' the lady's grave grew a bonny red rose,
    And out o' the knight's a brier.

And they twa met, and they twa plat,
    And fain they wad be near;
And a' the warld might ken right weel,
    They were twa lovers dear.

But bye and rade the Black Douglas,
    And wow but he was rough!
For he pull'd up the bonny brier,
    And flang'd in St Mary's Loch.

LORD RANDAL

'O where ha you been, Lord Randal, my son?
And where ha you been, my handsome young man?'
'I ha been at the greenwood; mother, mak my bed soon,
For I'm wearied wi huntin, and fain wad lie down.'

'An wha met ye there, Lord Randal, my son?
An wha met you there, my handsome young man?'
'O I met wi my true-love; mother, mak my bed soon,
For I'm wearied wi huntin, and fain wad lie down.'

'And what did she give you, Lord Randal, my son?
And what did she give you, my handsome young man?'
'Eels fried in a pan; mother, mak my bed soon,
For I'm wearied wi huntin, and fain wad lie down.'

flang'd flung it

'And wha gat your leavins, Lord Randal, my son?
And wha gat your leavins, my handsome young man?'
'My hawks and my hounds; mother, mak my bed soon,
For I'm wearied wi huntin, and fain wad lie down.'

'And what becam of them, Lord Randal, my son?
And what becam of them, my handsome young man?'
'They stretched their legs out an died; mother, mak my bed
 soon,
For I'm wearied wi huntin, and fain wad lie down.'

'O I fear you are poisoned, Lord Randal, my son!
I fear you are poisoned, my handsome young man!'
'O yes, I am poisoned; mother, make my bed soon,
For I'm sick at the heart, and I fain wad lie down.'

'What d'ye leave to your mother, Lord Randal, my son?
What d'ye leave to your mother, my handsome young man?'
'Four and twenty milk kye; mother, mak my bed soon,
For I'm sick at the heart, and I fain wad lie down.'

'What d'ye leave to your sister, Lord Randal, my son?
What d'ye leave to your sister, my handsome young man?'
'My gold and my silver; mother, mak my bed soon,
For I'm sick at the heart, and I fain wad lie down.'

'What d'ye leave to your brother, Lord Randal, my son?
What d'ye leave to your brother, my handsome young man?'
'My houses and my lands; mother, mak my bed soon,
For I'm sick at the heart, and I fain wad lie down.'

'What d'ye leave to your true-love, Lord Randal, my son?
What d'ye leave to your true-love, my handsome young man?'
'I leave her hell and fire; mother, mak my bed soon,
For I'm sick at the heart, and I fain wad lie down.'

THE DOWIE HOUMS O' YARROW

Late at e'en, drinkin' the wine,
　And ere they paid the lawin',
They set a combat them between,
　To fight it in the dawin'.

'O stay at hame, my noble lord!
　O stay at hame, my marrow!
My cruel brother will you betray,
　On the dowie houms o' Yarrow.'

'O fare ye weel, my lady gaye!
　O fare ye weel, my Sarah!
For I maun gae, tho' I ne'er return
　Frae the dowie banks o' Yarrow.'

She kiss'd his cheek, she kamed his hair,
　As she had done before, O;
She belted on his noble brand,
　An' he's awa to Yarrow.

O he's gane up yon high, high hill –
　I wat he gaed wi' sorrow –
An' in a den spied nine arm'd men,
　I' the dowie houms o' Yarrow.

'O ir ye come to drink the wine,
　As ye hae done before, O?
Or ir ye come to wield the brand,
　On the bonnie banks o' Yarrow?

dowie tragic, doleful　　*marrow* mate, equal
houms banks　　　　　　*kamed* combed
lawin' scot　　　　　　*ir* are

'I am no come to drink the wine,
  As I hae done before, O,
But I am come to wield the brand,
  On the dowie houms o' Yarrow.

'If I see all, ye're nine to ane;
  And that's an unequal marrow;
Yet will I fight, while lasts my brand,
  On the bonnie banks o' Yarrow.'

Four he hurt, an' five he slew,
  On the dowie houms o' Yarrow,
Till that stubborn knight came him behind,
  An' ran his body thorrow.

'Gae hame, gae hame, good-brother John,
  An' tell your sister Sarah
To come an' lift her noble lord,
  Who's sleepin' sound on Yarrow.'

'Yestreen I dream'd a dolefu' dream;
  I ken'd there wad be sorrow
I dream'd I pu'd the heather green,
  On the dowie banks o' Yarrow.'

She gaed up yon high, high hill –
  I wat she gaed wi' sorrow —
An' in a den spy'd nine dead men,
  On the dowie houms o' Yarrow.

She kiss'd his cheek, she kam'd his hair,
  As oft she did before, O,
She drank the red blood frae him ran,
  On the dowie houms o' Yarrow.

thorrow through

'O haud your tongue, my douchter dear,
　　For what needs a' this sorrow?
I'll wed you on a better lord
　　Than him you lost on Yarrow.'

'O haud your tongue, my father dear,
　　An' dinna grieve your Sarah;
A better lord was never born
　　Than him I lost on Yarrow.

'Tak hame your ousen, tak hame your kye,
　　For they hae bred our sorrow;
I wiss that they had a' gane mad
　　When they cam first to Yarrow.'

CLERK SAUNDERS

Clerk Saunders and may Margaret
　　Walked ower yon garden green;
And sad and heavy was the love
　　That fell thir twa between.

'A bed, a bed,' Clerk Saunders said,
　　A bed for you and me!'
'Fye na, fye na,' said may Margaret,
　　'Till anes we married be.

'For in may come my seven bauld brothers,
　　Wi' torches burning bright;
They'll say – 'We hae but ae sister,
　　And behold she's wi' a knight!'

ousen oxen　　　　　　*thir twa* these two
kye cattle　　　　　　*anes* once
may virgin

'Then take the sword frae my scabbard,
  And slowly lift the pin;
And you may swear, and safe your aith,
  Ye never let Clerk Saunders in.

'And take a napkin in your hand,
  And tie up baith your bonny een;
And you may swear, and safe your aith,
  Ye saw me na since late yestreen.'

It was about the midnight hour,
  When they asleep were laid,
When in and came her seven brothers,
  Wi' torches burning red.

When in and came her seven brothers,
  Wi' torches burning bright;
They said, 'We hae but ae sister,
  And behold her lying with a knight!'

Then out and spake the first o' them,
  'I bear the sword shall gar him die!'
And out and spake the second o' them,
  'His father has nae mair than he!'

And out and spake the third o' them,
  'I wot that they are lovers dear!'
And out and spake the fourth o' them,
  'They hae been in love this mony a year!'

Then out and spake the fifth o' them,
  'It were great sin true love to twain!'
And out and spake the sixth o' them,
  'It were shame to slay a sleeping man!'

aith oath   *twain* come between
gar cause

Then up and gat the seventh o' them,
  And never a word spake he;
But he has striped his bright brown brand
  Out through Clerk Saunders' fair bodye.

Clerk Saunders he started, and Margaret she turned
  Into his arms as asleep she lay;
And sad and silent was the night
  That was atween thir twae.

And they lay still and sleeped sound,
  Until the day began to daw;
And kindly to him she did say,
  'It is time, true-love, you were awa'.'

But he lay still, and sleeped sound,
  Albeit the sun began to sheen;
She looked atween her and the wa',
  And dull and drowsie were his een.

Then in and came her father dear,
  Said – 'Let a' your mourning be;
I'll carry the dead corpse to the clay,
  And I'll come back and comfort thee.'

'Comfort weel your seven sons;
  For comforted will I never be:
I ween 'twas neither knave nor loon
  Was in the bower last night wi' me.'

The clinking bell gaed through the town,
  To carry the dead corse to the clay;
And Clerk Saunders stood at may Margaret's window,
  I wot, an hour before the day.

'Are ye sleeping, Margaret?' he says,
  'Or are ye waking presentlie?
Give me my faith and troth again,
  I wot, true love, I gied to thee.'

'Your faith and troth ye sall never get,
  Nor our true love sall never twin,
Until ye come within my bower,
  And kiss me cheik and chin.'

'My mouth it is full cold, Margaret,
  It has the smell now of the ground;
And if I kiss thy comely mouth,
  Thy days of life will not be lang.

'O cocks are crowing a merry midnight,
  I wot the wild fowls are boding day;
Give me my faith and troth again,
  And let me fare me on my way.'

'Thy faith and troth thou sall na get,
  And our true love sall never twin,
Until ye tell what comes of women,
  I wot, who die in strong traivelling?'

'Their beds are made in the heavens high,
  Down at the foot of our good Lord's knee,
Weel set about wi' gillyflowers;
  I wot sweet company for to see.

'O cocks are crowing a merry midnight,
  I wot the wild fowl are boding day;
The psalms of heaven will soon be sung,
  And I, ere now, will be missed away.'

traivelling labour

Then she has ta'en a crystal wand,
   And she has stroken her troth thereon,
She has given it him out at her shot-window,
   Wi' mony a sad sigh, and heavy groan.

'I thank ye, Marg'ret; I thank ye, Marg'ret;
   And aye I thank ye heartilie;
Gin ever the dead come for the quick,
   Be sure, Marg'ret, I'll come for thee.'

It's hosen and shoon, and gown alone,
   She climbed the wall, and followed him,
Until she came to the green forest,
   And there she lost the sight o' him.

'Is there ony room at your head, Saunders,
   Is there ony room at your feet?
Or ony room at your side, Saunders,
   Where fain, fain, I wad sleep?'

'There's nae room at my head, Marg'ret,
   There's nae room at my feet;
My bed it is full lowly now:
   Amang the hungry worms I sleep.

'Cauld mould is my covering now,
   But and my winding-sheet;
The dew it falls nae sooner down,
   Than my resting-place is weet.

'But plait a wand o' bonnie birk,
   And lay it on my breast;
And shed a tear upon my grave,
   And wish my saul gude rest.

'And fair Marg'ret, and rare Marg'ret,
   And Marg'ret o' veritie,
Gin ere ye love another man,
   Ne'er love him as ye did me.'

Then up and crew the milk-white cock
. And up and crew the gray,
Her lover vanish'd in the air,
   And she gaed weeping away.

TRUE THOMAS

True Thomas lay on Huntlie bank;
   A ferlie he spied wi' his ee;
And there he saw a ladye bright,
   Come riding down by the Eildon Tree.

Her shirt was o' the grass-green silk,
   Her mantle o' the velvet fyne;
At ilka tett of her horse's mane,
   Hung fifty siller bells and nine.

True Thomas, he pull'd aff his cap,
   And louted low down to his knee,
'All hail, thou mighty Queen of Heaven!
   For thy peer on earth I never did see.'

'O no, O no, Thomas,' she said,
   'That name does not belong to me;
I am but the Queen of fair Elfland,
   That am hither come to visit thee.

'Harp and carp, Thomas,' she said,
   'Harp and carp along wi' me;
And if ye dare to kiss my lips,
   Sure of your bodie I will be.'

gaed went	*louted* stooped
ferlie marvel	*carp* converse
tett tassle	

'Betide me weal, betide me woe,
　That weird shall never daunton me;'
Syne he has kiss'd her rosy lips,
　All underneath the Eildon Tree.

'Now, ye maun go wi' me,' she said,
　'True Thomas, ye maun go wi' me;
And ye maun serve me seven years,
　Thro' weal or woe as may chance to be.'

She's mounted on her milk-white steed;
　She's ta'en true Thomas up behind:
And aye, whene'er her bridle rung,
　The steed flew swifter than the wind.

O they rade on, and farther on;
　The steed gaed swifter than the wind;
Until they reach'd a desert wide,
　And living land was left behind.

'Light down, light down, now, true Thomas,
　And lean you head upon my knee;
Abide and rest a little space,
　And I will show you ferlies three.

'O see ye not yon narrow road,
　So thick beset with thorns and briars?
That is the path of righteousness,
　Though after it but few enquires.'

'And see ye not that braid, braid road,
　That lies across that lily leven?
That is the path of wickedness,
　Though some call it the road to Heaven.

weird fate　　　　　　　　*leven* meadow

'And see not ye that bonny road
   That winds about the fernie brae?
That is the road to fair Elfland,
   Where thou and I this night maun gae.

'But Thomas, ye maun hold your tongue,
   Whatever ye may hear or see;
For if you speak word in Elflyn land
   Ye'll ne'er get back to your ain countrie.'

O they rade on, and farther on,
   And they waded through rivers aboon the knee;
And they saw neither sun nor moon,
   But they heard the roaring of the sea.

It was mirk, mirk night, and there was nae starn light,
   And they waded through red blude to the knee;
For a' the blude that's shed on earth
   Rins through the springs o' that countrie.

Syne they came to a garden green,
   And she pu'd an apple frae a tree –
'Take this for thy wages, true Thomas;
   It will give thee the tongue that can never lie.'

'My tongue is mine ain,' true Thomas said;
   A gudely gift ye wad gie to me!
I neither dought to buy nor sell
   At fair or tryst where I may be.

'I dought neither speak to prince or peer,
   Nor ask of grace from fair ladye!' –
'Now hold thy peace!' the lady said,
   'For as I say, so must it be.'

starn star   *dought* fear

He has gotten a coat of the even cloth,
    And a pair of shoes of velvet green;
And till seven years were gane and past,
    True Thomas on earth was never seen.

THE WIFE OF USHER'S WELL

There lived a wife at Usher's Well,
    And a wealthy wife was she!
She had three stout and stalwart sons,
    And sent them oer the sea.

They hadna been a week from her,
    A week but barely ane,
Whan word came to the carlin wife
    That her three sons were gane.

They hadna been a week from her,
    A week but barely three,
Whan word came to the carlin wife
    That her sons she'd never see.

'I wish the wind may never cease,
    Nor fashes in the flood,
Till my three sons come hame to me,
    In earthly flesh and blood.'

It fell about the Martinmass,
    When nights are lang and mirk,
The carlin wife's three sons came hame,
    And their hats were o the birk.

carlin old woman   *birk* birch
fashes agitations

It neither grew in syke nor ditch,
   Nor yet in any sheugh;
But at the gates o Paradise,
   That birk grew fair eneugh.

     *   *   *

'Blow up the fire, my maidens,
   Bring water from the well;
For a' my house shall feast this night,
   Since my three sons are well.'

And she has made to them a bed,
   She's made it large and wide,
And she's taen her mantle her about,
   Sat down at the bed-side.

     *   *   *

Up then crew the red, red cock,
   And up and crew the gray;
The eldest to the youngest said,
   'Tis time we were away.'

The cock he hadna crawd but once,
   And clappd his wings at a',
When the youngest to the eldest said,
   'Brother, we must awa,

'The cock doth craw, the day doth daw,
   The channerin worm doth chide;
Gin we be mist out o our place,
   A sair pain we maun bide.

'Fare ye weel, my mother dear!
   Fareweel to barn and byre!
And fare ye weel, the bonny lass
   That kindles my mother's fire!'

syke grove   *channerin* plaintive
sheugh dell   *byre* cowshed

THE TWA SISTERS

There was twa sisters in a bowr,
　　Binnorie, O Binnorie.
There was twa sisters in a bowr,
　　By the bonnie milldams o Binnorie.
There was twa sisters in a bowr,
　　Binnorie, O Binnorie,
There cam a knight to be their wooer,
　　By the bonnie milldams o Binnorie.

He courted the eldest wi glove an ring,
But he lovd the youngest above a' thing.

He courted the eldest wi brotch an knife,
But lovd the youngest as his life.

The eldest she was vexed sair,
An much envi'd her sister fair.

Into her bowr she could not rest,
Wi grief an spite she almos brast.

Upon a morning fair an clear,
She cried upon he' sister dear:

'O sister, come to yon sea stran,
An see our father's ships come to lan.'

She's taen her by the milk-white han,
An led her down to yon sea stran.

The younges[t] stood upon a stane,
The eldest came an threw her in.

brast burst

She tooke her by the middle sma,
An dashd her bonny back to the jaw.

'O sister, sister, tak my han,
An Ise mack you heir to a' my lan.

'O sister, sister, tak my middle,
An yes get my goud and my gouden girdle.

'O sister, sister, save my life
An I swear Ise never be nae man's wife.'

'Foul fa the han that I should tacke,
It twin'd me an my wardles make.

'Your cherry cheeks an yellow hair
Gars me gae maiden for evermair.'

Sometimes she sank, an sometimes she swam,
Till she came down yon bonny milldam.

O out it came the miller's son,
An saw the fair maid swimmin in.

'O father, father, draw your dam,
Here's either a mermaid or a swan.'

The miller quickly drew the dam,
An there he found a drownd woman.

You coudna see her middle sma
For gouden girdle that was sae braw.

You coudna see her fingers white,
For gouden rings that was sae gryte.

jaw wave	*make* mate
fa happen to	*gars* causes
wardles world's	*gryte* great

An by there came a harper fine,
That harped to the king at dine.

When he did look that lady upon,
He sighd and made a heavy moan.

He's taen three locks o her yellow hair,
An wi them strung his harp sae fair.

The first tune he did play and sing,
Was, 'Farewell to my father the king.'

The nextin tune that he played syne,
Was, 'Farewell to my mother the queen.'

The lasten tune that he playd then,
Was, 'Wae to my sister, fair Ellen.'

EDWARD

'Why dois your brand sae drap wi bluid,
                    Edward, Edward,
Why dois your brand sae drap wi bluid,
  And why sae gang yee O?'
'O I hae killed my hauke sae guid,
                    Mither, mither,
O I hae killed my hauke sae guid,
  And I had nae mair bot hee O.'

'Your haukis blud was nevir sae reid,
                    Edward, Edward,
Your haukis bluid was nevir sae reid,
  My deir son I tell thee O.'
'O I hae killed my reid-roan steid,
                    Mither, mither,
O I hae killed my reid-roan steid,
  That erst was sae fair and frie O.'

'Your steid was auld, and ye hae gat mair,
Edward, Edward,
Your steid was auld, and ye hae gat mair,
    Sum other dule ye drie O.'
'O I hae killed my fadir deir,
Mither, mither,
O I hae killed my fadir deir,
    Alas, and wae is mee O!'

'And whatten penance wul ye drie for that,
Edward, Edward?
And whatten penance will ye drie for that?
    My deir son, now tell me O.'
'Ile set my feit in yonder boat,
Mither, mither,
Ile set my feit in yonder boat,
    And Ile fare ovir the sea O.'

'And what wul ye doe wi your towirs and your ha,
Edward, Edward?
And what wul ye doe wi your towirs and your ha,
    That were sae fair to see O?'
'Ile let thame stand tul they doun fa,
Mither, mither,
Ile let thame stand tul they doun fa,
    For here nevir mair maun I bee O.'

'And what wul ye leive to your bairns and your wife,
Edward, Edward?
And what wul ye leive to your bairns and your wife,
    When ye gang ovir the sea O?'
'The warldis room, late them beg thrae life,
Mither, mither,
The warldis room, late them beg thrae life,
    For thame nevir mair wul I see O.'

'And what wul ye leive to your ain mither deir,
                              Edward, Edward?
And what wul ye leive to your ain mither deir?
  My deir son, now tell me O.'
'The curse of hell frae me sall ye beir,
                              Mither, mither,
The curse of hell frae me sall ye beir,
  Sic counseils ye gave to me O.'

Sir Robert Sempill
of Beltrees

?1595–?1660

THE LIFE AND DEATH
OF THE
PIPER OF KILBARCHAN

or

The Epitaph of Habbie Simson,
Who on his drone bore mony flags;
He made his cheeks as red as crimson,
And babbèd when he blew his bags.

Kilbarchan now may say alas!
For she hath lost her game and grace,
Both Trixie, and the Maiden Trace:
    But what remead?
For no man can supply his place,
    Hab Simson's dead.

Now who shall play, the Day it Daws?
Or Hunts Up, when the Cock he Craws?
Or who can for our Kirk-town-cause,
    Stand us in stead?
On bagpipes [now] no body blaws,
    Sen Habbie's dead.

drone drone of a bag-pipe   *babbèd* bobbed

Or wha will cause our shearers shear?
Wha will bend up the brags of weir,
Bring in the bells, or good play meir,
                    In time of need?
Hab Simson cou'd, what needs you spear?
                    But now he's dead.

So kindly to his neighbours neast,
At Beltan and Saint Barchan's feast,
He blew, and then held up his breast,
                    As he were weid;
But now we need not him arrest,
                    For Habbie's dead.

At fairs he play'd before the Spear-men,
All gaily graithed in their gear-men:
Steel bonnets, jacks, and swords so clear then,
                    Like any bead.
Now wha will play before such weir-men,
                    Sen Habbie's dead?

At Clark-plays when he wont to come,
His pipe play'd trimly to the drum;
Like bikes of bees he gart it bum,
                    And tun'd his reed.
Now all our pipers may sing dumb,
                    Sen Habbie's dead.

bend up, etc. embolden morale
    with military tunes
play meir hobby-horse
spear enquire
neast next
weid mad

graithed dressed
bead ring of onlookers
weir-men men of war
bikes hives
gart it bum made it buzz

And at Horse Races many a day,
Before the black, the brown, the gray,
He gart his pipe, when he did play,
    Baith skirl and skreed;
Now all such pastime's quite away,
    Sen Habbie's dead.

He counted was a weil'd wight-man,
And fiercely at Foot-ball he ran:
At every game the gree he wan,
    For pith and speed.
The like of Habbie was na than,
    But now he's dead.

And than, besides his valiant acts,
At bridals he wan many placks,
He bobbed ay behind fo'ks backs,
    And shook his head.
Now we want many merry cracks,
    Sen Habbie's dead.

He was convoyer of the bride,
With Kittock hinging at his side:
About the Kirk he thought a pride
    The ring to lead.
But now we may gae but a guide,
    For Habbie's dead.

So well's he keeped his *decorum*,
And all the stots of *Whip-meg-morum*,
He slew a man, and wae's me for him,
    And bure the fead!
But yet the man wan hame before him,
    And was not dead!

weil'd chosen	*placks* coins
wight-man stalwart	*Kittock* Kitty
gree prize	*stots, etc.* tempi of dance
than then	*bure the fead* bore the feud

And whan he play'd, the lasses leugh,
To see him teethless, auld and teugh.
He wan his pipes beside Barcleugh,
                    Withouten dread:
Which after wan him gear eneugh,
                    But now he's dead.

Ay whan he play'd, the gaitlings gedder'd,
And whan he spake, the carl bledder'd:
On Sabbath days his cap was fedder'd,
                    A seemly weid.
In the kirk-yeard, his mare stood tedder'd.
                    Where he lies dead.

Alas! for him my heart is sair,
For of his springs I gat a skair,
At every play, race, feast and fair,
                    But guile or greed.
We need not look for piping mair,
                    Sen Habbie's dead.

leugh laughed	*bledder'd* talked nonsense
gaitlings kids (children)	*skair* share
carl old man	

Francis Sempill of Beltrees

?1616–?1685

MAGGIE LAUDER

Wha wadna be in love
  Wi' bonnie Maggie Lauder?
A piper met her gaun to Fife,
  And spier'd what was't they ca'd her:
Richt scornfully she answered him,
  Begone, you hallanshaker!
Jog on your gate, you bladderskate!
  My name is Maggie Lauder.

Maggie! quoth he; and, by my bags,
  I'm fidgin' fain to see thee!
Sit doun by me, my bonnie bird;
  In troth I winna steer thee;
For I'm a piper to my trade;
  My name is Rob the Ranter:
The lasses loup as they were daft,
  When I blaw up my chanter.

Piper, quo Meg, hae ye your bags,
  Or is your drone in order?
If ye be Rob, I've heard o' you;
  Live you upo' the Border?

gaun going	*fidgin' fain* excited
spier'd enquired	*steer* interfere with
hallanshaker tramp	*loup* leap
gate way	*chanter* pipe of bagpipe
bladderskate windbag, gossiper	*drone* i.e. of bagpipe

The lasses a', baith far and near,
  Have heard o' Rob the Ranter;
I'll shake my foot wi' richt gude will,
  Gif ye'll blaw up your chanter.

Then to his bags he flew wi' speed;
  About the drone he twisted:
Meg up and wallop'd ower the green;
  For brawly could she frisk it!
Weel done! quo he. Play up! quo she.
  Weel bobb'd! quo Rob the Ranter;
It's worth my while to play, indeed,
  When I hae sic a dancer!

Weel hae ye play'd your part! quo Meg;
  Your cheeks are like the crimson!
There's nane in Scotland plays sae weel,
  Sin' we lost Habbie Simson.
I've lived in Fife, baith maid and wife,
  This ten years and a quarter;
Gin ye should come to Anster Fair,
  Spier ye for Maggie Lauder.

brawly bravely   *bobb'd* danced

James Graham
Marquis of Montrose

1612–50

HIS METRICAL PRAYER
(On the Eve of his Own Execution)

Let them bestow on ev'ry Airth a Limb;
Open all my Veins, that I may swim
To Thee my Saviour, in that Crimson Lake;
Then place my par-boil'd Head upon a Stake;
Scatter my Ashes, throw them in the Air:
Lord (since Thou know'st where all these Atoms are)
I'm hopeful, once Thou'lt recollect my Dust,
And confident Thou'lt raise me with the Just.

FROM TO HIS MISTRESS

My dear and only Love, I pray
This noble World of thee,
Be govern'd by no other Sway
But purest Monarchie.
For if Confusion have a Part,
Which vertuous Souls abhore,
And hold a Synod in thy Heart,
I'll never love thee more.

ev'ry airth north, south, east and   *synod* meeting of kirk dignitaries
west

Like *Alexander* I will reign,
    And I will reign alone,
My Thoughts shall evermore disdain
    A Rival on my Throne.
He either fears his Fate too much.
    Or his Deserts are small,
That puts it not unto the Touch,
    To win or lose it all.

Anonymous

17th Century

THE GABERLUNZIE MAN

The pawky auld carle cam ower the lea
Wi' mony good-e'ens and days to me,
Saying, 'Gudewife, for your courtesie,
   Will you lodge a silly poor man?'
The night was cauld, the carle was wat,
And down ayont the ingle he sat;
My dochter's shoulders he 'gan to clap,
   And cadgily ranted and sang.

'O wow!' quo' he, 'were I as free
As first when I saw this countrie,
How blyth and merry wad I be!
   And I wad nevir think lang.'
He grew canty, and she grew fain,
But little did her auld minny ken
What thir slee twa togither were say'n
   When wooing they were sa thrang.

'And O!' quo' he, 'and ye were as black
As e'er the crown of my daddy's hat,
'Tis I wad lay thee by my back,
   And awa' wi' me thou should gang.'

gaberlunzie packman's haversack	*fain* seductive
pawky funny, shrewd	*minny* mother
carle old man	*thir* these
clap caress	*slee twa* sly two
cadgily gaily	*thrang* busy
canty merry	*gang* go

'And O!' quo' she, 'and I were as white
As e'er the snaw lay on the dike,
I'd clead me braw and lady-like,
 And awa' wi' thee I would gang.'

Between the twa was made a plot;
They raise a wee before the cock,
And wilily they shot the lock,
 And fast to the bent are they gane.
Up in the morn the auld wife raise,
And at her leisure pat on her claise,
Syne to the servant's bed she gaes,
 To speir for the silly poor man.

She gaed to the bed where the beggar lay,
The strae was cauld, he was away;
She clapt her hand, cried 'Waladay!
 For some of our gear will be gane.'
Some ran to coffers and some to kist,
But nought was stown that cou'd be mist;
She danced her lane, cried 'Praise be blest,
 I have lodg'd a leal poor man.

'Since naething's awa', as we can learn,
The kirn's to kirn and milk to earn;
Gae butt the house, lass, and waken my bairn,
 And bid her come quickly ben.'
The servant gaed where the dochter lay,
The sheets were cauld, she was away,
And fast to her goodwife did say,
 'She's aff with the gaberlunzie man.'

dike ditch-wall	*kist* chest
clead clothe	*stown* stolen
bent moor	*leal* true-hearted
syne then	*kirn* churn
speir ask	*butt* parlour-bedroom
strae straw	*ben* kitchen
gear belongings	

'O fy gar ride an fy gar rin,
And haste ye find these traitors again;
For she's be burnt, and he's be slain,
    The wearifu' gaberlunzie man.'
Some rade upo' horse, some ran afit,
The wife was wud, and out o' her wit:
She could na gang, nor yet could she sit,
    But aye she curs'd and she bann'd.

Meantime far 'hind out o'er the lea,
Fu' snug in a glen, where nane could see,
The twa, with kindly sport and glee,
    Cut frae a new cheese a whang:
The priving was gude, it pleas'd them baith,
To lo'e her for ay, he ga'e her his aith.
Quo' she, 'To leave thee I will be laith,
    My winsome gaberlunzie man.

'O kend my minny I were wi' you,
Ill-fardly wad she crook her mou';
Sic a poor man she'd never trow,
    After the gaberlunzie man.'
'My dear,' quo' he, 'ye're yet ower young,
And hae na learned the beggar's tongue,
To follow me frae toun to toun,
    And carry the gaberlunzie on.'

'Wi' cauk and keel I'll win your bread,
And spindles and whorls for them wha need,
Whilk is a gentle trade indeed,
    To carry the Gaberlunzie on.

O fy gar ride O shame, make chase	*aith* oath
wearifu' bothersome	*laith* loath
wud mad	*kend* if knew
bann'd swore	*ill-fardly* bad-temperedly
whang slice	*cauk* chalk
priving sampling	*keel* ruddle
	whilk which

I'll bow my leg, and crook my knee,
And draw a black clout ower my e'e;
A cripple or blind they will ca' me,
　　While we sail be merry and sing.'

TAK' YOUR AULD CLOAK ABOUT YE

In winter when the rain rain'd cauld,
　　And frost and snaw on ilka hill;
And Boreas wi' his blasts sae bauld
　　Was threat'ning a' our kye to kill.
Then Bell, my wife, who lo'es na strife,
　　She said to me right hastily,
'Get up, gudeman, save crummie's life,
　　And tak' your auld cloak about ye.

'My crummie is a usefu' cow,
　　An' she has come o' a gude kin',
Aft has she wet the bairns' mou',
　　And I am laith that she should tyne.
Get up, gudeman, it is fu' time,
　　The sun shines in the lift sae hie;
Sloth never made a gracious end,
　　Gae tak' your auld cloak about ye.'

'My cloak was ance a gude grey cloak,
　　When it was fitting for my wear;
But now 'tis scantly worth a groat,
　　For I ha'e worn't this thretty year.

clout cloth　　　　　*tyne* be lost
cauld cold　　　　　*lift* sky
ilka each　　　　　*sae hie* so high
kye cattle　　　　　*thretty* thirty
crummie pet-cow

Let's spend the gear that we ha'e won,
   We little ken the day we'll dee;
Then I'll be proud, sin' I ha'e sworn
   To ha'e a new cloak about me.'

'In days when our King Robert rang,
   His trews they cost but half-a-croun;
He said they were a groat ower dear,
   And ca'd the tailor thief and loon.
He was the king that wore the croun,
   And thou'rt a man of laich degree;
'Tis pride puts a' the country doun,
   Sae tak' thy auld cloak about thee.'

'Every land has its ain laugh,
   Ilk kind o' corn it has its hool;
I think the warld is a' run wrang,
   When ilka wife her man wad rule.
Do ye no see Rob, Jock, and Hab,
   How they are girded gallantlie;
While I sit hurklin' i' the ase?
   I'll ha'e a new cloak about me!'

'Gudeman, I wat 'tis thretty year
   Sin' we did ane anither ken;
An' we ha'e had atween us twa
   Of lads and bonnie lasses ten;
Now they are women grown and men,
   I wish and pray well may they be;
And if you prove a good husband,
   E'en tak' your auld cloak about ye.'

gear capital	*hool* husk
rang reigned	*girded* girt themselves, dressed
trews trousers	*hurklin'* crouching
loon rascal	*ase* ashes
laich low	*ken* know

Bell, my wife, she lo'es na strife,
  But she would guide me if she can;
And to maintain an easy life,
  I aft maun yield, though I'm gudeman.
Nocht's to be won at woman's han',
  Unless you gie her a' the plea;
Then I'll leave aff where I began,
  And tak' my auld cloak about me.

a' the plea right of the argument

Lady Grizel Baillie

1665–1746

WERE NA MY HEART LIGHT I WAD DIE

There was ance a may, and she lo'ed na men,
She biggit her bonny bow'r down in yon glen;
But now she cries dool! and well-a-day!
Come down the green gate, and come here away.
   But now she cries dool! etc.

When bonny young Johnny came o'er the sea,
He said he saw naething sae lovely as me;
He hecht me baith rings and mony braw things;
And were na my heart light, I wad die.
   He hecht, etc.

He had a wee titty that lo'ed na me,
Because I was twice as bonny as she;
She rais'd sic a pother 'twixt him and his mother,
That were na my heart light, I wad die.
    She rais'd, etc.

The day it was set, and the bridal to be,
The wife took a dwam, and lay down to die;
She main'd and she grain'd out of dolour and pain,
Till he vow'd he never wad see me again.
    She main'd, etc.

may maid	*titty* sister
biggit built	*dwam* swoon
dool woe	*main'd* moaned
hecht promised	*grain'd* groaned

His kin was for ane of a higher degree,
Said, 'What had he to do with the like of me?'
Albeit I was bonny, I was na for Johnny;
And were na my heart light, I wad die.
     Albeit I was, etc.

They said I had neither cow nor calf,
Nor dribbles of drink rins thro' the draff,
Nor pickles of meal rins thro' the mill-eye;
And were na my heart light, I wad die.
     Nor pickles of, etc.

His titty she was baith wylie and slee;
She spy'd me as I came o'er the lea;
And then she ran in and made a loud din;
Believe your ain een, an ye trow na me.
     And then she, etc.

His bonnet stood ay fu' round on his brow;
His auld ane looks ay as well as some's new:
But now he lets 't wear ony gate it will hing,
And casts himsel dowie upo' the corn-bing.
     But now he, etc.

And now he gaes drooping about the dykes,
And a' he dow do is to hund the tykes;
The live-lang night he ne'er steeks his eye;
And were na my heart light, I wad die.
     The live-lang, etc.

draff malt-grain
pickles small amounts
slee sly, subtle
ony gate any manner
hing hang
dowie depressed

corn-bing heap of corn
dykes field-walls
dow dares
hund hound
tykes curs
steeks shuts

Were I young for thee, as I hae been,
We shou'd hae been galloping down on yon green,
And linking out o'er yon lily-white lea;
And wow gin I were but young for thee.
    And linking, etc.

William Hamilton of Gilbertfield

?1665–1751

THE LAST DYING WORDS OF
BONNIE HECK, A FAMOUS GREY-HOUND
IN THE SHIRE OF FIFE

Alas, alas, quo' bonnie Heck,
On former days when I reflec'!
I was a dog much in respec'
    For doughty deed:
But now I must hing by the neck
    Without remead.

O fy, sirs, for black burning shame,
Ye'll bring a blunder on your name!
Pray tell me wherein I'm to blame.
    Is't in effec',
Because I'm cripple, auld and lame?
    Quo' bonnie Heck.

What great feats have I done mysel
Within clink of Kilrenny bell,
When I was souple, young, and fell,
    But fear or dread;
John Ness and Paterson can tell,
    Whose hearts may bleed.

fell keen

They'll witness that I was the vier
Of all the dogs within the shire;
I'd run all day and never tire;
  But now my neck,
It must be stretched for my hire,
  Quo' bonnie Heck.

How nimbly could I turn the hare,
Then serve myself; that was right fair!
For still it was my constant care
  The van to lead,
Now what could sery Heck do mair?
  Syne kill her dead.

At the King's-muir, and Kelly-law,
Where good stout hares gang fast awa',
So cleverly I did it claw,
  With pith and speed;
I bure the bell before them a'
  As clear's a bead.

I ran alike on a' kind grunds;
Yea, in the midst of Ardry whins,
I gripp'd the maukins by the buns,
  Or by the neck;
When naething could slay them but guns,
  Save bonnie Heck.

I wily, witty was, and gash,
With my auld fellin pawky pash;
Nae man might ance buy me for cash
  In some respec':
Are they not then confounded rash,
  That hangs poor Heck?

sery shrewd   *gash* wise
maukins hares   *fellin pawky pash* very shrewd
buns tails   head

I was a bardy tyke, and bauld;
Tho' my beard's grey, I'm not so auld.
Can any man to me unfauld
　　What is the feid,
To stane me ere I be well cauld?
　　A cruel deed!

Now honesty was ay my drift,
An innocent and harmless shift,
A kail-pot lid gently to lift
　　Or aumrie sneck:
Shame fa' the chafts dare call that thift,
　　Quo' bonnie Heck.

So well's I cou'd play Hocus Pocus,
And of the servants mak Jodocus,
And this I did in every Locus
　　Throw their neglec':
And was not this a merry Jocus?
　　Quo' bonnie Heck.

But now, good sirs, this day is lost
The best dog in the East-Neuk coast;
For never ane durst brag nor boast
　　Me, for their neck.
But now I must yield up the ghost,
　　Quo' bonnie Heck,

And put a period to my talking;
For I'm unto my exit making:
Sirs, ye may a' gae to the hawking,
　　And there reflec'
Ye'll ne'er get sic a dog for maukin
　　As bonnie Heck.

bardy forward	*aumrie sneck* cupboard-latch
feid feud	*chafts* jaws

But if my puppies ance were ready,
Which I gat on a bonnie lady,
They'll be baith clever, keen, and beddy,
    And ne'er neglec'
To clink it like their ancient daddy,
    The famous Heck.

beddy responsive

Allan Ramsay

1684/5–1758

THE TWA BOOKS

Two Books, near Neighbours in a Shop,
The tane a guilded *Turky* Fop,
The tither's Face was weather-beaten,
And Caf-skin Jacket sair worm-eaten.
The Corky, proud of his braw Suit,
Curl'd up his Nose, and thus cry'd out,

'Ah! place me on some fresher Binks,
'Figh! how this mouldy Creature stinks!
'How can a gentle Book like me
'Endure sic scoundrel Company?
'What may Fowk say to see me cling
'Sae close to this auld ugly thing;
'But that I'm of a simple Spirit,
'And disregard my proper Merit?'

Quoth Gray-baird, *'Whish, Sir, with your Din,*
'For a' your meritorious Skin,
'I doubt if you be worth within,
'For as auld-fashion'd as I look,
'May be I am the better Book.

tane the one   *tither* the other
Turky bound with Turkish   *binks* shelves
   leather

'O Heavens! I canna thole the Clash
'Of this impertinent auld Hash;
'I winna stay ae Moment langer.'
'*My Lord, please to command your Anger;*
'*Pray only let me tell you that –*'
'What wad this Insolent be at!
'Rot out your Tongue – Pray, Master *Symmer,*
'Remove me frae this dinsome *Rhimer:*
'If you regard your Reputation,
'And us of a distinguish'd Station,
'Hence frae this Beast let me be hurried,
'For with his Stour and Stink I'm worried.'

Scarce had he shook his paughty Crap,
When in a Customer did pap;
He up douse *Stanza* lifts, and ey's him,
Turns o'er his Leaves, admires, and buys him:
'*This Book*', said he, '*is good and scarce,
The Saul of Sense in sweetest Verse.*'
But reading Title of gilt cleathing,
Cries, '*Gods! wha buys this bonny naithing?
Nought duller e'er was put in Print:
Wow! what a deal of Turky's tint!*'

Now, Sir, t'apply what we've invented,
You are the Buyer represented:
And, may your Servant hope
My Lays shall merit your Regard,
I'll thank the Gods for my Reward,
And smile at ilka Fop.

clash talking   *crap* crop, head
hash mess   *pap* pop
stour dust   *douse* humble
paughty proud   *tint* lost

LUCKY SPENCE'S LAST ADVICE

Three times the carline grain'd and rifted,
Then frae the cod her pow she lifted,
In bawdy policy well gifted,
    When she now fan
That death nae longer wad be shifted,
    She thus began:

'My loving lasses, I maun leave ye;
But dinna wi' your greeting grieve me,
Nor wi your draunts and droning deave me,
    But bring's a gill;
For faith, my bairns, ye may believe me,
    'Tis 'gainst my will.

'O black-ey'd Bess, and mim-mou'd Meg,
O'er good to work, or yet to beg,
Lay sunkets up for a sair leg;
    For when ye fail,
Ye'r face will not be worth a feg,
    Nor yet ye'r tail.

'Whane'er ye meet a fool that's fou,
That ye're a maiden gar him trow,
Seem nice, but stick to him like glue
    And when set down,
Drive at the jango till he spew,
    Syne he'll sleep sown.

carline old woman
grain'd groaned
rifted belched
cod bolster
pow head
fan found
greeting weeping
draunts drawlings

bairns children
mim-mou'd prissy mouthed
sunkets provisions
feg fig
fou drunk
gar cause
Drive, etc. make him come fast
sown sound

'When he's asleep, then dive and catch
His ready cash, his rings, or watch;
And gin he likes to light his match
    At your spunk-box,
Ne'er stand to let the fumbling wretch
    E'en take the pox.

'Cleek a' ye can by hook or crook,
Rype ilka pouch frae nook to nook;
Be sure to truff his pocket-book –
    Saxty pounds Scots
Is nae deaf nits; in little bouk
    Lie great bank notes.

'To get amends of whinging fools
That's frighted for repenting-stools,
Wha often whan their metal cools
    Turn sweer to pay;
Gar the kirk-boxie hale the dools
    Anither day.

'But dawt red-coats, and let them scoup
Free for the fou of cutty stoup;
To gee them up, ye needna hope
    E'er to do weel;
They'll rive ye'r brats, and kick your doup,
    And play the deel.

cleek clutch	*hale the dools* win the game
rype search	*dawt* pet
truff steal	*scoup* fuck
deaf nits hollow nuts	*fou* fill
bouk bulk	*cutty stoup* small tankard
whinging whining	*gee . . . up* reject
repenting-stools for exposing	*rive* tear
sinners in kirk	*brats* underclothes
sweer reluctant	*doup* backside
gar cause	*deel* devil

'There's ae sair cross attends the craft,
That curst correction-house, where aft
Wild hangy's tawse ye'er riggings saft
    Makes black and blae,
Enough to put a body daft;
    But what'll ye say?

'Nane gaithers gear withouten care,
Ilk pleasure has of pain a share;
Suppose then they should tirle ye bare,
    And gar ye sike,
E'en learn to thole; 'tis very fair,
    Ye're nibour-like.

'Forby, my loves, count upo' losses,
Ye'r milk-white teeth, and cheeks like roses,
Whan jet-black hair and brigs of noses
    Fa' doon wi' dads,
To keep your hearts up 'neath sic crosses,
    Set up for bawds.

'Wi' well-creeshed loofs I hae been canty.
Whan e'er the lads wad fain ha'e faun t'ye,
To try the auld game taunty-raunty,
    Like coosers keen,
They took advice of me, your aunty,
    If ye were clean.

sair sore		*forby* besides
hangy the hangman		*brigs* bridges
tawse leather lashes		*dads* lumps
riggings back, backside		*well-creeshed* well-greased
gear capital		*loofs* palms
tirle strip		*canty* happy
sike sigh, weep		*faun* fallen
thole endure		*coosers* stallions
nibour-like neighbourly		

'Then up I took my siller ca',
And whistl'd benn, whiles ane whiles twa;
Roun'd in his lug that there was a
      Poor country Kate,
As halesome as the well of Spa,
      But unca blate.

'Sae when e'er company came in,
And were upon a merry pin,
I slade awa' wi' little din
      And muckle mense,
Lest conscience judge, it was a' ane
      To Lucky Spence.

'My bennison come on good doers
Wha spend their cash on bawds and whores;
May they ne'er want the wale of cures
      For a sair snout;
Foul fa' the quacks wha that fire smoors,
      And puts nae out.

'My malison light ilka day
On them that drink and dinna pay,
But tak' a snack and run away;
      May't be their hap
Never to want a gonorrhea
      Or rotten clap.

'Lass, gi'e us in anither gill,
A mutchken, jo, let's tak' our fill;
Let Death syne registrate his bill
      Whan I want sense,
I'll slip awa' wi' better will' –
      Quo' Lucky Spence.

siller ca' silver whistle   *mense* discretion
roun'd whispered   *wale* choice
lug ear   *foul fa'* may ill befall
unca blate very shy   *smoors* smothers
pin mood   *jo* dear

Alexander Ross

1699–1784

WOO'D AND MARRIED AND A'

Wooed and married and a',
   Married and wooed and a';
The dandilly toast of the parish
   Is wooed and married and a'.
The wooers will now ride thinner,
   And by, when they wonted to ca';
'Tis needless to speer for the lassie
   That's wooed and married and a'.

The girss had na freedom of growing
   As lang as she wasna awa',
Nor in the town could there be stowing
   For wooers that wanted to ca'.
For drinking and dancing and brulyies,
   And boxing and shaking of fa's,
The town was for ever in tulyies;
   But now the lassie's awa'.

But had they but ken'd her as I did,
   Their errand it wad ha'e been sma';
She neither kent spinning nor carding,
   Nor brewing nor baking ava'.

dandilly over-admired   *brulyies* brawls
speer enquire   *tulyies* turmoils
girss grass   *ava'* at all
stowing accommodation

But wooers ran all mad upon her,
   Because she was bonnie and braw,
And sae I dread will be seen on her,
   When she's byhand and awa'.

He'll roose her but sma' that has married her,
   Now when he's gotten her a',
And wish, I fear, he had miscarry'd her,
   Tocher and ribbons and a',
For her art it lay all in her dressing;
   But gin her braws ance were awa',
I fear she'll turn out o' the fashion,
   And knit up her moggans with straw.

For yesterday I yeed to see her,
   And O she was wonderous braw,
Yet she cried to her husband to gie her
   An ell of red ribbons or twa.
He up and he set doun beside her
   A reel and a wheelie to ca';
She said, Was he this gate to guide her?
   And out at the door and awa'.

Her neist road was hame till her mither,
   Who speer'd at her now, How was a'?
She says till her, 'Was't for nae ither
   That I was married awa',
But gae and sit down to a wheelie,
   And at it baith night and day ca',
And ha'e the yarn reeled by a cheelie,
   That ever was crying to draw?'

byhand decided, gone
roose value
tocher dowry
moggans stockings

yeed went
reel, etc. to drive a spinning wheel
gate manner
cheelie small man

Her mother says till her, 'Hech, lassie,
   He's wisest, I fear, of the twa;
Ye'll ha'e little to put in the bassie,
   Gin ye be backward to draw.
'Tis now ye should work like a tiger
   And at it baith wallop and ca',
As lang's ye ha'e youthhead and vigour,
   And little anes and debt are awa'.

'Sae swythe awa' hame to your hadding,
   Mair fool than when ye came awa';
Ye maunna now keep ilka wedding,
   Nor gae sae clean-fingered and braw;
But mind with a neiper you're yokit,
   And that ye your end o't maun draw,
Or else ye deserve to be dockit;
   Sae that is an answer for a'.'

Young lucky now finds herself nidder'd,
   And wist na well what gate to ca';
But with hersel even considered
   That hamewith were better to draw,
And e'en tak her chance of her landing,
   However the matter might fa';
Folk need not on frets to be standing
   That's wooed and married and a'.

bassie basket	*dockit* spanked
swythe hurry	*lucky* wife
hadding holding	*nidder'd* held down
neiper partner	*frets* petty wrongs

James Thomson

1700–1748

FROM WINTER

The keener tempests come: and, fuming dun
From all the livid east or piercing north,
Thick clouds ascend, in whose capacious womb
A vapoury deluge lies, to snow congealed.
Heavy they roll their fleecy world along,
And the sky saddens with the gathered storm.
Through the hushed air the whitening shower descends,
At first thin-wavering; till at last the flakes
Fall broad and wide and fast, dimming the day
With a continual flow. The cherished fields
Put on their winter-robe of purest white.
'Tis brightness all; save where the new snow melts
Along the mazy current. Low the woods
Bow their hoar head; and, ere the languid sun
Faint from the west emits his evening ray,
Earth's universal face, deep-hid and chill,
Is one wild dazzling waste, that buries wide
The works of man. Drooping, the labourer-ox
Stands covered o'er with snow, and then demands
The fruit of all his toil. The fowls of heaven,
Tamed by the cruel season, crowd around
The winnowing store, and claim the little boon
Which Providence assigns them. One alone,
The redbreast, sacred to the household gods,
Wisely regardful of the embroiling sky,
In joyless fields and thorny thickets leaves
His shivering mates, and pays to trusted man

His annual visit. Half afraid, he first
Against the window beats; then brisk alights
On the warm hearth; then hopping o'er the floor,
Eyes all the smiling family askance,
And pecks, and starts, and wonders where he is –
Till, more familiar grown, the table-crumbs
Attract his slender feet. The foodless wilds
Pour forth their brown inhabitants. The hare,
Though timorous of heart, and hard beset
By death in various forms, dark snares, and dogs,
And more unpitying men, the garden seeks,
Urged on by fearless want. The bleating kind
Eye the bleak heaven, and next the glistening earth,
With looks of dumb despair; then, sad-dispersed,
Dig for the withered herb through heaps of snow.

Adam Skirving

1719–1803

JOHNNIE COPE

Hey, Johnnie Cope, are ye wauking yet?
Or are your drums a-beating yet?
If ye were wauking I wad wait
 To gang to the coals i' the morning.

Cope sent a challenge frae Dunbar:
'Charlie, meet me an ye daur,
And I'll learn you the art o' war
 If you'll meet me i' the morning.'

When Charlie looked the letter upon
He drew his sword the scabbard from:
'Come, follow me, my merry merry men,
 And we'll meet Johnnie Cope i' the morning!

'Now Johnnie, be as good's your word;
Come, let us try both fire and sword;
And dinna rin like a frighted bird,
 That's chased frae its nest i' the morning.'

When Johnnie Cope he heard of this,
He thought it wadna be amiss
To hae a horse in readiness
 To flee awa' i' the morning.

wauking waking

Fy now, Johnnie, get up and rin;
The Highland bagpipes mak a din;
It's best to sleep in a hale skin,
        For 'twill be a bluidy morning.

When Johnnie Cope to Dunbar came,
They speered at him, 'Where's a' your men?'
'The deil confound me gin I ken,
        For I left them a' i' the morning.

'Now Johnnie, troth, ye are na blate
To come wi' the news o' your ain defeat,
And leave your men in sic a strait
        Sae early in the morning.

'I' faith,' quo' Johnnie, 'I got a fleg
Wi' their claymores and philabegs;
If I face them again, deil break my legs!
        Sae I wish you a gude morning'.

speered enquired   *fleg* fright
blate shy   *philabegs* kilts

William Wilkie

1721–72

THE HARE AND THE PARTAN

A hare, ae morning, chanc'd to see
A partan creepin on a lee;
A fishwife wha was early oot
Had drapt the creature thereaboot.
Mawkin bumbas'd and drighted sair
To see a thing but hide and hair,
Which if it stur'd not might be taen
For naething ither than a stane:
A squunt-wife wambling, sair beset
Wi gerse and rashes like a net;
First thought to rin for't; (for bi kind
A hare's nae fechter, ye maun mind).
But seeing that, wi aw its strength
It scarce cou'd creep a tether length,
The hare grew baulder and cam near,
Turn'd playsome, and forgat her fear.
Quoth Mawkin, was there ere in nature
Sae feckless and sae poor a creature?
It scarcely kens, or am mistaen,
The way to gang or stand its lane.

partan edible crab	*squunt-wife* misshapen woman
mawkin puss, the hare	*wambling* walking clumsily
bumbas'd startled	*gerse* grass
but without	*rashes* rushes
stur'd stirred	*fechter* fighter
taen taken	*maun* must

See how it steitters; a'll be bund
To rin a mile of up-hill grund
Before it gets a rig-braid frae
The place it's in, though doon the brae.

Mawkin wi this began to frisk,
And there was little risk,
Clapt baith her feet on partan's back,
And turn'd him awald in a crack.
To see the creature sprawl, her sport
Grew twice as good, yet prov'd but short.
For patting wi her fit, in play,
Just whaur the partan's nippers lay,
He gript it fast, which made her squeel,
And think she bourded wi the deil.
She strave to rin, and made a fistle:
The tither catch'd a tough bur-thristle,
Which held them baith, till o'er a dyke
A herd came stending wi his tyke,
And fell'd poor Mawkin, sairly ruein
Whan forc'd to drink of her ain brewin.

steitters staggers
rig-braid furrow-breadth
awald upside-down
bourded japed
fistle whistling cry
bur-thristle thistle

stending striding
tyke mongrel dog
sairly ruein etc. proverb – to
  drink of one's own brewing,
  i.e., to be caught in one's
  own trap.

John Skinner

1721–1807

TULLOCHGORUM

Come gie's a sang, Montgomery cry'd,
And lay your disputes all aside,
What signifies 't for folks to chide
    For what was done before them:
Let Whig and Tory all agree,
    Whig and Tory, Whig and Tory,
    Whig and Tory all agree,
        To drop their Whig-mig-morum;
Let Whig and Tory all agree
To spend the night wi' mirth and glee,
And cheerful sing alang wi' me
    The Reel o' Tullochgorum.

O Tullochgorum's my delight,
It gars us a' in ane unite,
And ony sumph that keeps a spite,
    In conscience I abhor him:
For blythe and cheerie we's be a',
    Blythe and cheerie, blythe and cheerie,
    Blythe and cherrie we's be a',
        And make a happy quorum,
For blythe and cheerie we's be a'
As lang as we hae breath to draw,
And dance till we be like to fa'
    The Reel o' Tullochgorum.

Whig-mig-morum political   *gars* makes
  nonsense   *sumph* fool

What needs there be sae great a fraise
Wi' dringing dull Italian lays,
I wadna gie our ain Strathspeys
     For half a hunder score o' them;
They're dowf and dowie at the best,
    Dowf and dowie, dowf and dowie,
    Dowf and dowie at the best,
     Wi' a' their variorum;
They're dowf and dowie at the best,
Their *allegros* and a' the rest,
They canna' please a Scottish taste
     Compar'd wi' Tullochgorum.

Let warldly worms their minds oppress
Wi' fears o' want and double cess,
And sullen sots themsells distress
     Wi' keeping up decorum:
Shall we sae sour and sulky sit,
    Sour and sulky, sour and sulky,
    Sour and sulky shall we sit,
     Like old philosophorum!
Shall we sae sour and sulky sit,
Wi' neither sense, nor mirth, nor wit,
Nor ever try to shake a fit
     To th' Reel o' Tullochgorum?

May choicest blessings ay attend
Each honest, open-hearted friend,
And calm and quiet be his end,
     And a' that's good watch o'er him;
May peace and plenty be his lot,
    Peace and plenty, peace and plenty,
    Peace and plenty be his lot,
     And dainties a great store o' them;

fraise fracas   *dowf* woeful
dringing wearisome   *dowie* depressing

May peace and plenty be his lot,
Unstain'd by any vicious spot,
And may he never want a groat,
    That's fond o' Tullochgorum!

But for the sullen frumpish fool,
That loves to be oppression's tool,
May envy gnaw his rotten soul,
    And discontent devour him;
May dool and sorrow be his chance,
  Dool and sorrow, dool and sorrow,
  Dool and sorrow be his chance,
    And nane say, wae's me for him!
May dool and sorrow be his chance,
Wi' a' the ills that come frae France,
Wha e'er he be that winna dance
    The Reel o' Tullochgorum.

dool woe

Jean Elliot

1727–1805

THE FLOWERS OF THE FOREST

I've heard the lilting at our yowe-milking,
    Lasses a-lilting before the dawn o' day;
But now they are moaning on ilka green loaning;
    'The Flowers of the Forest are a' wede away.'

At buchts, in the morning, nae blythe lads are scorning;
    The lasses are lonely, and dowie, and wae;
Nae daffin', nae gabbin', but sighing and sabbing:
    Ilk ane lifts her leglen, and hies her away.

In hairst, at the shearing, nae youths now are jeering,
    The bandsters are lyart, and runkled and grey;
At fair or at preaching, nae wooing, nae fleeching:
    The Flowers of the Forest are a' wede away.

At e'en, in the gloaming, nae swankies are roaming
    'Bout stacks wi' the lasses at bogle to play,
But ilk ane sits drearie, lamenting her dearie:
    The Flowers of the Forest are a' wede away.

yowe	ewe	*hairst*	harvest
wede	withered	*bandsters*	binders
buchts	cattle-pens	*lyart*	grizzled
dowie	sad	*fleeching*	coaxing
daffin'	dallying	*swankies*	young bucks
leglen	stool	*bogle*	peek-a-boo

Dule and wae for the order sent our lads to the Border;
  The English, for ance, by guile wan the day:
The Flowers of the Forest, that foucht aye the foremost,
  The prime o' our land are cauld in the clay.

Anonymous Pasquils on the Treaty of Union 1707

VERSES ON THE SCOTS PEERS 1706

Our Duiks were deills, our Marquesses wer mad,
Our Earls were evills, our Viscounts yet more bad,
Our Lords were villains, and our Barons knaves
    Who with our burrows did sell us for slaves.

They sold the church, they sold the State and Nation,
They sold their honour, name and reputation,
They sold their birthright, peerages and places
    And now they leave the House with angrie faces.

And now they frown, and fret, and curse their fate,
And still in vain lost libertie regrate,
And are not these rare merchants nicelie trickt,
    Who were old Peers, but now are deils belikt.

Barons and burrows equally rewarded,
They were cajoled by all, but now by none regarded,
O may our God, who rules both heaven and earth
    Avert sad judgements – from us turn his wrath.

Let all true Scots with God importunat be
That he may yet restore our pristine libertie;
That he who rules the hearts of kings alone
    May settle James at length upon the throne.

A LITANIE ANENT THE UNION

From a forced and divided Union
And from the church and kirk communion
Where Lordly prelates have dominion
                              Deliver us, Lord.

From a new transubstantiation
Of the old Scots into ane English nation
And from all the foes to Reformation
                              Deliver us, Lord.

From selling Kingdoms, Kings and Crowns
For groats ill payed by Southeron lowns,
From mitres, surplices, long sleev'd gowns
                              Deliver us, Lord.

From a November powder treason
To blow up Parliament at this season,
Tho without powder, rhyme or reason,
                              Deliver us, Lord.

From Pets, and men of Posts and Pensions,
Sole managers of state conventions,
And from all interest in contentions
                              Deliver us, Lord.

From heavie taxes laid on salt,
On blinked (sour) ale, on beer or malt,
And herrieing us without a fault
                              Deliver us, Lord.

From trading with ane emptie purse
And meriting the old wife's curse,
And from all changes to the worse
                              Deliver us, Lord.

From paying debts we doe not owe,
Equivalents we do not know,
From being mad and still kept low
                    Deliver us, Lord.

From Patriots to Presbytery
Who to it bear antipathy,
And such friends as old Cromarty*
                    Deliver us, Lord.

From Patriots who for pious ends
Keep kirks unplanted that the teinds
They may secure to their best friends
                    Deliver us, Lord.

From bartering the ancient nation
For a new trade communication,
From English acts of navigation,
                    Deliver us, Lord.

From Burrows, Barons, and our Peers
Who bring ane old house o'er their ears,
For which they shall pay, some folk swears,
                    Deliver us, Lord.

From Holy Wars and hellish plots,
From faithless Christians, brutish Scots
And the disease that noses rots
                    Deliver us, Lord.

From rebell ruleing corporations
And headles Mobs governing nations
And acting out of their stations,
                    Deliver us, Lord.

* George MacKenzie, Earl of Cromarty

From paying us our Darien costs
By laying on cess and new imposts,
From the English ruling the Scots rosts
                    Deliver us, Lord.

From a free trade with prohibitions,
Restriction's heavie impositions,
Union on base unjust conditions
                    Deliver us, Lord.

From Peers whose state's a sepulchre,
Who vote the nation to interre,
And enemies to fast and prayer
                    Deliver us, Lord.

From pillor'd Poets* and Scots Pedlars†
For souldering kingdoms, busie meddlers,
From Organs and Cathedral Fiddlers
                    Deliver us, Lord.

From old Scots nobles in the rear
Of each new upstart English Peer,
And rouping Parliament robes next year
                    Deliver us, Lord.

From oaths and Tests which bar the just,
From Offices of place and trust
To satisfy the Clergy's lust
                    Deliver us, Lord.

From Esau Merchants and Trustees
Who serve them best, who give best fees,
And men whose heads are full of bees
                    Deliver us, Lord.

* Daniel Defoe   † Paterson the Banker

From Pride, Poverty and greed
United, and from old Scots feed (feud)
From making more haste than good speed
                         Deliver us, Lord.

From all religious compositions
Of old and modern superstitions,
From boots and thumbkin inquisitions
                         Deliver us, Lord.

From innocent men laying snares
And killing Glenco-men by pairs,
From sudden death, like the Earl of Stair's
                         Deliver us, Lord.

James Beattie

1735–1803

TO MR ALEXANDER ROSS

O Ross, thou wale of hearty cocks,
Sae crouse and canty with thy jokes!
Thy hamely auldwarl'd muse provokes
    Me for awhile
To ape our guid plain countra' folks
    In verse and stile.

Sure never carle was haff sae gabby
E'er since the winsome days o' Habby:
O mayst thou ne'er gang clung, or shabby,
    Nor miss thy snaker!
Or I'll ca' fortune nasty drabby,
    And say – pox take her!

O may the roupe ne'er roust thy weason,
May thirst thy thrapple never gizzen!
But bottled ale in mony a dizzen,
    Aye lade thy gantry!
And fouth o' vivres a' in season,
    Plenish thy pantry!

wale choice
crouse keen
canty merry
carle old man
gabby gossipy
Habby Habbie Simson
clung hungry
snaker ? sly drink

roupe head-cold
roust roughen
weason throat
thrapple gullet
gizzen parch
gantry wine-cellar
fouth lots
vivres victuals

Lang may thy stevin fill wi' glee
The glens and mountains of Lochlee,
Which were right gowsty but for thee,
　　Whase sangs enamour
Ilk lass, and teach wi' melody
　　The rocks to yamour.

Ye shak your head, but, o' my fegs,
Ye've set old Scota on her legs,
Lang had she lyen wi' beffs and flegs,
　　Bumbaz'd and dizzie;
Her fiddle wanted strings and pegs,
　　Waes me! poor hizzie!

Since Allan's death naebody car'd
For anes to speer how Scota far'd,
Nor plack nor thristled turner war'd
　　To quench her drouth;
For frae the cottar to the laird
　　We a' rin South.

The Southland chiels indeed hae mettle,
And brawley at a sang can ettle,
Yet we right couthily might settle
　　O' this side Forth.
The devil pay them wi' a pettle
　　That slight the North.

stevin vocal noise　　　*turner* small coin
gowsty desolate　　　　*war'd* spent
beffs blows　　　　　　*chiels* fellows
flegs terrors　　　　　*ettle* have a go
bumbaz'd confused　　　*couthily* cosily
Allan Allan Ramsay　　*pettle* plough-staff
plack small coin

Our countra leed is far frae barren,
It's even right pithy and aulfarren,
Oursells are neiper-like, I warren,
    For sense and smergh;
In kittle times when faes are yarring,
    We're no thought ergh.

Oh! bonny are our greensward hows,
Where through the birks the birny rows,
And the bee bums, and the ox lows,
    And saft winds rusle;
And shepherd lads on sunny knows
    Blaw the blythe fusle.

It's true, we Norlans manna fa'
To eat sae nice or gang sac bra',
As they that come from far awa,
    Yet sma's our skaith;
We've peace (and that's well worth it a')
    And meat and claith.

Our fine newfangle sparks, I grant ye,
Gi'e poor auld Scotland mony a taunty;
They're grown sae ugertfu' and vaunty,
    And capernoited,
They guide her like a canker'd aunty
    That's deaf and doited.

leed language	*rows* ripples
aulfarren old-fashioned	*fusle* whistle
neiper-like neighbourly	*manna* must not
smergh marrow	*fa'* happen
kittle unsettled	*skaith* harm
yarring snarling	*sparks* wits
ergh timid	*ugertfu'* squeamish
hows hollows	*capernoited* ill-tempered
birks birches	*doited* half-witted

Sae comes of ignorance I trow,
It's this that crooks their ill fa'r'd mou'
Wi' jokes sae course, they gar fouk spue
    For downright skonner;
For Scotland wants na sons enew
    To do her honour.

I here might gie a skreed o' names,
Dawties of Heliconian dames!
The foremost place Gawin Douglas claims,
    That canty priest;
And wha can match the fifth King James
    For sang or jest!

Montgomery grave, and Ramsay gay,
Dunbar, Scot, Hawthornden, and mae
Than I can tell; for o' my fae,
    I maun break aff;
'Twould take a live lang simmer day
    To name the haff.

The saucy chiels – I think they ca' them
Criticks, the muckle sorrow claw them,
(For mense nor manners ne'er could awe them
    Frae their presumption)
They need nae try thy jokes to fathom;
    They want rumgumption.

But ilka Mearns and Angus bearn,
Thy tales and sangs by heart shall learn,
And chiels shall come frae yont the Cairn –
    – Amounth, right yousty,
If Ross will be so kind as share in
    Their pint at Drousty.

ill fa'r'd ill-shaped	*mense* good sense, judgement
skonner revulsion, nausea	*rumgumption* initiative
dawties darlings	*bearn* native
mae more	*yousty* talkative
fae faith	*Drousty* alehouse in Lochlee

Robert Graham of Gartmore

c. 1735–97

O TELL ME HOW TO WOO THEE

If doughty deeds my lady please,
    Right soon I'll mount my steed;
And strong his arm, and fast his seat,
    That bears frae me the meed.
I'll wear thy colours in my cap,
    Thy picture in my heart;
And he that bends not to thine eye
    Shall rue it to his smart.

      Then tell me how to woo thee, love;
        O tell me how to woo thee!
      For thy dear sake, nae care I'll take,
        Tho' ne'er another trow me.

If gay attire delight thine eye,
    I'll dight me in array;
I'll tend thy chamber door all night,
    And squire thee all the day.
If sweetest sounds can win thine ear,
    These sounds I'll strive to catch;
Thy voice I'll steal to woo thysel',
    That voice that nane can match.

      Then tell me how to woo thee, etc.

But if fond love thy heart can gain,
    I never broke a vow;

Nae maiden lays her skaith to me;
  I never loved but you.
For you alone I ride the ring,
  For you I wear the blue;
For you alone I strive to sing,
  O tell me how to woo!

  Then tell me how to woo thee, etc.

Alexander Geddes

1737–1802

FROM THE EPISTLE TO THE
PRESIDENT, VICE-PRESIDENTS, AND
MEMBERS OF THE SCOTTISH SOCIETY
OF ANTIQUARIES: ON BEING CHOSEN A
CORRESPONDENT MEMBER

Nor will the search be hard or long:
For tho' 'tis true that Mither-tongue
Has had the melancholy fate
To be neglekit by the great,
She still has fun an open door
Amang the uncurruptit poor,
Wha be na weent to treat wi' scorn
A gentlewoman bred and born,
But bid her, thoch in tatters drest,
A hearty welcome to their best.

There aft on benmaist bink she sits,
And sharps the edge of cuintry wits,
Wi' routh of gabby saws, an' says,
An' jokes, an' gibes of uther days:
That gi'e si'k gust to rustic sport,
And gar the langsome night leuk short,

fun found	*routh* plenty
weent accustomed	*si'k* such
benmaist inmost	*gust* spice
bink bench	*gar* cause

At uther times in some warm neuk
She to the cutchok ha'ds a beuk,
And reids in si'k a magic tone,
The deeds that our forebeirs ha' done:
That – as 'tis said of that faim't Greek
Wha gaed to hell his wife to seek,
Sa sweet he sang, Ixion's wheel
And Sysiphus's stane stood still:
Nay mair; those greedy gleds, that iver
'Till nou had peck't Prometheus' Liver,
Forgat their prey, opt' wide their throats,
And lent their lugs to Orpheus' notes.
Sa here, gif ye attention gi'e,
Si'k auld-warld wunders ye may see;
May see the maiden stap her wheel;
The mistress cease to turn the reel;
Lizzy, wi' laddle in her hand,
Til pot boil over, gapand stand:
Ev'n hungry Gib his speun depose
And, for a mament, spare his brose.

Let bragart England in disdain
Ha'd ilka lingo, but her a'in:
Her a'in, we wat, say what she can,
Is like her true-born Englishman,*
A vile promiscuous mungrel† seed
Of Danish, Dutch, an' Norman breed,
An' prostituted, since, to a'
The jargons on this earthly ba'!
Bedek't, 'tis true, an' made fu' smart
Wi' mekil learning, pains an' art;

cutchok fire	*brose* kind of broth
ha'ds holds	*a'in* own
gleds kites	*is like, etc.* (reference to Defoe's
lugs ears	*True-born Englishman*)
laddle ladle	*mekil* much

* Defoe
† *Hybrida quidem lingua Anglicana est:* Hickes

An' taught to baik, an' benge, an' bou
As dogs an' dancin'-masters do:
Wi' fardit cheeks an' pouder't hair,
An' brazen confidential stare –
While ours, a blate an' bashfu' maid
Conceals her blushes wi' her plaid;
And is unwillan' to display
Her beuties in the face o' day.

    Bot strip them baith – an' see wha's shape
Has least the semblance of an ape?
Wha's lim's are straughtest? Wha can sheu
The whiter skin, an' fairer heu
An' whilk, in short, is the mair fit
To gender genuine manly wit?
I'll pledge my pen, you'll judgment pass
In favor of the Scottis lass.

benge fawn   *blate* shy
fardit painted   *whilk* which

Robert Fergusson

1750–74

BRAID CLAITH

Ye wha are fain to hae your name
Wrote in the bonny book of fame,
Let merit nae pretension claim
    To laurel'd wreath,
But hap ye weel, baith back and wame,
    In gude Braid Claith.

He that some ells o' this may fa,
An' slae-black hat on pow like snaw,
Bids bauld to bear the gree awa',
    Wi' a' this graith,
Whan bienly clad wi' shell fu' braw
    O' gude Braid Claith.

Waesuck for him wha has na fek o't!
For he's a gowk they're sure to geck at,
A chiel that ne'er will be respekit
    While he draws breath,
Till his four quarters are bedeckit
    Wi' gude Braid Claith.

hap wrap   *bienly* respectably
wame belly   *waesuck* pity
fa obtain   *fek* plenty
gree prize   *geck* mock
graith attire   *chiel* fellow

On Sabbath-days the barber spark,
When he has done wi' scrapin wark,
Wi' siller broachie in his sark,
    Gangs trigly, faith!
Or to the Meadow, or the Park,
    In gude Braid Claith.

Weel might ye trow, to see them there,
That they to shave your haffits bare,
Or curl an' sleek a pickle hair,
    Wou'd be right laith,
Whan pacing wi' a gawsy air
    In gude Braid Claith.

If ony mettl'd stirrah green
For favour frae a lady's ein
He maunna care for being seen
    Before he sheath
His body in a scabbard clean
    O' gude Braid Claith.

For, gin he come wi' coat thread-bare,
A feg for him she winna care,
But crook her bonny mou' fu' sair,
    And scald him baith.
Wooers shou'd ay their travel spare
    Without Braid Claith.

Braid Claith lends fock an unco heese,
Makes mony kail-worms butter-flies,
Gies mony a doctor his degrees
    For little skaith:
In short, you may be what you please
    Wi' gude Braid Claith.

spark chap		*green* yearn	
sark shirt		*feg* fig	
haffits side-whiskers		*scald* scold	
pickle little		*heese* uplift	
gawsy proud		*kail-worms* caterpillars	
stirrah gallant		*skaith* harm	

For thof ye had as wise a snout on
As *Shakespeare* or *Sir Isaac Newton*
Your judgment fouk wou'd hae a doubt on,
    I'll tak my aith,
Till they cou'd see ye wi' a suit on
      O' gude Braid Claith.

HALLOW-FAIR

At *Hallowmas*, whan nights grow lang,
  And *starnies* shine fu' clear,
Whan fock, the nippin cald to bang,
  Their winter *hap-warms* wear,
Near Edinbrough a fair there hads,
  I wat there's nane whase name is,
For strappin dames and sturdy lads,
  And cap and stoup, mair famous
      Than it that day.

Upo' the tap o' ilka lum
  The sun began to keek,
And bad the trig made maidens come
  A sightly joe to seek
At *Hallow-fair*, whare browsters rare
  Keep gude ale on the gantries,
And dinna scrimp ye o' a skair
  O' kebbucks frae their pantries,
      Fu' saut that day.

thof though if	*lum* chimney
starnies stars	*joe* lover
bang defeat	*browsters* brewers
hads holds	*skair* share
cap cup	*kebbucks* cheeses
mair more	*fu' saut* very salty

Here country John in bonnet blue,
  An' eke his Sunday claise on,
Rins efter Meg wi' *rokelay* new,
  An' sappy kisses lays on;
She'll tauntin say, Ye silly coof!
  Be o' your gab mair spairin;
He'll tak the hint, and criesh her loof
  Wi' what will buy her fairin,
      To chow that day.

Here chapman billies tak their stand,
  An' shaw their *bonny wallies*;
Wow, but they lie fu' gleg aff hand
  To trick the silly fallows:
Heh, Sirs! what cairds and tinklers come,
  An' *ne'er-do-weel* horse-coupers,
An' spae-wives fenzying to be dumb,
  Wi' a' siclike landloupers,
      To thrive that day.

Here Sawny cries, frae Aberdeen;
  'Come ye to me fa need:
'The brawest *shanks* that e'er were seen
  'I'll sell ye cheap an' guid.
'I wyt they are as protty hose
  'As come fae *weyr* or *leem*:
'Here tak a rug, and shaw's your pose:
  'Forseeth, my ain's but teem
      'An' light this day.'

rokelay mantle	*landloupers* vagabonds
coof fool	*fa* who
gab mouth	*shanks* hose
criesh grease	*weyr* wire
loof palm	*leem* loom
fairin lunch	*rug* bargain
chapman billies packman fellows	*pose* money
wallies wares	*ain* own
gleg readily	*teem* empty
spae-wives fortune-tellers	

Ye wives, as ye gang thro' the fair,
    O mak your bargains hooly!
O' a' thir wylie lowns beware,
    Or fegs they will ye spulyie.
For fairn-year *Meg Thamson* got,
    Frae thir mischievous villains,
A scaw'd bit o' a penny note,
    That lost a score o' shillins
       To her that day.

The dinlin drums alarm our ears,
    The serjeant screechs fu' loud,
'A' gentlemen and volunteers
    'That wish your country gude,
'Come here to me, and I shall gie
    'Twa guineas and a crown,
'A bowl o' *punch*, that like the sea
    'Will soum a lang dragoon
       'Wi' ease this day.'

Without the cuissers prance and nicker,
    An' our the ley-rig scud;
In tents the carles bend the bicker,
    An' rant an' roar like wud.
Then there's sic yellowchin and din,
    Wi' wives and wee-anes gablin,
That ane might true they were a-kin
    To a' the tongues at Babylon,
       Confus'd that day.

gang go	*ley-rig* grass-field
thir these	*scud* drive
lowns fellows	*carles* elders
spulyie spoil	*bicker* tankard
fairn-year last year	*wud* mad
scaw'd bit worthless scrap	*yellowchin* yelling
soum swim	*wee-anes* children
cuissers lancers	*true* believe

Whan *Phoebus* ligs in *Thetis* lap,
   Auld Reekie gies them shelter;
Whare cadgily they kiss the cap,
   An' ca't round helter-skelter.
Jock Bell gaed furth to play his freaks,
   Great cause he had to rue it,
For frae a stark Lochaber aix
   He gat a *clamihewit*
      Fu' sair that night.

'Ohon!' quo' he, 'I'd rather be
   'By *sword* or *bagnet* stickit,
'Than hae my crown or body wi'
   'Sic deadly weapons nicket.'
Wi' that he gat anither straik
   Mair weighty than before,
That gar'd his feckless body aik,
   An' spew the reikin gore,
      Fu' red that night.

He peching on the cawsey lay,
   O' kicks and cuffs weel sair'd;
A *Highland* aith the serjeant gae,
   'She maun pe see our guard.'
Out spak the weirlike corporal,
   'Pring in ta drunken sot.'
They trail'd him ben, an' by my saul,
   He paid his drunken groat,
      For that neist day.

cadgily gaily	*reikin* steaming
freaks pranks	*cawsey* pavement
clamihewit heavy blow	*sair'd* served
bagnet bayonet	*maun pe see* must be seeing
niket cut	*weirlike* warlike
straik stroke	*ben* in
feckless useless	*groat* small coin

Good fock, as ye come frae the fair,
   Bide yont frae this black squad;
There's nae sic savages elsewhere
   Allow'd to wear cockade.
Than the strong lion's hungry maw,
   Or tusk o' Russian bear,
Frae their wanruly fellin paw
   Mair cause ye hae to fear
       Your death that day.

A wee soup drink dis unco weel
   To had the heart aboon;
It's good as lang's a canny chiel
   Can stand steeve in his shoon.
But gin a birkie's owr weel sair'd,
   It gars him aften stammer
To *pleys* that bring him to the guard,
   An' eke the *Council-chawmir*,
       Wi' shame that day.

TO DR SAMUEL JOHNSON

Food for a new Edition of his Dictionary

Great Pedagogue, whose literanian lore,
With syllable and syllable conjoin'd
To transmutate and varyfy, has learn'd
The whole revolving scientific names
That in the alphabetic columns lie,
Far from the knowledge of mortalic shapes,
As we, who never can peroculate
The miracles by thee miraculiz'd,
The Muse, silential long, with mouth apert

bide yont stay far from   *aboon* above
wanruly unruly   *steeve* upright
unco weel very well   *birkie* chap

Would give vibration to stagnatic tongue,
And loud encomiate thy puissant name,
Eulogiated from the green decline
Of Thames's bank to Scoticanian shores,
Where Loch-Lomondian liquids undulize.

To meminate thy name in after times,
The mighty Mayor of each regalian town
Shall consignate thy work to parchment fair
In roll burgharian, and their tables all
Shall fumigate with fumigation' strong:
Scotland, from perpendicularian hills,
Shall emigrate her fair muttonian store,
Which late had there in pedestration walk'd,
And o'er her airy heights perambuliz'd.

Oh, blackest execrations on thy head,
Edina shameless! tho' he came within
The bounds of your notation, tho' you knew
His honorific name, you noted not,
But basely suffer'd him to chariotize
Far from tow'rs, with smoke that nubilate,
Nor drank one amicitial swelling cup
To welcome him convivial. Bailies all,
With rage inflated, Catenations tear,
Nor ever after be you vinculiz'd,
Since you that sociability denied
To him whose potent Lexiphanian stile
Words can prolongate, and inswell his page
With what in others to a line's confin'd.

Welcome, thou verbal potentate and prince!
To hills and vallies, where emerging oats
From earth assurge our pauperty to bay,
And bless thy name, thy dictionarian skill,
Which there definitive will still remain,
And oft be speculiz'd by taper blue,
While youth studentious turn thy folio page.

Bailies councillors

Have you as yet, in per'patetic mood,
Regarded with the texture of the eye
The cave cavernick, where fraternal bard,
Churchill, depicted pauperated swains
With thraldom and black want, reducted sore,
Where Nature, coloriz'd, so coarsely fades,
And puts her russet par'phernalia on?
Have you as yet the way explorified,
To let lignarian chalice, swell'd with oats,
Thy orifice approach? Have you as yet,
With skin fresh rubified by scarlet spheres,
Apply'd brimstonic unction to your hide,
To terrify the salamandrian fire
That from involuntary digits asks
The strong allaceration? Or can you swill
The usquebalian flames of whisky blue
In fermentation strong? Have you apply'd
The kelt aerian to your Anglian thighs,
And with renunciation assigniz'd
Your breeches in Londona to be worn?
Can you, in frigor of Highlandian sky,
On healthy summits take nocturnal rest?
It cannot be – you may as well desire
An alderman leave plumb-puddenian store,
And scratch the tegument from pottage-dish,
As bid thy countrymen, and thee conjoin'd,
Forsake stomachic joys. Then hie you home,
And be a malcontent, that naked hinds,
On lentiles fed, can make your kingdom quake,
And tremulate Old England libertiz'd.

usquebalian from 'usquebae', whisky

THE GHAISTS: A KIRK-YARD ECLOGUE

> Did you not say, on good ANN's day,
>   And vow and did protest, Sir,
> That when HANOVER should come o'er,
>   We surely should be blest, Sir?
>   *An auld sang made new again*

Whare the braid planes in dowy murmurs wave
Their antient taps out o'er the cald, cald grave,
Whare *Geordie Girdwood*, mony a lang-spun day,
Houkit for gentlest banes the humblest clay,
Twa sheeted ghaists, sae grizly and sae wan,
'Mang lanely tombs their douff discourse began.

WATSON

Cauld blaws the nippin north wi' angry sough,
And showers his hailstanes frae the Castle Cleugh
O'er the Greyfriars, whare, at mirkest hour,
Bogles and spectres wont to tak their tour,
Harlin the pows and shanks to hidden cairns,
Amang the hamlocks wild, and sun-burnt fearns
But nane the night save you and I hae come
Frae the dern mansions of the midnight tomb,
Now whan the dawning's near, whan cock maun craw,
And wi his angry bougil gar's withdraw,
Ayont the kirk we'll stap, and there tak bield,
While the black hours our nightly freedom yield.

dowy sad	*harlin* dragging
houkit dug	*pows* heads
ghaists ghosts	*dern* secret
douff mournful	*bougil* bugle
cleugh cliff	*bield* shelter
bogles ghosts, spirits	

HERRIOT

I'm weel content; but binna cassen down,
Nor trow the cock will ca' ye hame o'er soon,
For tho' the eastern lift betakens day,
Changing her rokelay black for mantle grey,
Nae weirlike bird our knell of parting rings,
Nor sheds the caller moisture frae his wings.
NATURE has chang'd her course; the birds o' day
Dosin' in silence on the bending spray,
While owlets round the craigs at noon-tide flee,
And bludey bawks sit singand on the tree.
Ah, CALEDON! the land I yence held dear,
Sair mane mak I for thy destruction near;
And thou, EDINA! anes my dear abode,
Whan royal JAMIE sway'd the sovereign rod,
In thae blest days, weel did I think bestow'd,
To blaw thy poortith by wi' heaps o' gowd;
To mak thee sonsy seem wi' mony a gift,
And gar thy stately turrets speel the lift:
In vain did Danish Jones, wi' gimcrack pains,
In Gothic sculpture fret the pliant stanes:
In vain did he affix my statue here,
Brawly to busk wi' flow'rs ilk coming year;
My tow'rs are sunk, my lands are barren now,
My fame, my honour, like my flow'rs maun dow.

lift sky	*anes* once
rokely cloak	*thae* those
wierlike warlike	*poortith* poverty
caller fresh	*sonsy* wealthy
craigs rocks	*speel* climb
bawks bats	*busk* deck
sair mane sore moan	*dow* fade

WATSON

Sure *Major Weir*, or some sic warlock wight,
Has flung beguilin' glamer o'er your sight;
Or else some kittle cantrup thrown, I ween,
Has bound in mirlygoes my ain twa ein,
If ever aught frae sense cou'd be believed
(And seenil hae my senses been deceiv'd),
This moment, o'er the tap of Adam's tomb,
Fu' easy can I see your chiefest dome:
Nae corbie fleein' there, nor croupin' craws,
Seem to forspeak the ruin of thy haws,
But a' your tow'rs in wonted order stand,
Steeve as the rocks that hem our native land.

HERRIOT

Think na I vent my well-a-day in vain,
Kent ye the cause, ye sure wad join my mane.
Black be the day that e'er to England's ground
Scotland was eikit by the UNION's bond;
For mony a menzie of destructive ills
The country now maun brook frae *mortmain bills*,
That void our test-ments, and can freely gie
Sic will and scoup to the ordain'd trustee,
That he may tir our stateliest riggins bare,
Nor acres, houses, woods, nor fishins spare,
Till he can lend the stoitering state a lift
Wi' gowd in gowpins as a grassum gift;
In lieu o' whilk, we maun be weel content
To tyne the capital at three *per cent*.

kittle deceitful	*steeve* hard
cantrup trick	*menzie* crowd
mirlygoes delusions	*scoup* scope
seenil seldom	*tir* strip
corbie crow	*stoitering* staggering
haws halls	*tyne* lose

A doughty sum indeed, whan now-a-days
They raise provisions as the stents they raise,
Yoke hard the poor, and lat the rich chiels be,
Pamper'd at ease by ither's industry.
    Hale interest for my fund can scantly now
Cleed a' my callants backs, and stap their mou'.
How maun their weyms wi' sairest hunger slack,
Their duds in targets flaff upo' their back,
Whan they are doom'd to keep a lasting Lent,
Starving for England's weel at *three per cent*.

WATSON

    Auld Reekie than may bless the gowden times,
Whan honesty and poortith baith are crimes;
She little kend, whan you and I endow'd
Our hospitals for back-gaun burghers gude,
That e'er our siller or our lands shou'd bring
A gude bien living to a back-gaun king.
Wha, thanks to ministry! is grown sae wise,
He douna chew the bitter cud of vice;
For gin, frae Castlehill to Netherbow,
Wad honest houses baudy-houses grow,
The crown wad never spier the price o' sin,
Nor hinder younkers to the de'il to rin;
But gif some mortal grien for pious fame,
And leave the poor man's pray'r to sane his name,
His geer maun a' be scatter'd by the claws
O' ruthless, ravenous, and harpy laws.
Yet, shou'd I think, altho' the bill tak place,
The council winna lack sae meikle grace

stents lots		*siller* silver
chiels fellows		*bien* comfortable
cleed clothe		*douna* dare not
callants boys		*spier* ask for
weyms bellies		*grien* yearn
duds clothes		*sane* bless
targets rags		*geer* goods
back-gaun needy		*meikle* much

As lat our heritage at wanworth gang,
Or the succeeding generations wrang
O' braw bien maintenance and walth o' lear,
Whilk else had drappit to their children's skair;
For mony a deep, and mony a rare engyne
Ha'e sprung frae Herriot's wark, and sprung frae mine.

HERRIOT

I find, my friend, that ye but little ken,
There's einow on the earth a set o' men,
Wha' if they get their private pouches lin'd,
Gie na a winnelstrae for a' mankind;
They'll sell their country, flae their conscience bare,
To gar the weigh-bauk turn a single hair.
The government need only bait the line
Wi' the prevailing flee, the gowden coin,
Then our executors, and wise trustees,
Will sell them fishes in forbiddon seas,
Upo' their dwining country girn in sport,
Laugh in their sleeve, and get a place at court.

WATSON

Ere that day come, I'll 'mang our spirits pick
Some ghaist that trokes and conjures wi' Auld Nick,
To gar the wind wi' rougher rumbles blaw,
And weightier thuds than ever mortal saw:
Fire-flaught and hail, wi' tenfald fury's fires,
Shall lay yird-laigh Edina's airy spires:

at wanworth gang go worthless	*flee* fly
lear learning	*dwining* dwindling
skair share	*girn* complain
engyne genius	*trokes* deals
einow even now	*fire-flaught* lightning
weigh-bauk scales	*yird-laigh* earth-low

Tweed shall rin rowtin' down his banks out o'er,
Till Scotland's out o' reach o' England's pow'r;
Upo' the briny Borean jaws to float,
And mourn in dowy saughs her dowy lot.

HERRIOT

Yonder's the tomb of wise *Mackenzie* fam'd,
Whase laws rebellious bigotry reclaim'd,
Freed the hail land frae convenanting fools,
Wha erst ha'e fash'd us wi' unnumber'd dools;
Till night we'll tak the swaird aboon our pows,
And than, whan she her ebon chariot rows,
We'll travel to the vaut wi' stealing stap,
And wauk Mackenzie frae his quiet nap:
Tell him our ails, that he, wi' wonted skill,
May fleg the schemers o' the *mortmain-bill.*

FROM AULD REIKIE

Now morn, with bonny purpie-smiles,
Kisses the air-cock o' St Giles;
Rakin their ein, the servant lasses
Early begin their lies and clashes;
Ilk tells her friend of saddest distress
That still she brooks frae scouling mistress;
And wi' her joe in Turnpike Stair
She'd rather snuff the stinking air
As be subjected to her tongue,
When justly censur'd in the wrong.

rowtin' roaring
saughs willows
fash'd annoyed
dools woes
fleg frighten

purpie purple
rakin rubbing
clashes gossips
scouling scowling
joe sweetheart

On stair wi' tub, or pat, in hand,
The barefoot housemaids looe to stand,
That antrin folk may ken how snell
Auld Reikie will at morning smell:
Then with an inundation big as
The burn that neath the Nor' Loch brig is,
They kindly shower Edina's Roses
To quicken and regale our noses.
Now some for this, wi' satyre's leesh,
Ha'e gi'en auld Edinburgh a creesh;
But without souring nocht is sweet;
The morning smells that hail our street
Prepare, and gently lead the way
To simmer canty, braw and gay.
Edina's sons mair eithly share
Her spices and her dainties rare
Than he that's never yet been call'd
Aff frae his plaidie or his fauld.

Now stairhead critics, senseless fools,
Censure their aim, and pride their rules,
In Luckenbooths, wi' glouring eye,
Their neighbours sma'est faults descry:
If ony loun should dander there,
Of aukward gate and foreign air,
They trace his steps till they can tell
His pedigree as weel's himsell.

pat pot
antrin other, passing-by
Nor' Loch now the railway at
  Waverley Station
Edina's Roses contents of the
  chamber-pots
leesh lash
creesh thrashing
simmer summer

canty merry
eithly easily
aff frae, etc. i.e. from the rural
  life
Luckenbooths tenements of shops
  in the High Street
loun fellow
dander lounge, wander
gate manner

When Phoebus blinks wi' warmer ray,
And schools at noonday get the play,
Then bus'ness, weighty bus'ness comes;
The trader glours; he doubts, he hums;
The lawyers eke to Cross repair,
Their wigs to shaw, and toss an air;
While busy agent closely plies,
And a' his kittle cases tries.

glours scowls   *shaw* exhibit
eke also   *kittle* subtle

Lady Anne Lindsay

1750–1825

AULD ROBIN GRAY

When the sheep are in the fauld, and the kye a' at hame,
When a' the weary warld to sleep are gane,
The waes o' my heart fa' in showers frae my e'e,
While my gudeman lies sound by me.

Young Jamie lo'ed me weel, and sought me for his bride;
But saving a croun he had naething else beside.
To mak the croun a pound, my Jamie gaed to sea,
And the croun and the pound, they were baith for me.

He hadna been awa' a week but only twa,
When my mither she fell sick and the cow was stown awa';
My father brak his arm – my Jamie at the sea;
And auld Robin Gray cam a-courtin' me.

My father couldna wark, my mither couldna spin;
I toil'd day and nicht, but their bread I couldna win:
Auld Rob maintain'd them baith, and wi' tears in his e'e,
Said, 'Jeanie, for their sakes, will ye marry me?'

My heart it said na – I look'd for Jamie back;
But the wind it blew hie, and the ship it was a wrack;
His ship it was a wrack – why didna Jamie dee?
And why do I live to cry, Wae's me?

fauld sheepfold   *gudeman* husband
kye cattle   *hie* high

My father urged me sair; my mither didna speak,
But she looked in my face till my heart was like to break.
They gied him my hand – my heart was at the sea;
Sae auld Robin Gray, he was gudeman to me.

I hadna been a wife a week but only four,
When, mournfu' as I sat on the stane at the door,
I saw my Jamie's wraith – I couldna think it he,
Till he said, 'I'm come hame, my love, to marry thee.'

O sair did we greet, and meikle did we say:
We took but ae kiss, and I bade him gang away.
I wish that I were dead, but I'm no like to dee;
And why was I born to say, Wae's me?

I gang like a ghaist, and I carena to spin;
I daurna think o' Jamie, for that wad be a sin.
But I'll do my best a gude wife to be,
For auld Robin Gray, he is kind to me.

sair sorely   *meikle* much
greet weep

Robert Burns

1759–96

TO A MOUSE

Wee, sleeket, cowran, tim'rous beastie,
O' what a panic's in thy breastie!
Thou need na start awa sae hasty
   Wi' bickering brattle!
I wad be laith to rin an' chase thee,
   Wi' murdering pattle!

I'm truly sorry man's dominion
Has broken Nature's social union,
An' justifies that ill opinion
   Which makes thee startle
At me, thy poor, earth-born companion
   An' fellow mortal!

I doubt na, whyles, but thou may thieve,
What then? poor beastie, thou maun live!
A daimen-icker in a thrave
   'S a sma' request;
I'll get a blessin wi' the lave,
   An' never miss't!

sleeket sly, smooth-haired
cowran cowering
bickering brattle anxious chiding
pattle ploughstaff

whyles occasionally
daimen-icker stray ear of corn
thrave sheaf
lave remainder

Thy wee bit housie, too, in ruin!
Its silly wa's the win's are strewin!
An' naething, now, to big a new ane,
   O' foggage green!
An' bleak December's win's ensuin,
   Baith snell an' keen!

Thou saw the fields laid bare an' wast,
An' weary winter comin fast,
An' cozie here, beneath the blast,
   Thou thought to dwell,
Till crash! the cruel coulter past
   Out thro' thy cell.

That wee-bit heap o' leaves an' stibble,
Has cost thee monie a wearie nibble!
Now thou's turned out, for a' thy trouble,
   But house or hald,
To thole the winter's sleety dribble,
   An' cranreuch cauld!

But Mousie, thou art no thy lane,
In proving foresight may be vain:
The best-laid schemes o' Mice an' Men
   Gang aft agley,
An, lea'e us nocht but grief an' pain,
   For promis'd joy!

Still thou art blest, compar'd wi' me!
The present only toucheth thee:
But och! I backward cast my e'e,
   On prospects drear!
An' forward, tho' I canna see,
   I guess an' fear!

big build
foggage foliage
coulter plough-share blade
but house, etc. with nowhere to
  shelter

thole endure
cranreuch frosty
no thy lane not alone
gang aft agley go often awry

TAM O' SHANTER

A TALE

Of Brownys and of Bogillis full is this Buke.
Gawin Douglas

When chapman billies leave the street,
And drouthy neebors neebors meet;
As market-days are wearing late,
An' folk begin to tak the gate:
While we sit bousing at the nappy,
An' getting fou and unco happy,
We think na on the lang Scots miles,
The mosses, waters, slaps, and styles,
That lie between us and our hame
Whare sits our sulky sullen dame,
Gathering her brows like gathering storm,
Nursing her wrath to keep it warm.

This truth fand honest Tam o' Shanter,
As he frae Ayr ae night did canter;
(Auld Ayr, wham ne'er a town surpasses,
For honest men and bonie lasses).

O Tam, had'st thou but been sae wise,
As taen thy ain wife Kate's advice!
She tauld thee weel thou was a skellum,
A blethering, blustering, drunken blellum;
That frae November till October,
Ae market-day thou was na sober,

Bogillis ghosts
chapman billies packman fellows
drouthy thirsty
gate way
fand found

taen taken
skellum good-for-nothing
blethering gossiping
blellum babbler

That ilka melder wi' the miller,
Thou sat as lang as thou had siller;
That ev'ry naig was ca'd a shoe on,
The smith and thee gat roaring fou on;
That at the Lord's house, even on Sunday,
Thou drank wi' Kirkton Jean till Monday.
She prophesied, that, late or soon,
Thou would be found deep drown'd in Doon,
Or catch'd wi' warlocks in the mirk
By Alloway's auld, haunted kirk.
Ah, gentle dames! it gars me greet,
To think how monie counsels sweet,
How monie lengthen'd, sage advices
The husband frae the wife despises!

But to our tale:— Ae market-night,
Tam had got planted unco right,
Fast by an ingle, bleezing finely,
Wi' reaming swats, that drank divinely;
And at his elbow, Souter Johnie,
His ancient, trusty, drouthy cronie:
Tam lo'ed him like a very brither;
They had been fou for weeks thegither.
The night drave on wi' sang and clatter;
And ay the ale was growing better:
The landlady and Tam grew gracious
Wi' secret favours, sweet and precious:
The Souter tauld his queerest stories;
The landlord's laugh was ready chorus:
The storm without might rair and rustle,
Tam did na mind the storm a whistle.

melder amount of grain for
    milling
siller silver
ca'd hammered
fou drunk
warlocks wizards

gars me greet makes me weep
reaming swats frothing drinks
Souter Shoemaker
cronie pal
clatter chat

Care, mad to see a man sae happy,
E'en drown'd himsel amang the nappy.
As bees flee hame wi' lades o' treasure,
The minutes wing'd their way wi' pleasure.
Kings may be blest but Tam was glorious,
O'er a' the ills o' life victorious!

But pleasures are like poppies spread:
You seize the flow'r, its bloom is shed;
Or like the snow falls in the river,
A moment white – then melts for ever;
Or like the borealis race,
That flit ere you can point their place;
Or like the rainbow's lovely form
Evanishing amid the storm.
Nae man can tether time or tide;
The hour approaches Tam maun ride:
That hour, o' night's black arch the key-stane,
That dreary hour Tam mounts his beast in,
And sic a night he taks the road in,
As ne'er poor sinner was abroad in.

The wind blew as 'twad blawn its last;
The rattling showers rose on the blast;
The speedy gleams the darkness swallow'd;
Loud, deep, and lang the thunder bellow'd;
That night, a child might understand,
The Deil had business on his hand.

Weel mounted on his gray mare Meg,
A better never lifted leg,
Tam skelpit on thro' dub and mire,
Despising wind, and rain, and fire;
Whiles holding fast his guid blue bonnet,

lades loads   *skelpit* galloped
maun must

Whiles crooning o'er some auld Scots sonnet,
Whiles glow'ring round wi' prudent cares,
Lest bogles catch him unawares:
Kirk-Alloway was drawing nigh,
Whare ghaists and houlets nightly cry.
By this time he was cross the ford,
Whare in the snaw the chapman smoor'd;
And past the birks and meikle stane,
Whare drunken Charlie brak's neck-bane;
And thro' the whins, and by the cairn,
Where hunters fand the murder'd bairn;
And near the thorn, aboon the well,
Whare Mungo's mither hang'd hersel.
Before him Doon pours all his floods;
The doubling storm roars thro' the woods;
The lightnings flash from pole to pole;
Near and more near the thunders roll:
When, glimmering thro' the groaning trees,
Kirk-Alloway seem'd in a bleeze,
Thro' ilka bore the beams were glancing,
And loud resounded mirth and dancing.

Inspiring bold John Barleycorn,
What dangers thou canst make us scorn!
Wi' tippenny, we fear nae evil;
Wi' usquabae, we'll face the Devil!
The swats sae reamed in Tammie's noddle,
Fair play, he car'd na deils a boddle.
But Maggie stood, right sair astonish'd,
Till, by the heel and hand admonish'd,
She ventur'd forward on the light;
And, wow! Tam saw an unco sight!

bogles ghosts
houlets owls
smoor'd smothered
birks birch-trees

bore hole
tippenny ale
usquabae whisky
boddle small coin

Warlocks and witches in a dance:
Nae cotillion, brent new frae France,
But hornpipes, jigs, strathspeys, and reels,
Put life and mettle in their heels.
A winnock-bunker in the east,
There sat Auld Nick, in shape o' beast;
A tousie tyke, black, grim, and large,
To gie them music was his charge:
He screw'd the pipes and gart them skirl,
Till roof and rafters a' did dirl.
Coffins stood round, like open presses,
That shaw'd the dead in their last dresses;
And, by some devilish cantraip sleight,
Each in its cauld hand held a light:
By which heroic Tam was able
To note upon the haly table,
A murderer's banes, in gibbet-airns;
Twa span-lang, wee, unchristen'd bairns;
A thief new-cutted frae a rape –
Wi' his last gasp his gab did gape;
Five tomahawks wi' blude red-rusted;
Five scimitars wi' murder crusted;
A garter which a babe had strangled;
A knife a father's throat had mangled –
Whom his ain son o' life bereft –
The grey hairs yet stack to the heft;
Wi' mair o' horrible and awfu',
Which even to name wad be unlawfu'.
Three lawyers' tongues, turned inside out,
Wi' lies seamed like a beggar's clout;
Three Priests' hearts, rotten, black as muck,
Lay stinking, vile, in every neuk.

winnock-bunker window-seat   *cantraip* trick
tyke cur   *gibbet-airns* gibbet-irons
dirl resound   *rape* rope

As Tammie glowr'd, amazed, and curious,
The mirth and fun grew fast and furious;
The piper loud and louder blew,
The dancers quick and quicker flew,
They reel'd, they set, they cross'd, they cleekit,
Till ilka carlin swat and reekit,
And coost her duddies to the wark,
And linket at it in her sark!

Now Tam, O Tam! had thae been queans,
A' plump and strapping in their teens!
Their sarks, instead o' creeshie flannen,
Been snaw-white seventeen hunder linen! –
Thir breeks o' mine, my only pair,
That ance were plush, o' gude blue hair,
I wad hae gi'en them off my hurdies
For ae blink o' the bonie burdies!

But wither'd beldams, auld and droll,
Rigwoodie hags wad spean a foal,
Louping and flinging on a crummock,
I wonder did na turn thy stomach!

But Tam kend what was what fu' brawlie:
There was ae winsome wench and wawlie,
That night enlisted in the core,
Lang after kend on Garrick shore

(For monie a beast to dead she shot,
An' perish'd monie a bonie boat,
And shook baith meikle corn and bear,

carlin old woman	*creeshie flannen* greasy flannel
swat sweated	*hurdies* hips
reekit steamed	*rigwoodie* stringy
coost cast	*spean* wean
duddies clothes, rags	*crummock* stick
linket danced	*wawlie* spirited
sark shift	*bear* barley

And kept the country-side in fear).
Her cutty sark, o' Paisley harn,
That while a lassie she had worn,
In longitude tho' sorely scanty,
It was her best, and she was vauntie . . .
Ah! little kend thy reverend grannie,
That sark she coft for her wee Nannie,
Wi' twa pund Scots ('twas a' her riches),
Wad ever grac'd a dance o' witches!
But here my Muse her wing maun cour,
Sic flights are far beyond her power:
To sing how Nannie lap and flang
(A souple jade she was and strang),
And how Tam stood like ane bewitch'd,
And thought his very een enrich'd;
Ev'n Satan glowr'd, and fidg'd fu' fain,
And hotch'd and blew wi' might and main;
Till first ae caper, syne anither,
Tam tint his reason a' thegither,
And roars out: 'Weel done, Cutty-sark!'
And in an instant all was dark;
And scarcely had he Maggie rallied,
When out the hellish legion sallied.

As bees bizz out wi' angry fyke,
When plundering herds assail their byke;
As open pussie's mortal foes,
When, pop! she starts before their nose;
As eager runs the market-crowd,
When 'Catch the thief!' resounds aloud:
So Maggie runs, the witches follow,
Wi' monie an eldritch skriech and hollo.
Ah, Tam! Ah, Tam! thou'll get thy fairin!

cutty diminutive	*fidg'd* itched randily
harn linen	*fyke* fuss
vauntie proud	*byke* hive
coft bought	*pussie* a hare
cour cower	*eldritch* unearthly

In hell they'll roast thee like a herrin!
In vain thy Kate awaits thy comin!
Kate soon will be a woefu' woman!
Now, do thy speedy utmost, Meg,
And win the key-stane of the brig;
There, at them thou thy tail may toss,
A running stream they dare na cross!
But ere the key-stane she could make,
The fient a tail she had to shake;
For Nannie, far before the rest,
Hard upon noble Maggie prest,
And flew at Tam wi' furious ettle;
But little wist she Maggie's mettle!
Ae spring brought off her master hale,
But left behind her ain grey tail:
The carlin claught her by the rump,
And left poor Maggie scarce a stump.

Now, wha this tale o' truth shall read,
Ilk man, and mother's son, take heed;
Whene'er to drink you are inclin'd,
Or cutty sarks run in your mind,
Think! ye may buy the joys o'er dear:
Remember Tam o' Shanter's mare.

HOLY WILLIE'S PRAYER

And send the godly in a pet to pray.
        Pope.

O Thou that in the Heavens does dwell,
Wha, as it pleases best Thysel,
Sends ane to Heaven an' ten to Hell
    A' for thy glory,
And no for onie gude or ill
    They've done before Thee!

brig bridge   *ettle* intention
fient a tail no tail at all   *onie* any

I bless and praise Thy matchless might,
When thousands Thou has left in night,
That I am here before Thy sight
    For gifts an' grace
A burning and a shining light
      To a' this place.

What was I, or my generation,
That I should get sic exaltation?
I, wha deserv'd most just damnation
    For broken laws
Sax thousand years ere my creation,
      Thro' Adam's cause!

When from my mither's womb I fell,
Thou might hae plung'd me deep in hell
To gnash my gooms, and weep, and wail
    In burning lakes,
Where damned devils roar and yell,
      Chain'd to their stakes.

Yet I am here, a chosen sample,
To show Thy grace is great and ample:
I'm here a pillar o' Thy temple,
    Strong as a rock,
A guide, a buckler, and example
      To a' Thy flock!

But yet, O Lord! confess I must:
At times I'm fash'd wi' fleshly lust;
An' sometimes, too, in warldly trust
    Vile self gets in;
But Thou remembers we are dust,
    Defiled wi' sin.

gooms gums   *fash'd* troubled

O Lord! yestreen, Thou kens, wi' Meg –
Thy pardon I sincerely beg –
O' may't ne'er be a living plague
    To my dishonour!
An' I'll ne'er lift a lawless leg
    Again upon her.

Besides, I farther maun avow –
Wi' Leezie's lass, three times, I trow –
But, Lord, that Friday I was fou,
    When I cam near her,
Or else, Thou kens, Thy servant true
    Wad never steer her.

Maybe Thou lets this fleshly thorn
Buffet Thy servant e'en and morn,
Lest he owre-proud and high should turn
    That he's sae gifted:
If sae, Thy han' maun e'en be borne
    Until Thou lift it.

Lord, bless Thy chosen in this place,
For here Thou has a chosen race!
But God confound their stubborn face
    An' blast their name,
Wha brings Thy elders to disgrace
    An' open shame!

Lord, mind Gau'n Hamilton's deserts:
He drinks, an' swears, an' plays at cartes,
Yet has sae monie takin arts
    Wi' great and sma',
Frae God's ain Priest the people's hearts
    He steals awa.

fou drunk   *cartes* cards
steer interfere with, fuck

And when we chasten'd him therefore,
Thou kens how he bred sic a splore,
And set the warld in a roar
   O' laughin at us:
Curse Thou his basket and his store,
    'Kail an' potatoes!

Lord, hear my earnest cry and pray'r
Against that Presbyt'ry of Ayr!
Thy strong right hand, Lord, make it bare
   Upo' their heads!
Lord, visit them, an' dinna spare
   For their misdeeds!

O Lord, my God! that glib-tongu'd Aiken,
My vera heart and flesh are quakin
To think how we stood sweatin, shakin,
  An' pish'd wi' dread,
While Auld, wi' hingin lip gaed sneaking
  And hid his head.

Lord, in Thy day o' veangeance try him!
Lord, visit him wha did employ him!
And pass not in Thy mercy by them
   Nor hear their pray'r,
But for Thy people's sake destroy them,
   An' dinna spare!

But Lord, remember me and mine
Wi' mercies temporal and divine,
That I for grace an' gear may shine
   Excell'd by nane;
And a' the glory shall be Thine –
   Amen, Amen!

splore riot   *gear* capital
Auld Daddy Auld the minister:
  Hamilton and Aiken were
  friends of Burns

AULD LANG SYNE

Should auld acquaintance be forgot,
   And never brought to mind?
Should auld acquaintance be forgot,
   And auld lang syne?

   For auld lang syne, my jo,
     For auld lang syne,
   We'll tak a cup o' kindness yet
     For auld lang syne.

And surely you'll be your pint-stowp,
   And surely I'll be mine,
And we'll tak a cup o' kindness yet
   For auld lang syne!

   For auld lang syne, etc.

We twa hae run about the braes,
   And pu'd the gowans fine,
But we've wander'd monie a weary fit
   Sin' auld lang syne.

   For auld lang syne, etc.

We twa hae paidl'd in the burn
   Frae morning sun til dine,
But seas between us braid hae roar'd
   Sin' auld lang syne.

   For auld land syne, etc.

auld lang syne former days and
   friends
jo dear
stowp tankard
gowans daisies
fit foot
braid broad

And there's a hand, my trusty fiere,
  And gie's a hand o' thine,
And we'll tak a right guid-willie waught
  For auld lang syne!

For auld lang syne, etc.

SCOTS, WHA HAE

Scots, wha hae wi' Wallace bled,
Scots, wham Bruce has aften led,
Welcome to your gory bed
        Or to victorie!

Now's the day, and now's the hour:
See the front o' battle lour,
See approach proud Edward's power –
        Chains and slaverie!

Wha will be a traitor knave?
Wha can fill a coward's grave?
Wha sae base as be a slave? –
        Let him turn, and flee!

Wha for Scotland's King and Law
Freedom's sword will strongly draw,
Freeman stand, or freeman fa',
        Let him follow me!

By Oppression's woes and pains,
By your sons in servile chains,
We will drain our dearest veins
        But they shall be free!

guid-willie waught friendly draught   *aften* often
wha hae wi, etc. who have bled   *lour* loom up
  with Wallace

Lay the proud usurpers low!
Tyrants fall in every foe!
Liberty's in every blow!
    Let us do, or die!

CORN RIGGS

It was upon a Lammas night
  When corn riggs are bonie,
Beneath the moon's unclouded light,
  I held awa to Annie:
The time flew by, wi' tentless heed,
  Till 'tween the late and early;
Wi' sma' persuasion she agreed,
  To see me thro' the barley.

The sky was blue, the wind was still,
  The moon was shining clearly;
I set her down, wi' right good will,
  Amang the rigs o' barley:
I ken't her heart was a' my ain;
  I lov'd her most sincerely;
I kiss'd her owre and owre again,
  Amang the rigs o' barley.

I lock'd her in my fond embrace;
  Her heart was beating rarely:
My blessing on that happy place,
  Amang the rigs o' barley!
But by the moon and stars so bright,
  That shone that night so clearly!
She ay shall bless that happy night,
  Amang the rigs o' barley.

riggs fields   *tentless* heedless, careless

I hae been blythe wi' comrades dear;
  I hae been merry drinking;
I hae been joyfu' gath'rin gear;
  I hae been happy thinking:
But a' the pleasures e'er I saw,
  Tho' three times doubl'd fairly,
That happy night was worth them a',
  Amang the rigs o' barley.

  Corn rigs, an' barley rigs,
    An' corn rigs are bonie:
  I'll ne'er forget that happy night,
    Amang the rigs wi' Annie.

WILLIE BREW'D A PECK O' MAUT

O Willie brew'd a peck o' maut,
  And Rob and Allan cam to see;
Three blyther hearts that lee-lang night
  Ye wad na found in Christendie.

  We are na fou, we're nae that fou,
    But just a drappie in our e'e!
  The cock may craw, the day may daw,
    And ay we'll taste the barley-bree!

Here are we met three merry boys,
  Three merry boys I trow are we;
And monie a night we've merry been,
  And monie mae we hope to be!

gear possessions   fou drunk
Maut malt whisky   drappie little crop
lee-lang livelong   bree brewing, liquor

It is the moon, I ken her horn,
    That's blinkin in the lift sae hie:
She shines sae bright to wyle us hame,
    But, by my sooth, she'll wait a wee!

Wha first shall rise to gang awa,
    A cuckold, coward loun is he!
Wha first beside his chair shall fa',
    He is the King amang us three!

ADDRESS TO THE DEIL

O Prince, O chief of many throned pow'rs,
That led th'embattl'd Seraphim to war –
                      Milton

O Thou, whatever title suit thee!
Auld Hornie, Satan, Nick, or Clootie,
Wha in yon cavern grim an' sooty
    Clos'd under hatches,
Spairges about the brunstane cootie,
    To scaud poor wretches!

Hear me, auld Hangie, for a wee,
An' let poor, damned bodies bee;
I'm sure sma' pleasure it can gie,
    Ev'n to a deil,
To skelp an' scaud poor dogs like me,
    An' hear us squeel!

hie high		*brunstane* brimstone	
wyle beguile		*cootie* vessel	
wee little time		*scaud* scald	
gang go		*wee* little time	
loun fellow		*skelp* thrash	
spairges spatters			

Great is thy pow'r, an' great thy fame;
Far ken'd, an' noted is thy name;
An' tho' yon lowan heugh's thy hame,
 Thou travels far;
An' faith! thou's neither lag nor lame,
 Nor blate nor scaur.

Whyles, ranging like a roaring lion,
For prey, a' holes an' corners tryin;
Whyles, on the strong-wing'd Tempest flyin,
 Tirlan the kirks;
Whyles, in the human bosom pryin,
 Unseen thou lurks.

I've heard my rev'rend Graunie say,
In lanely glens ye like to stray;
Or where auld, ruin'd castles, gray,
 Nod to the moon,
Ye fright the nightly wand'rer's way,
 Wi' eldritch croon.

When twilight did my Graunie summon,
To say her pray'rs, douse, honest woman,
Aft 'yont the dyke she's heard you bumman,
 Wi' eerie drone;
Or, rustling, thro' the boortries coman,
 Wi' heavy groan.

Ae dreary, windy, winter night,
The stars shot down wi' sklentan light,
Wi' you, mysel, I gat a fright

lowan	flaming	*tirlan*	striking, rattling
heugh	abyss	*eldritch*	unearthly
blate	shy	*bumman*	buzzing
scaur	scared	*boortries*	elders
whyles	at times	*sklentan*	glancing

  Ayont the lough;
Ye, like a rash-buss, stood in sight,
  Wi' waving sugh:

The cudgel in my nieve did shake,
Each bristl'd hair stood like a stake,
When wi' an eldritch stoor quaick, quaick,
  Amang the springs,
Awa ye squatter'd like a drake,
  On whistling wings.

Let Warlocks grim, an' wither'd Hags,
Tell, how wi' you, on ragweed nags,
They skim the muirs an' dizzy crags,
  Wi' wicked speed;
And in kirk-yards renew their leagues,
  Owre howket dead.

Thence, countra wives, wi toil an' pain,
May plunge an' plunge the kirn in vain;
For Och! the yellow treasure's taen,
  By witching skill;
An' dawtit, twal-pint Hawkie's gane
  As yell's the Bill.

Thence, mystic knots mak great abuse,
On Young-Guidmen, fond, keen an' croose;
When the best warklume i' the house,
  By cantraip wit,
Is instant made no worth a louse,
  Just at the bit.

lough lake	*dawtit* petted
sugh noise of wind in trees	*hawkie* cow
nieve fist	*as yell's, etc.* as milkless as bull
stoor noise	*guidmen* husbands
warlocks wizards	*croose* happy
owre over	*warklume* tool
howket dug-up	*cantraip* tricky
kirn churn	*bit* crucial moment

When thowes dissolve the snawy hoord,
An' float the jinglan icy boord,
Then, water-kelpies haunt the foord,
    By your direction,
An' nighted trav'llers are allur'd
    To their destruction.

An' aft your moss-traversing spunkies
Decoy the wight that late an' drunk is:
The bleezan, curst, mischievous monkies
    Delude his eyes,
Till in some miry slough he sunk is,
    Ne'er mair to rise.

When Masons' mystic word an' grip,
In storms an' tempests raise you up,
Some cock, or cat, your rage maun stop,
    Or, strange to tell!
The youngest Brother ye wad whip
    Aff straught to Hell.

Lang syne in Eden's bonie yard,
When youthfu' lovers first were pair'd,
An' all the soul of love they shar'd,
    The raptur'd hour,
Sweet on the fragrant, flow'ry swaird,
    In shady bow'r:

Then you, ye auld, snick-drawing dog!
Ye cam to Paradise incog,
An' play'd on man a cursed brogue,
    (Black be your fa'!)
An' gied the infant warld a shog,
    'Maist ruin'd a'.

thowes thaws   *snick-drawing* stealthily entering
hoord hoard   *brogue* trick
kelpies water-spirits   *shog* jolt
spunkies will-o-the-wisps

D'ye mind that day, when in a bizz,
Wi' reeket duds, an' reestet gizz,
Ye did present your smoutie phiz
    'Mang better folk,
An' sklented on the man of Uz
    Your spitefu' joke?

An' how ye gat him i' your thrall,
An' brak him out o' house an' hal',
While scabs an' botches did him gall,
    Wi' bitter claw,
An' lows'd his ill-tongu'd, wicked scawl
    Was warst ava?

But a' your doings to rehearse,
Your wily snares an' fechtin fierce,
Sin' that day Michael did you pierce,
    Down to this time,
Wad ding a' Lallan tongue, or Erse,
    In prose or rhyme.

An' now, auld Cloots, I ken ye're thinkan,
A certain bardie's rantin, drinkin,
Some luckless hour will send him linkan,
    To your black pit;
But faith! he'll turn a corner jinkan,
    An' cheat you yet.

But fare you weel, auld Nickie-ben!
O wad ye tak a thought an' men'!
Ye aiblins might – I dinna ken –
    Still hae a stake –
I'm wae to think upo' yon den,
    Ev'n for your sake.

reeket smoked
reestet gizz roasted face
smoutie phiz smutty muzzle
sklented on turned on
scawl scold (woman)

ava of all
ding defeat
linkan stepping quickly
aiblins perhaps

SUCH A PARCEL OF ROGUES IN A NATION

Fareweel to a' our Scottish fame,
  Fareweel our ancient glory!
Fareweel ev'n to the Scottish name,
  Sae famed in martial story!
Now Sark rins o'er the Solway sands,
  An' Tweed rins to the ocean,
To mark where England's province stands –
  Such a parcel of rogues in a nation!

What force or guile could not subdue
  Thro' many warlike ages
Is wrought now by a coward few
  For hireling traitor's wages.
The English steel we could disdain,
  Secure in valour's station;
But English gold has been our bane –
  Such a parcel of rogues in a nation!

O, would, or I had seen the day
  That Treason thus could sell us,
My auld grey head had lien in clay
  Wi' Bruce and loyal Wallace!
But pith and power, till my last hour
  I'll mak this declaration: –
'We're bought and sold for English gold' –
  Such a parcel of rogues in a nation!

A RED, RED ROSE

O, my luve's like a red, red rose,
  That's newly sprung in June.
O, my luve's like the melodie,
  That's sweetly play'd in tune.

As fair art thou, my bonnie lass,
   So deep in luve am I,
And I will luve thee still, my dear,
   Till a' the seas gang dry.

Till a' the seas gang dry, my dear,
   And the rocks melt wi' the sun!
And I will luve thee still, my dear,
   While the sands o' life shall run.

And fare thee weel, my only luve,
   And fare thee weel a while!
And I will come again, my luve,
   Tho, it were ten thousand mile!

A MAN'S A MAN FOR A' THAT

Is there for honest poverty
   That hings his head, an' a' that?
The coward slave, we pass him by -
   We dare be poor for a' that!
For a' that, an' a' that!
   Our toils obscure, an' a' that,
The rank is but the guinea's stamp,
   The man's the gowd for a' that.

What though on hamely fare we dine,
   Wear hoddin grey an' a' that?
Gie fools their silks, and knaves their wine -
   A man's a man for a' that.
For a' that, an' a' that,
   Their tinsel show, an' a' that,
The honest man, tho' e'er sae poor,
   Is king o' men for a' that.

hoddin grey tweed

Ye see yon birkie ca'd 'a lord',
    Wha struts, an' stares, an' a' that?
Tho' hundreds worship at his word,
    He's but a cuif for a' that,
For a' that, an' a' that,
    His ribband, star, an' a' that,
The man o' independent mind,
    He looks an' laughs at a' that.

A prince can mak a belted knight,
    A marquis, duke, an' a' that!
But an honest man's aboon his might --
    Guid faith, he mauna fa' that.
For a' that, an' a' that,
    Their dignities, an' a' that,
The pith o' sense an' pride o' worth
    Are higher rank than a' that.

Then let us pray that come it may
    (As come it will for a' that)
That Sense and Worth o'er a' the earth
    Shall bear the gree an' a' that!
For a' that, an' a' that,
    It's comin yet for a' that,
That man and man the world o'er
    Shall brothers be for a' that.

O, WERT THOU IN THE CAULD BLAST

O wert thou in the cauld blast
    On yonder lea, on yonder lea,
My plaidie to the angry airt,
    I'd shelter thee, I'd shelter thee.

birkie dandy   *bear the gree* take the prize
cuif fool   *airt* quarter of earth, direction of
fa' cause   wind

Or did Misfortune's bitter storms
   Around thee blaw, around thee blaw,
Thy bield should be my bosom,
   To share it a', to share it a'.

Or were I in the wildest waste,
   Sae black and bare, sae black and bare,
The desert were a Paradise,
   If thou wert there, if thou wert there.
Or were I monarch of the globe,
   Wi' thee to reign, wi' thee to reign,
The brightest jewel in my crown
   Wad be my queen, wad be my queen.

RANTIN, ROVIN ROBIN

There was a lad was born in Kyle,
But what na day o' what na style,
I doubt it's hardly worth the while
   To be sae nice wi' Robin.

   Robin was a rovin boy,
      Rantin, rovin, rantin, rovin,
   Robin was a rovin boy,
      Rantin, rovin Robin!

Our monarch's hindmost year but ane
Was five-and-twenty days begun,
'Twas then a blast o' Janwar' win'
   Blew hansel in on Robin!

   Robin was a rovin boy, etc.

bield shelter   *hansel* birth-gift

The gossip keekit in his loof,
Quo' she: – 'Wha lives'll see the proof,
This waly boy will be nae coof:
    I think we'll ca' him Robin.'

        Robin was a rovin boy, etc.

'He'll hae misfortunes great an' sma',
But ay a heart aboon them a'.
He'll gie his Daddie's name a blaw,
    We'll a' be proud o' Robin.'

        Robin was a rovin boy, etc.

'But sure as three times three mak nine
I see by ilka score and line,
This chap will dearly like our kin',
    Sae leeze me on thee, Robin!'

        Robin was a rovin boy, etc.

'Guid faith', quo' she, 'I doubt you, Stir,
Ye'll gar the lassies lie aspar,
But twenty fauts ye may hae waur –
    So blessins on thee, Robin.'

        Robin was a rovin boy, etc.

gossip midwife   *Stir* gallant
loof palm   *gar* make
waly fine   *aspar* astride
coof fool

TO A LOUSE

Ha! whare ye gaun, ye crowlan ferlie!
Your impudence protects you fairly:
I canna say but ye strunt rarely,
    Owre gawze and lace;
Tho' faith, I fear ye dine but sparely
    On sic a place.

Ye ugly, creepan, blastet wonner,
Detestet, shunn'd, by saunt an' sinner,
How daur ye set your fit upon her,
    Sae fine a Lady!
Gae somewhere else and seek your dinner,
    On some poor body.

Swith, in some beggar's haffet squattle;
There ye may creep, and sprawl, and sprattle,
Wi' ither kindred, jumping cattle,
    In shoals and nations;
Whare horn nor bane ne'er daur unsettle
    Your thick plantations.

Now haud you there, ye're out o' sight,
Below the fatt'rels, snug and tight,
Na faith ye yet! ye'll no be right,
    Till ye've got on it,
The vera tapmost, towrin height
    O' Miss's bonnet.

crowlan ferlie crawling wonder	*fit* foot
strunt strut	*swith* quick
wonner creature	*haffet* whisker
daur dare	*fatt'rels* ribbons

My sooth! right bauld ye set your nose out,
As plump an' gray as onie grozet:
O for some rank, mercurial rozet,
  Or fell, red smeddum,
I'd gie you sic a hearty dose o't,
  Wad dress your droddum!

I wad na been surpriz'd to spy
You on an auld wife's flainen toy;
Or aiblins some bit duddie boy,
  On's wylecoat;
But Miss's fine Lunardi, fye!
  Haw daur ye do't?

O Jenny dinna toss your head,
An' set your beauties a' abread!
Ye little ken what cursed speed
  The blastie's makin!
Thae winks and finger-ends, I dread,
  Are notice takin!

O wad some Pow'r the giftie gie us
To see oursels as others see us!
It wad frae monie a blunder free us
  An' foolish notion:
What airs in dress an' gait wad lea'e us,
  And ev'n Devotion!

grozet gooseberry	*duddie* ragged
rozet resin	*wylecoat* waistcoat
smeddum powder	*a' abread* all abroad
droddum backside	*blastie* dwarf
flainen toy flannel mutch-cap	*thae* those
aiblins perhaps	*gait* manner, carriage

TO WILLIAM SIMSON,
SCHOOLMASTER OF OCHILTREE

I gat your letter, winsome Willie;
Wi' gratefu' heart I thank you brawlie;
Tho' I maun say't, I wad be silly,
    An' unco vain,
Should I believe, my coaxin billie,
    Your flatterin strain.

But I'se believe ye kindly meant it,
I sud be laith to think ye hinted
Ironic satire, sidelins sklented,
    On my poor Musie;
Tho' in sic phraisin terms ye've penn'd it,
    I scarce excuse ye.

My senses wad be in a creel,
Should I but dare a hope to speel,
Wi' Allan, or wi' Gilbertfield,
    The braes o' fame;
Or Ferguson, the writer-chiel,
    A deathless name.

(O Ferguson! thy glorious parts,
Ill-suited law's dry, musty arts!
My curse upon your whunstane hearts,
    Ye E'nbrugh Gentry!
The tythe o' what ye waste at cartes
    Wad stow'd his pantry!)

billie fellow   *Wi' Allan, etc.* Allan Ramsay,
sklented angled   Hamilton of Gilbertfield the
phraisin flattering   poet, and Robert Fergusson
creel basket   *cartes* cards
speel climb

Yet when a tale comes i' my head,
Or lasses gie my heart a screed,
As whiles they're like to be my dead,
   (O sad disease!)
I kittle up my rustic reed;
   It gies me ease.

Auld Coila, now, may fidge fu' fain,
She's gotten Bardies o' her ain,
Chiels wha their chanters winna hain,
   But tune their lays,
Till echoes a' resound again,
   Her weel-sung praise.

Nae Poet thought her worth his while,
To set her name in measur'd style;
She lay like some unkend-of isle
   Beside New Holland,
Or whare wild-meeting oceans boil
   Besouth Magellan.

Ramsay an' famous Ferguson
Gied Forth an' Tay a lift aboon;
Yarrow an' Tweed, to mony a tune
   Owre Scotland rings,
While Irwin, Lugar, Aire, an' Doon,
   Naebody sings.

Th' Illissus, Tiber, Thames an' Seine,
Glide sweet in monie a tunefu' line;
But Willie set your fit to mine,
   An' cock your crest,
We'll gar our streams an' burnies shine
   Up wi' the best.

screed twist   *hain* spare
kittle tickle   *burnies* streamlets

We'll sing auld Coila's plains an' fells,
Her moors red brown wi' heather bells,
Her banks an' braes, her dens an' dells,
    Where glorious Wallace
A'ft bure the gree, as story tells,
    Frae Suthron billies.

At *Wallace'* name, what Scottish blood
But boils up in a spring-time flood!
Oft have our fearless fathers strode
    By *Wallace'* side,
Still pressing onward, red-wat-shod,
    Or glorious dy'd!

O sweet are COILA's haughs an' woods,
When lintwhites chant amang the buds,
And jinkin hares, in amorous whids,
    Their loves enjoy,
While thro' the braes the cushat croods
    With wailfu' cry!

Ev'n winter bleak has charms to me
When winds rave thro' the naked tree;
Or frosts on hills of Ochiltree
    Are hoary gray;
Or blinding drifts wild-furious flee,
    Dark'ning the day!

O Nature! a' thy shews an' forms
To feeling, pensive hearts hae charms!
Whether the Summer kindly warms,
    Wi' life an' light,
Or Winter howls, in gusty storms,
    The lang, dark night!

bure the gree bore the prize
red-wat-shod with bloody feet
haughs meadows
lintwhites linnets

whids gambols
cushat wood-pigeon
croods croons, coos

The Muse, nae Poet ever fand her,
Till by himsel he learn'd to wander,
Adown some trottin burn's meander
   An' no think lang;
O sweet, to stray an' pensive ponder
   A heart-felt sang!

The warly race may drudge an' drive,
Hog-shouther, jundie, stretch an' strive,
Let me fair *Nature's* face descrive,
   And I, wi' pleasure,
Shall let the busy, grumbling hive
   Bum owre their treasure.

Fareweel, 'my rhyme-composing' brither!
We've been owre lang unkenn'd to ither:
Now let us lay our heads thegither
   In love fraternal:
May Envy wallop in a tether,
   Black fiend, infernal!

While Highlandmen hate tolls an' taxes;
While moorlan herds like guid, fat braxies;
While Terra firma, on her axis,
   Diurnal turns,
Count on a friend, in faith an' practice,
   In ROBERT BURNS.

MARY MORISON

O Mary, at thy window be!
   It is the wish'd, the trysted hour.
Those smiles and glances let me see,

jundie jostle   *braxies* sheep
bum buzz

That make the miser's treasure poor,
  How blithely wad I bide the stoure,
A weary slave frae sun to sun,
  Could I the rich reward secure –
The lovely Mary Morison.

Yestreen, when to the trembling string
  The dance gaed thro, the lighted ha',
To thee my fancy took its wing,
  I sat, but neither heard nor saw:
  Tho' this was fair, and that was braw,
And yon the toast of a' the town,
  I sigh'd and said amang them a':–
'Ye are na Mary Morison.'

O Mary canst thou wreck his peace
  Wha for thy sake wad gladly die?
Or canst thou break that heart of his
  Whase only faut is loving thee?
  If love for love thou wilt na gie,
At least be pity to me shown:
  A thought ungentle canna be
The thought o' Mary Morison.

DEATH AND DOCTOR HORNBOOK
A TRUE STORY

Some books are lies frae end to end,
And some great lies were never penn'd:
Ev'n ministers they hae been kenn'd,
    In holy rapture,
A rousing whid, at times, to vend,
    And nail't wi' Scripture.

stoure strife   *whid* lie
kenn'd known

But this that I am gaun to tell,
Which lately on a night befel,
Is just as true's the Deil's in hell,
    Or Dublin city:
That e'er he nearer comes oursel
    'S a muckle pity.

The clachan yill had made me canty,
I was na fou, but just had plenty;
I stacher'd whyles, but yet took tent ay
    To free the ditches;
An' hillocks, stanes, an' bushes kenn'd ay
    Frae ghaists an' witches.

The rising moon began to glowr
The distant Cumnock hills out-owre;
To count her horns, wi' a' my pow'r,
    I set mysel,
But whether she had three or four,
    I cou'd na tell.

I was come round about the hill,
And todlin down on Willie's mill,
Setting my staff wi' a' my skill,
    To keep me sicker;
Tho' leeward whyles, against my will,
    I took a bicker.

I there wi' something does forgather,
That pat me in an eerie swither;
An awfu' scythe, out-owre ae shouther,
    Clear-dangling, hang;
A three-tae'd leister on the ither
    Lay, large an' lang.

clachan yill village ale	*sicker* surefooted
canty happy	*bicker* lurch
fou drunk	*swither* dilemma
stacher'd staggered	*leister* trident
tent care	

Its stature seem'd lang Scotch ells twa,
The queerest shape that e'er I saw,
For fient a wame it had ava,
  And then its shanks,
They were as thin, as sharp an' sma'
  As cheeks o' branks.

'Guid-een,' quo' I; 'Friend! hae ye been mawin,
'When ither folk are busy sawin?'
It seem'd to mak a kind o' stan',
  But naething spak;
At length, says I, 'Friend, whare ye gaun,
  'Will ye go back?'

It spak right howe – '**My name is Death,**
'But be na' fley'd.' – **Quoth I, 'Guid faith,**
'Ye're maybe come to **stap** my breath;
  'But tent me, billie;
'I red ye weel, tak care o' skaith,
  'See, there's a gully!'

'Gudeman,' quo' he, 'put up your whittle,
'I'm no design'd to try its mettle;
'But if I did, I wad be kittle
  'To be mislear'd,
'I wad na' mind it, no that spittle
  'Out-owre my beard.'

'Weel, weel!' says I, 'a bargain be't;
'Come, gies your hand, an' sae we're gree't;
'We'll ease our shanks an' tak a seat,

or fient, etc. for no belly it had at *fley'd* afraid
 all   *tent* heed
branks bridles   *red* advise
mawin mowing   *skaith* harm
sawin sowing   *gully* gully-knife
gaun going   *whittle* knife
howe hollow   *kittle* amused

'Come, gies your news!
'This while ye hae been mony a gate,
    'At mony a house.'

'Ay, ay!' quo' he, an' shook his head,
'It's e'en a lang, lang time indeed
'Sin' I began to nick the thread,
    'An' choke the breath:
'Folk maun do something for their bread,
    'An' sae maun Death.

'Sax thousand years are near hand fled
'Sin' I was to the butching bred,
'And mony a scheme in vain's been laid,
    'To stap or scar me;
'Till ane Hornbook's ta'en up the trade,
    'And faith, he'll waur me.

'Ye ken Jock Hornbook i' the clachan,
'Deil mak his king's-hood in a spleuchan!
'He's grown sae weel acquaint wi' Buchan,
    'And ither chaps,
'The weans haud out their fingers laughin,
    'And pouk my hips.

'See, here's a scythe, and there's a dart,
'They hae pierc'd mony a gallant heart;
'But Doctor Hornbook, wi' his art
    'And cursed skill,
'Has made them baith no worth a fart,
    'Damn'd haet they'll kill!

mony many	*spleuchan* tobacco-pouch
gate way, time	*Buchan* Wm Buchan's **book**
maun must	*Domestic Medicine*
scar scare	*weans* children
waur outdo	*pouk* poke
king's-hood bowels	*haet* jot

'Twas but yestreen, nae farther gaen,
'I threw a noble throw at ane;
'Wi' less, I'm sure, I've hundreds slain;
   'But deil-ma-care!
'It just play'd dirl on the bane,
   'But did nae mair.

'Hornbook was by, wi' ready art,
'And had sae fortify'd the part,
'That when I looked to my dart,
   'It was sae blunt,
'Fient haet o't wad hae pierc'd the heart
   'Of a kail-runt.

'I drew my scythe in sic a fury,
'I nearhand cowpit wi' my hurry.
'But yet the bauld apothecary
   'Withstood the shock;
'I might as weel hae try'd a quarry
   'O' hard whin-rock.

'Ev'n them he canna get attended,
'Altho' their face he ne'er had kenn'd it,
'Just shit in a kail-blade and send it,
   'As soon's he smells 't,
'Baith their disease, and what will mend it,
   'At once he tells't.

'And then a' doctor's saws and whittles,
'Of a' dimensions, shapes, an' mettles,
'A' kinds o' boxes, mugs, an' bottles,
   'He's sure to hae;
'Their Latin names as fast he rattles
   'As A B C.

dirl jolt	*kail-runt* cabbage-stalk
fient haet no bit	*cowpit* overturned

'Calces o' fossils, earths, and trees,
'True Sal-marinum o' the seas;
'The farina of beans and pease,
      'He has't in plenty;
'Aqua-fontis, what you please,
      'He can content ye.

'Forbye some new, uncommon weapons,
'Urinus Spiritus of capons;
'Or mite-horn shavings, filings, scrapings,
      'Distill'd *per se*;
'Sal-alkali o' midge-tail clippings,
      'And mony mae.'

'Waes me for Johnny Ged's-Hole* now,'
Quoth I, 'if that thae news be true!
'His braw calf-ward whare gowans grew,
      'Sae white an' bonie,
'Nae doubt they'll rive it wi' the plew;
      'They'll ruin Johnie!'

The creature grain'd an eldritch laugh,
And says, 'Ye needna yoke the pleugh,
'Kirk-yards will soon be till'd eneugh,
      'Tak ye nae fear:
'They'll a' be trench'd wi' mony a sheugh,
      'In twa-three year.

'Whare I kill'd ane, a fair strae-death,
'By loss o' blood, or want o' breath,
'This night I'm free to tak my aith,

thae those	*sheugh* drill
calf-ward meadow for calves	*strae* straw, i.e. bed
pleugh, plew plough	*aith* oath

* Grave-digger

'That Hornbook's skill
'Has clad a score i' their last claith,
 'By drap and pill.

'An honest wabster to his trade,
'Whase wife's twa nieves were scarce weel-bred,
'Gat tippence-worth to mend her head,
 'When it was sair;
'The wife slade cannie to her bed,
 'But ne'er spak mair.

'A countra Laird had ta'en the batts,
'Or some curmurring in his guts,
'His only son for Hornbook sets,
 'And pays him well,
'The lad, for twa guid gimmer-pets,
 'Was Laird himsel.

'A bonie lass, ye kenn'd her name,
'Some ill-brewn drink had hov'd her wame,
'She trusts hersel, to hide the shame,
 'In Hornbook's care;
'Horn sent her aff to her lang hame,
 'To hide it there.

'That's just a swatch o' Hornbook's way,
'Thus goes he on from day to day,
'Thus does he poison, kill, an' slay,
 'An's weel pay'd for't;
'Yet stops me o' my lawfu' prey,
 'Wi' his damn'd dirt!

claith cloth	*slade cannie* slid gently
drap drop	*batts* colic
wabster weaver	*curmurring* rumbling
nieves fists	*gimmer-pets* ewes
sair sore	*hov'd* swelled

'But hark! I'll tell you of a plot,
'Tho' dinna ye be speakin o't,
'Ill nail the self-conceited sot,
    'As dead's a herrin:
'Niest time we meet, I'll wad a groat,
    'He gets his fairin!'

But just as he began to tell,
The auld kirk-hammer strak the bell
Some wee, short hour ayont the twal,
    Which rais'd us baith:
I took the way that pleas'd mysel,
    And sae did Death.

MY BONY MARY

Go fetch to me a pint o' wine,
    And fill it in a silver tassie;
That I may drink, before I go,
    A service to my bonie lassie.
The boat rocks at the Pier o' Leith,
    Fu' loud the wind blaws frae the Ferry;
The ship rides by the Berwick-law,
    And I maun leave my bony Mary.

The trumpets sound, the banners fly,
    The glittering spears are ranked ready;
The shouts o' war are heard afar,
    The battle closes deep and bloody.
It's not the roar o' sea or shore,
    Wad make me langer wish to tarry;
Nor shouts o' war that's heard afar –
    It's leaving thee, my bony Mary!

wad bet   *tassie* tankard
twal twelve

TAM GLEN

My heart is a breaking, dear Tittie,
  Some counsel unto me come len';
To anger them a' is a pity,
  But what will I do wi' Tam Glen?

I'm thinking, wi' sic a braw fellow,
  In poortith I might mak a fen':
What care I in riches to wallow,
  If I mauna marry Tam Glen.

There's Lowrie the laird o' Dumeller,
  'Gude day to you (brute)' he comes ben:
He brags and he blaws o' his siller,
  But when will he dance like Tam Glen.

My Minnie does constantly deave me,
  And bids me beware o' young men;
They flatter, she says, to deceive me,
  But wha can think sae o' Tam Glen.

My Daddie says, gin I'll forsake him,
  He'll gie me gude hunder marks ten:
But, if it's ordained I maun take him,
  O wha will I get but Tam Glen?

Yestreen at the Valentines' dealing,
  My heart to my mou gied a sten;
For thrice I drew ane without failing,
  And thrice it was written, Tam Glen.

tittie sister	*minnie* mother
poortith poverty	*deave* deafen
mak a fen' manage	*maun* must
ben into the kitchen	*sten* start

The last Halloween I was waukin
  My droukit sark-sleeve, as ye ken;
His likeness cam up the house staukin,
  And the very grey breeks o' Tam Glen!

Come counsel, dear Tittie, don't tarry;
  I'll gie you my bonie black hen,
Gif ye will advise me to marry
  The lad I lo'e dearly, Tam Glen.

LOVE AND LIBERTY

—

FROM THE JOLLY BEGGARS

A CANTATA (FINALE)

Air: *For A' That an' A' That*

I am a bard of no regard,
  Wi' gentle folk an' a' that;
But Homer like the glowran byke,
  Frae town to town I draw that.

Chorus

  For a' that an' a' that,
    An' twice as muckle's a' that,
  I've lost but ane, I've twa behin',
    I've wife eneugh for a' that.

I never drank the Muses' stank,
  Castalia's burn an' a' that,
But there it streams an' richly reams,
  My Helicon I ca' that.
    For a' that, etc.

waukin drying		*byke* crowd	
droukit drenched		*stank* well	
staukin stalking		*reams* foams	
glowran glaring			

Great love I bear to all the fair,
　　Their humble slave an' a' that;
But lordly will, I hold it still
　　A mortal sin to thraw that.
　　　　For a' that, etc.

In raptures sweet this hour we meet,
　　Wi' mutual love an' a' that;
But for how lang the flie may stang,
　　Let inclination law that.
　　　　For a' that, etc.

Their tricks an' craft hae put me daft,
　　They've ta'en me in, an' a' that,
But clear your decks an' here's the sex!
　　I like the jads for a' that.
　　　　For a' that an' a' that
　　　　　　An' twice as muckle's a' that,
　　　　My dearest bluid to do them guid,
　　　　　　They're welcome till't for a' that.

RECITATIVO

So sung the bard – and Nansie's waws
Shook with a thunder of applause
　　Re-echo'd from each mouth!
They toom'd their pocks, they pawn'd their duds,
They scarcely left to coor their fuds
　　To quench their lowan drouth:
Then owre again the jovial thrang
　　The poet did request

thraw endure	*duds* rags
flie fly	*coor* cover
stang sting	*fuds* loins
law determine	*lowan* flaming
toom'd emptied	*thrang* throng

To lowse his pack an' wale a sang,
  A ballad o' the best.
    He, rising, rejoicing,
      Between his twa Deborahs,
  Looks round him an' found them
    Impatient for the chorus.

Air: *Jolly Mortals, fill your glasses*

See the smoking bowl before us,
  Mark our jovial ragged ring!
Round and round take up the chorus,
  And in raptures let us sing –

Chorus

  A fig for those by law protected!
    Liberty's a glorious feast!
  Courts for Cowards were erected,
    Churches built to please the priest,

What is title, what is treasure,
  What is reputation's care?
If we lead a life of pleasure,
  'Tis no matter how or where.
    A fig, etc.

With the ready trick and fable
  Round we wander all the day;
And at night, in barn or stable,
  Hug our doxies on the hay.
    A fig, etc.

wale choose   *doxies* wenches

Does the train-attended carriage
　　Thro' the country lighter rove?
Does the sober bed of marriage
　　Witness brighter scenes of love?
　　　　A fig, etc.

Life is all a variorum,
　　We regard not how it goes;
Let them cant about decorum,
　　Who have character to lose.
　　　　A fig, etc.

Here's to budgets, bags and wallets!
　　Here's to all the wandering train!
Here's our ragged brats and callets!
　　One and all cry out, Amen!
　　　　A fig for those by law protected,
　　　　　Liberty's a glorious feast!
　　　　Courts for cowards were erected,
　　　　　Churches built to please the priest.

　　　　　callets light-of-loves

from *The Merry Muses*

THE BONNIEST LASS

The bonniest lass that ye meet neist
    Gie her a kiss and a' that,
In spite o' ilka parish priest,
    Repentin' stool an' a' that.

    For a' that an' a' that,
        Their mim-mou'd sangs an' a' that,
    In time and place convenient
        They'll do't themselves for a' that.

Your patriarchs in days o' yore
    Had their handmaids an' a' that,
O' bastard gets some had a score,
    And some had mair than a' that.
        For a' that, etc.

King Davie, when he waxed auld,
    An's bluid ran thin, an' a' that,
An' fand his cods were growin' cauld,
    Could not refrain, for a' that.
        For a' that, etc.

neist next   *gets* children
repentin' stool fornicators had   *cods* balls
    to sit on it in front of the
    congregation

Wha wadna pity thae sweet dames
 He fumbled at, an' a' that,
An' raised their bluid up into flames
 He couldna drown for a' that.
  For a' that, etc.

King Solomon, prince o' divines
 Wha proverbs made an' a' that,
Baith mistresses an' concubines
 In hundreds had, for a' that.
  For a' that, etc.

Then still I swear, a clever chiel
 Should kiss a lass an' a' that,
Tho priests consign him to the deil
 As reprobate an' a' that.
  For a' that, an' a' that,
   Their canting stuff an' a' that,
  They ken nae mair wha's reprobate
   Than you or I, for a' that.

GIE THE LASS HER FAIRIN

O gie the lass her fairin lad,
 O gie the lass her fairin,
An' something else she'll gie to you
 That's waly worth the wearin;
Syne coup her o'er amang the creels
 When ye hae taen your brandy,
The mair she bangs the less she squeels,
 An' hey for houghmagandie.

fairin proper food   *coup* tumble
waly worth well-aworth   *houghmagandie* copulation

Then gie the lass a fairin, lad,
 O gie the lass her fairin,
And she'll gie you a hairy thing,
 An' of it be na sparin.
But coup her o'er amang the creels
 An' bar the door wi baith your heels;
The mair she bangs the less she squeels,
 An' hey for houghmagandie.

GREEN GROW THE RASHES

O wat ye ought o fisher Meg,
 And how she trow'd the webster, O;
She loot me see her carrot cunt,
 And sell'd it for a labster, O.
  Green grow the rashes, O
   Green grow the rashes, O;
  The lassies they hae wimble-bores,
   The widows they hae gashes, O.

Mistress Mary cow'd her thing
 Because she wad be gentle, O
And span the fleece upon a rock
 To waft a highland mantle, O.
  Green grow, etc.

An' heard ye o the coat o arms
 The Lyon brought our lady, O?
The crest was couchant sable cunt,
 The motto *ready, ready*, O.
  Green grow, etc.

loot let   *rock* spingle-rock
labster lobster

An' ken ye Leezie Lundie, O,
   The godly Leezie Lundie, O?
She mows like reek thro a' the week,
   But finger-fucks on Sunday, O.
      Green grow, etc.

DUNCAN GRAY

Can ye play me *Duncan Gray*,
   Ha, ha, the girdin' o't;
O'er the hills an' far away,
   Ha, ha the girdin' o't.
Duncan cam our Meg to woo,
Meg was nice an' wadna do,
But like an ither puff'd an' blew
   At offer o' the girdin' o't.

Duncan, he cam here again,
   Ha, ha, the girdin' o't,
A' was out an' Meg her lane,
   Ha, ha, the girdin' o't.
He kiss'd her butt, he kiss'd her ben,
He bang'd a thing against her wame -
But troth, I now forget its name
   But I trow she gat the girdin' o't.

She took him to the cellar then,
   Ha, ha, the girdin' o't,
To see gif he could do't again,
   Ha, ha, the girdin' o't.

mows fucks   *ben* in the kitchen
girdin' fucking   *wame* belly
butt in the parlour

He kiss'd her ance, he kiss'd her twice,
An' by the bye he kiss'd her thrice
Till deil a mair the thing wad rise,
    To gie her the long girdin' o't.

But Duncan took her to his wife,
    Ha, ha, the girdin' o't,
To be the comfort o' his life,
    Ha, ha, the girdin' o't.
An' now she scauls baith night an' day
Except when Duncan's at the play –
An' that's as seldom as he may,
    He's weary o' the girdin' o't.

COMIN' THROU THE RYE

O gin a body meet a body,
    Comin' throu the rye,
Gin a body fuck a body,
    Need a body cry?
        Comin' throu the rye, my jo,
            An' comin' throu the rye;
            She fand a staun o staunin graith
            Comin' throu the rye.

Gin a body meet a body
    Comin' throu the glen,
Gin a body fuck a body,
    Need the warld ken?
        Comin' throu the rye, etc.

deil a mair no more at all   staun stand
scauls scolds   staunin standing
play copulation   graith growth, weapon

Gin a body meet a body
    Comin' throu the grain,
Gin a body fuck a body,
    Cunt's a body's ain.
        Comin' throu the rye, etc.

Gin a body meet a body
    By a body's sel,
Whatna body fucks a body.
    Wad a body tell?
        Comin' throu the rye, etc.

Mony a body meets a body
    They darena weel avow;
Mony a body fucks a body,
    Ye wadna think it true.
        Comin, throu the rye, my jo,
            An' comin throu the rye,
            She fand a staun o staunin graith
            Comin' throu the rye.

JOHN ANDERSON, MY JO

John Anderson, my jo, John,
    I wonder what ye mean,
To lie sae lang i' the mornin',
    And sit sae late at e'en?
Ye'll bleer a' your een, John,
    And why do ye so?
Come sooner to your bed at een,
    John Anderson, my jo.

John Anderson, my jo, John,
    When first that ye began,
Ye had as good a tail-tree,
    As ony ither man;

tail-tree penis

But now its waxen wan, John,
  And wrinkles to and fro;
I've twa gae-ups for ae gae-down,
  John Anderson, my jo.

I'm backit like a salmon,
  I'm breastit like a swan;
My wame it is a down-cod,
  My middle ye may span:
Frae my tap-knot to my tae, John,
  I'm like the new-fa'n snow;
And it's a' for your convenience,
  John Anderson, my jo.

O it is a fine thing
  To keep out o'er the dyke;
But it's a meikle finer thing,
  To see your hurdies fyke;
To see your hurdies fyke, John,
  And hit the rising blow;
It's then I like your chanter-pipe,
  John Anderson, my jo.

When ye come on before, John,
  See that ye do your best;
When ye begin to haud me,
  See that ye grip me fast;
See that ye grip me fast, John,
  Until that I cry 'Oh!'
Your back shall crack or I do that,
  John Anderson, my jo.

wame belly   *hurdies* hips
down-cod bolster   *fyke* jerk
tae toe

John Anderson, my jo, John,
   Ye're welcome when ye please;
It's either in the warm bed
   Or else aboon the claes:
Or ye shall hae the horns, John,
   Upon your head to grow;
An' that's the cuckold's mallison,
   John Anderson, my jo.

Carolina Oliphant
(Lady Nairne)
1766–1845

THE LAND O' THE LEAL

I'm wearin' awa', John,
Like snaw-wreaths in thaw, John,
I'm wearin' awa'
  To the land o' the leal.
There's nae sorrow there, John,
There's neither cauld nor care, John,
The day is aye fair
  In the land o' the leal.

Our bonnie bairn's there, John,
She was baith gude and fair, John,
And, oh! we grudged her sair
  To the land o' the leal.
But sorrow's sel' wears past, John,
And joy is comin' fast, John,
The joy that's aye to last
  In the land o' the leal.

Sae dear's that joy was bought, John,
Sae free the battle fought, John,
That sinfu' man e'er brought
  To the land o' the leal.
Oh! dry your glist'nin' e'e, John,

leal loyal   *sair* sore
bairn child

My saul langs to be free, John,
And angels beckon me
    To the land o' the leal.

Oh! haud ye leal an' true, John,
Your day it's wearin' thro', John,
And I'll welcome you
    To the land o' the leal.
Now fare ye weel, my ain John,
This warld's cares are vain, John,
We'll meet, and we'll be fain,
    In the land o' the leal.

CALLER HERRIN'

Wha'll buy my caller herrin'?
    They're bonnie fish and halesome farin';
Wha'll buy my caller herrin',
    New drawn frae the Forth.

When ye were sleepin' on your pillows,
    Dream'd ye aught o' our puir fellows,
Darkling as they fac'd the billows,
    A' to fill the woven willows?
        Buy my caller herrin',
        New drawn frae the Forth.

Wha'll buy my caller herrin'?
    They're no brought here without brave darin';
Buy my caller herrin',
    Haul'd through wind and rain.
        Wha'll buy my caller herrin'? etc.

fain happy   *halesum farin'* healthy food
caller fresh

Wha'll buy my caller herrin'?
  Oh, ye may ca' them vulgar farin' –
Wives and mithers, maist despairin',
  Ca' them lives o' men.
    Wha'll buy my caller herrin'? etc.

When the creel o' herrin' passes,
  Ladies clad in silks and laces,
Gather in their braw pelisses,
  Cast their heads and screw their faces,
    Wha'll buy my caller herrin'? etc.

Caller herrin's no got lightlie:–
  Ye can trip the spring fu' tightlie;
Spite o' tauntin', flauntin', flingin',
  Gow had set you a' a-singing
    Wha'll buy my caller herrin'? etc.

Neebour wives, now tent my tellin',
  When the bonnie fish ye're sellin',
At ae word be in yere dealin' –
  Truth will stand when a' thin's failin',
    Wha'll buy my caller herrin'?
      They're bonnie fish and halesome farin',
    Wha'll buy my caller herrin',
      New drawn frae the Forth?

---

creel basket
ye can trip, etc. you can dance the
  jig very neatly

Gow Neil Gow, a famous fiddler
tent heed

Anonymous

18th Century

CA' THE YOWES TO THE KNOWES

Ca' the yowes to the knowes,
Ca' them where the heather grows,
Ca' them where the burnie rowes,
My bonnie dearie.

'Will ye gang down yon water side,
That thro' the glen does saftly glide,
And I shall rowe thee in my plaid,
My bonnie dearie?'

'Ye sall hae rings and ribbons meet,
Calf-leather shoon upon your feet,
And in my bosom ye sall sleep,
My bonnie dearie.'

'I was brought up at nae sic school,
My shepherd lad, to play the fool,
Nor sit the livelong day in dool,
Lanely and eerie.'

'Yon yowes and lammies on the plain,
Wi' a' the gear my dad did hain,
I'se gie thee, if thoul't be mine ain,
My bonnie dearie.'

yowes ewes	*rowes* rolls
knowes knolls	*lammies* lambs
burnie streamlet	*hain* save

'Come weel, come wae, whate'er betide,
Gin ye'll prove true, I'se be your bride,
And ye sall rowe me in your plaid,
My winsome dearie.'

CANADIAN BOAT SONG

Fair these broad meads – these hoary woods are grand;
    But we are exiles from our fathers' land.

Listen to me, as when ye heard our father
    Sing long ago the song of other shores –
Listen to me, and then in chorus gather
    All your deep voices, as ye pull your oars.

From the lone shieling of the misty island
    Mountains divide us, and waste of seas –
Yet still the blood is strong, the heart is Highland,
    And we in dreams behold the Hebrides.

We ne'er shall tread the fancy-haunted valley,
    Where 'tween the dark hills creeps the small clear stream,
In arms around the patriarch banner rally,
    Nor see the moon on royal tombstones gleam.

When the bold kindred, in the time long vanish'd,
    Conquer'd the soil and fortified the keep –
No seer foretold the children would be banish'd,
    That a degenerate lord might boast his sheep.

Come foreign rage – let Discord burst in slaughter!
    O then for clansmen true, and stern claymore –
The hearts that would have given their blood like water,
    Beat heavily beyond the Atlantic roar.

shieling highland cottage   *claymore* broadsword

SOMEBODY

Och hon for somebody!
Och hey for somebody!
I wad do – what wad I not,
    For the sake o' somebody?

My heart is sair, I daurna tell
My heart is sair for somebody;
I wad walk a winter's night,
    For a sight o' somebody.

If somebody were come again,
Then somebody maun cross the main,
And ilka ane will get his ain,
    And I will see my somebody.

What need I kame my tresses bright,
Or why should coal or candle-light
E'er shine in my bower day or night,
    Since gane is my dear somebody?

Oh! I hae grutten mony a day
For ane that's banished far away;
I canna sing, and maunna say
    How sair I grieve for somebody.

somebody the banished Stewart king	*daurna* daren't
sair sore	*kame* comb
	grutten wept

James Hogg

1770–1835

McLEAN'S WELCOME

Come o'er the stream, Charlie, dear Charlie, brave Charlie;
Come o'er the stream, Charlie, and dine with McLean;
And though you be weary, we'll make your heart cheery,
And welcome our Charlie, and his loyal train.
We'll bring down the track deer, we'll bring down the black
    steer,
The lamb from the braken, and doe from the glen,
The salt sea we'll harry, and bring to our Charlie
The cream from the bothy and curd from the pen.

Come o'er the stream, Charlie, dear Charlie, brave Charlie;
Come o'er the stream, Charlie, and dine with McLean;
And you shall drink freely the dews of Glen-Sheerly,
That stream in the starlight when kings do not ken,
And deep be your meed of the wine that is red,
To drink to your sire, and his friend the McLean.

Come o'er the stream, Charlie, dear Charlie, brave Charlie;
Come o'er the stream, Charlie, and dine with McLean;
O'er heath-bells shall trace you the maids to embrace you,
And deck your blue bonnet with flowers of the brae;
And the loveliest Mari in all Glen M'Quarry
Shall lie in your bosom till break of the day.

Come o'er the stream, Charlie, dear Charlie, brave Charlie;
Come o'er the stream, Charlie, and dine with McLean;
If aught will invite you, or more will delight you,

'Tis ready, a troop of our bold Highlandmen,
All ranged on the heather, with bonnet and feather,
Strong arms and broad claymores, three hundred and ten!

LOCK THE DOOR, LARISTON

Lock the door, Lariston, lion of Liddisdale,
Lock the door, Lariston, Lowther comes on,
 The Armstrongs are flying,
 Their widows are crying,
The Castletown's burning, and Oliver's gone;
Lock the door, Lariston – high on the weather gleam
See how the Saxon plumes bob on the sky,
 Yeoman and carbineer,
 Billman and halberdier;
Fierce is the foray, and far is the cry.

Bewcastle brandishes high his broad scimitar,
Ridley is riding his fleet-footed grey,
 Hedley and Howard there,
 Wandale and Windermere –
Lock the door, Lariston, hold them at bay,
Why dost thou smile, noble Elliot of Lariston?
Why do the joy-candles gleam in thine eye?
 Thou bold Border ranger,
 Beware of thy danger –
Thy foes are relentless, determined, and nigh.

Jock Elliot raised up his steel bonnet and lookit,
His hand grasp'd the sword with a nervous embrace;
 'Ah, welcome, brave foemen,
 On earth there are no men
More gallant to meet in the foray or chase!
Little know you of the hearts I have hidden here,

Little know you of our moss-troopers' might –
    Linhope and Sorbie true,
    Sundhope and Milburn too,
Gentle in manner, but lions in fight!

I've Mangerton, Ogilvie, Raeburn and Netherby,
Old Sim of Whitram, and all his array;
    Come all Northumberland,
    Teesdale and Cumberland,
Here at the Breaken Tower end shall the fray.'
Scowl'd the broad sun o'er the links of green Liddisdale,
Red as the beacon-light tipp'd he the wold;
    Many a bold martial eye
    Mirror'd that morning sky,
Never more oped on his orbit of gold!

Shrill was the bugle's note, dreadful the warrior shout,
Lances and halberds in splinters were borne;
    Halberd and hauberk then
    Braved the claymore in vain,
Buckler and armlet in shivers were shorn.
See how they wane, the proud files of the Windermere,
Howard – Ah! woe to thy hopes of the day!
    Hear the wide welkin rend,
    While the Scots' shouts ascend,
'Elliot of Lariston, Elliot for aye!'

WHEN THE KYE COMES HAME

Come all ye jolly shepherds
    That whistle through the glen,
I'll tell ye of a secret
    That courtiers dinna ken:
What is the greatest bliss
    That the tongue o' man can name?

'Tis to woo a bonny lassie
　When the kye comes hame.
　　When the kye comes hame,
　　When the kye comes hame,
　　'Tween the gloaming and the mirk,
　　When the kye comes hame.

'Tis not beneath the coronet,
　Nor canopy of state,
'Tis not on couch of velvet,
　Nor arbour of the great —
'Tis beneath the spreading birk,
　In the glen without the name,
Wi' a bonny, bonny lassie,
　When the kye comes hame.
　　When the kye comes hame, etc.

There the blackbird bigs his nest,
　For the mate he loes to see,
And on the topmost bough,
　O, a happy bird is he;
Where he pours his melting ditty,
　And love is a' the theme,
And he'll woo his bonny lassie
　When the kye comes hame.
　　When the kye comes hame, etc.

When the blewart bears a pearl,
　And the daisy turns a pea,
And the bonny lucken gowan
　Has fauldit up her ee,
Then the laverock frae the blue lift

kye cattle, cows	*lucken gowan* globe-flower
mirk darkness	*fauldit* folded
bigs builds	*laverock* lark
blewart hairbell	*lift* sky

Drops down, an' thinks nae shame
To woo his bonny lassie
  When the kye comes hame.
    When the kye comes hame, etc.

See yonder pawkie shepherd,
  That lingers on the hill,
His ewes are in the fauld,
  An' his lambs are lying still;
Yet he downa gang to bed,
  For his heart is in a flame,
To meet his bonny lassie
  When the kye comes hame.
    When the kye comes hame, etc.

When the little wee bit heart
  Rises high in the breast,
An' the little wee bit starn
  Rises red in the east,
O there's a joy sae dear,
  That the heart can hardly frame,
Wi' a bonny, bonny lassie,
  When the kye comes hame!
    When the kye comes hame, etc.

Then since all nature joins
  In this love without alloy,
O, wha wad prove a traitor
  To Nature's dearest joy?
Or wha wad choose a crown,
  Wi' its perils and its fame,
And *miss* his bonny lassie
  When the kye comes hame?
    When the kye comes hame,
    When the kye comes hame,
    'Tween the gloaming and the mirk,
    When the kye comes hame!

downa daren't   *starn* star

A WITCH'S CHANT

Thou art weary, weary, weary,
Thou art weary and far away!
Hear me, gentle spirit, hear me;
Come before the dawn of day.

I hear a small voice from the hill,
The vapour is deadly, pale, and still –
A murmuring sough is on the wood,
And the witching star is red as blood.

And in the cleft of heaven I scan
The giant form of a naked man;
His eye is like the burning brand,
And he holds a sword in his right hand.

All is not well: by dint of spell,
Somewhere between the heaven and hell
There is this night a wild deray;
The spirits have wander'd from their way.

The purple drops shall tinge the moon,
As she wanders through the midnight noon;
And the dawning heaven shall all be red
With blood by guilty angels shed.

Be as it will, I have the skill
To work by good or work by ill;
Then here's for pain, and here's for thrall,
And here's for conscience, worst of all!

Another chant, and then, and then,
Spirits shall come or Christian men –
Come from the earth, the air or the sea:
Great Gil-Moules, I cry to thee!

deray disorder

Sleep'st thou, wakest thou, lord of the wind!
Mount thy steeds and gallop them blind;
And the long-tailed fiery dragon outfly,
The rocket of heaven, the bomb of the sky.

Over the dog-star, over the wain,
Over the cloud, and the rainbow's mane,
Over the mountain, and over the sea,
Haste – haste – haste to me!

Then here's for trouble and here's for smart,
And here's for the pang that seeks the heart;
Here's for madness, and here's for thrall,
And here's for conscience, the worst of all!

Walter Scott

1771–1832

FROM THE LAY OF THE LAST MINSTREL

(Canto VI, i)

Breathes there the man with soul so dead,
 Who never to himself hath said,
 This is my own, my native land!
Whose heart hath ne'er within him burn'd,
As home his footsteps he hath turn'd
 From wandering on a foreign strand!
If such there breathe, go, mark him well;
For him no Minstrel raptures swell;
High though his titles, proud his name,
Boundless his wealth as wish can claim;
Despite those titles, power, and pelf,
The wretch, concentred all in self,
Living, shall forfeit fair renown,
And, doubly dying, shall go down
To the vile dust, from whence he sprung,
Unwept, unhonour'd, and unsung.

JOCK OF HAZELDEAN

'Why weep ye by the tide, ladie,
 Why weep ye by the tide?
I'll wed ye to my youngest son,
 And ye sall be his bride:

And ye sall be his bride, ladie,
  Sae comely to be seen' –
But aye she loot the tears down fa'
  For Jock of Hazeldean.

'Now let this wilfu' grief be done,
  And dry that cheek so pale;
Young Frank is chief of Errington,
  And lord of Langley-dale;
His step is first in peaceful ha',
  His sword in battle keen' –
But aye she loot the tears down fa'
  For Jock of Hazeldean.

The kirk was deck'd at morning-tide,
  The tapers glimmer'd fair;
The priest and bridegroom wait the bride,
  And dame and knight are there.
They sought her baith by bower and ha';
  The ladie was not seen!
She's o'er the Border, and awa'
  Wi' Jock of Hazeldean.

FROM MARMION

(Canto V, xii)

—

LOCHINVAR

O Young Lochinvar is come out of the west,
Through all the wide Border his steed was the best:
And save his good broadsword he weapons had none.
He rode all unarm'd, and he rode all alone,
So faithful in love, and so dauntless in war,
There never was knight like the young Lochinvar.

loot let   *fa* fall

He staid not for brake, and he stopp'd not for stone,
He swam the Eske river where ford there was none;
But ere he alighted at Netherby gate,
The bride had consented, the gallant came late:
For a laggard in love, and a dastard in war,
Was to wed the fair Ellen of brave Lochinvar.

So boldly he enter'd the Netherby Hall,
Among bride's-men, and kinsmen, and brothers and all:
Then spoke the bride's father, his hand on his sword,
(For the poor craven bridegroom said never a word),
'O come ye in peace here, or come ye in war,
Or to dance at our bridal, young Lord Lochinvar?'

'I long woo'd your daughter, my suit you denied; –
Love swells like the Solway, but ebbs like its tide –
And now I am come, with this lost love of mine,
To lead but one measure, drink one cup of wine.
There are maidens in Scotland, more lovely by far,
That would gladly be bride to the young Lochinvar.'

The bride kiss'd the goblet: the knight took it up,
He quaff'd off the wine, and he threw down the cup.
She look'd down to blush, and she look'd up to sigh,
With a smile on her lips and a tear in her eye.
He took her soft hand, ere her mother could bar, –
'Now tread we a measure!' said young Lochinvar.

So stately his form, and so lovely her face,
That never a hall such a galliard did grace;
While her mother did fret, and her father did fume,
And the bridegroom stood dangling his bonnet and plume;
And the bride-maidens whisper'd, ''twere better by far
To have match'd our fair cousin with young Lochinvar.'

One touch to her hand, and one word in her ear,
When they reach'd the hall-door, and the charger stood near;
So light to the croupe the fair lady he swung,

So light to the saddle before her he sprung!
'She is won! we are gone, over bank, bush, and scaur;
They'll have fleet steeds that follow', quoth young Lochin-
    var.

There was mounting 'mong Graemes of the Netherby clan;
Forsters, Fenwicks, and Musgraves, they rode and they ran:
There was racing and chasing on Cannobie Lee,
But the lost bride of Netherby ne'er did they see.
So daring in love, and so dauntless in war,
Have ye e'er heard of gallant like young Lochinvar?

FROM THE LADY OF THE LAKE

'Now, yield thee, or by Him who made
The world, thy heart's blood dyes my blade!'
'Thy threats, thy mercy, I defy!
Let recreant yield, who fears to die.'
Like adder darting from his coil,
Like wolf that dashes through the toil,
Like mountain-cat who guards her young,
Full at Fitz-James' throat he sprung;
Received, but reck'd not of a wound,
And lock'd his arms his foeman round.
Now, gallant Saxon, hold thine own!
No maiden's hand is round thee thrown!
That desperate grasp thy frame might feel
Through bars of brass and triple steel!
They tug, they strain! down, down they go,
The Gael above, Fitz-James below.
The Chieftain's gripe his throat compress'd,
His knee was planted in his breast;
His clotted locks he backward threw,
Across his brow his hand he drew,
From blood and mist to clear his sight,
Then gleam'd aloft his dagger bright!

But hate and fury ill supplied
The stream of life's exhausted tide,
And all too late the advantage came,
To turn the odds of deadly game;
For, while the dagger gleam'd on high,
Reel'd soul and sense, reel'd brain and eye.
Down came the blow – but in the heath;
The erring blade found bloodless sheath.
The struggling foe may now unclasp
The fainting Chief's relaxing grasp;
Unwounded from the dreadful close,
But breathless all, Fitz-James arose.

PROUD MAISIE

Proud Maisie is in the wood,
　　Walking so early;
Sweet Robin sits on the bush,
　　Singing so rarely.

'Tell me, thou bonny bird,
　　When shall I marry me?'
'When six braw gentlemen
　　Kirkward shall carry ye.'

'Who makes the bridal bed,
　　Birdie, say truly?'
'The grey-headed sexton
　　That delves the grave duly.

'The glow-worm o'er grave and stone
　　Shall light thee steady.
The owl from the steeple sing,
　　Welcome, proud lady.'

BLUE BONNETS OVER THE BORDER

MARCH, march, Ettrick and Teviotdale,
Why the deil dinna ye march forward in order?
March, march, Eskdale and Liddesdale,
All the Blue Bonnets are bound for the Border.
  Many a banner spread
  Flutters above your head,
Many a crest that is famous in story.
  Mount and make ready then,
  Sons of the mountain glen,
Fight for the Queen and the old Scottish glory.

Come from the hills where your hirsels are grazing,
Come from the glen of the buck and the roe;
Come to the crag where the beacon is blazing,
Come with the buckler, the lance, and the bow.
  Trumpets are sounding,
  War-steeds are bounding,
Stand to your arms then, and march in good order;
  England shall many a day
  Tell of the bloody fray,
When the Blue Bonnets came over the Border.

Robert Tannahill

1774–1810

O! ARE YE SLEEPIN, MAGGIE?

'O! Are ye sleepin Maggie?
   O! are ye sleepin, Maggie?
Let me in, for loud the linn
   Is roaring o'er the warlock craigie!

'Mirk an rainy is the nicht,
   No a starn in a the carry;
Lightnin's gleam athwart the lift,
   An win's drive wi winter's fury.

'Fearfu' soughs the boor-tree bank,
   The rifted wood roars wild an dreary,
Loud the iron yett does clank,
   The cry o howlets mak's me eerie.

'Aboon my breath I daurna speak,
   For fear I rouse your waukrif daddie,
Caul's the blast upon my cheek, –
   O rise, rise my bonnie ladie!'

linn waterfall	*boor-tree* elder
craigie rock	*yett* gate
starn star	*howlets* owls
carry cloudy sky	*waukrif* wakeful
lift sky	*caul* cold

She oped the door, she loot him in:
　　He cuist aside his dreepin plaidie:
'Blaw your warst, ye rain an win,
　　Since, Maggie, now I'm in aside ye.

'Now, since ye're waukin, Maggie,
　　Now, since ye're waukin, Maggie,
What care I for howlet's cry,
　　For boor-tree bank, or warlock craigie?'

BONNIE WOOD O' CRAIGIELEA

Thou bonnie wood o' Craigielea!
　　Thou bonnie wood o' Craigielea!
Near thee I pass'd life's early day,
　　And won my Mary's heart in thee.

The brume, the brier, the birken bush,
　　Blume bonnie o'er thy flowery lee,
An a the sweets that ane can wish
　　Frae Nature's han, are strewed on thee.

Far ben thy dark green plantin's shade,
　　The cushat croodles am'rously,
The mavis, doon thy bughted glade,
　　Gars echo ring frae ev'ry tree.

Awa, ye thochtless, murd'rin gang
　　Wha tear the nestlins ere they flee!
They'll sing you yet a cantie sang,
　　Then, oh! in pity let them be!

loot let		*cushat* woodpigeon	
waukin waking		*mavis* song-thrush	
birken birch		*bughted* sheltered	
han hand		*gars* makes	
ben within		*cantie* tuneful!	

Whan Winter blaws, in sleety showers,
   Frae aff the Norlan hills sae hie,
He lichtly skiffs thy bonnie bow'rs,
   As laith tae harm a flow'r in thee.

Though fate should drag me south the line,
   Or o'er the wide Atlantic sea,
The happy hours I'll ever mind
   That I, in youth, hae spent in thee.

Allan Cunningham

1784–1842

THE WEE, WEE GERMAN LAIRDIE

Wha the deil hae we got for a King,
    But a wee, wee German lairdie!
An' whan we gaed to bring him hame,
    He was delving in his kail-yardie.
Sheughing kail an' laying leeks,
    But the hose and but the breeks,
Up his beggar duds he cleeks,
    The wee, wee German lairdie.

An' he's clapt down in our gudeman's chair,
    The wee, wee German lairdie;
An' he's brought fouth o' foreign leeks,
    An' dibblet them in his yardie.
He's pu'd the rose o' English louns,
    An' brak the harp o' Irish clowns,
But our thistle will jag his thumbs,
    The wee, wee German lairdie.

Come up amang the Highland hills,
    Thou wee, wee German lairdie;
An' see how Charlie's lang-kail thrive,

lairdie petty squire
kail-yardie cabbage patch
sheughing uplifting
but without
duds rags

gudeman king
fouth a lot
louns fellows
lang-kail swords of Prince
    Charles Edward's men

He dibblet in his yardie.
An' if a stock ye daur to pu',
 Or haud the yoking of a pleugh,
We'll break yere sceptre o'er yere mou',
 Thou wee bit German lairdie.

Our hills are steep, our glens are deep,
 Nae fitting for a yardie;
An' our norlan' thistles winna pu',
 Thou wee, wee German lairdie.
An' we've the trenching blades o' weir,
 Wad twine ye o' yere German gear;
An' pass ye 'neath the claymore's shear,
 Thou feckless German lairdie.

daur dare	*gear* belongings	
haud hold	*claymore* broadsword	
weir war	*feckless* useless	

Alexander Rodger

1784–1846

MY AULD BREEKS

My mither men't my auld breeks,
  An' wow! but they were duddy,
And sent me to get Mally shod
  At Robin Tamson's smiddy;
The smiddy stands beside the burn
  That wimples through the clachan,
I never yet gae by the door,
  But aye I fa' a-lauchin'.

For Robin was a walthy carle,
  An' had ae bonnie dochter,
Yet ne'er wad let her tak a man,
  Tho' mony lads had socht her;
But what think ye o' my exploit?
  The time our mare was shoeing,
I slippit up beside the lass,
  And briskly fell a-wooing.

An' aye she e'ed my auld breeks,
  The time that we sat crackin',
Quo' I, 'My lass, ne'er mind the clouts,

breeks breeches   *the time* while
duddy ragged   *crackin'* chatting
clachan village   *clouts* clothes
carle old man

I've new anes for the makin';
But gin ye'll just come hame wi' me,
   An' lea'e the carle, your father,
Ye'se get my breeks to keep in trim,
   Mysel, an' a' thegither.'

''Deed, lad', quo' she, 'Your offer's fair,
   I really think I'll tak it,
Sae, gang awa', get out the mare,
   We'll baith slip on the back o't:
For gin I wait my father's time,
   I'll wait till I be fifty;
But na! – I'll marry in my prime,
   An' mak a wife most thrifty.'

Wow! Robin was an angry man,
   At tyning o' his dochter:
Thro' a' the kintra-side he ran,
   An' far an' near he socht her;
But when he cam to our fire-end,
   An' fand us baith thegither,
Quo' I, 'Gudeman, I've ta'en your bairn,
   An' ye may tak my mither.'

Auld Robin girn'd an' sheuk his pow,
   'Guid sooth!' quo' he, 'Ye're merry,
But I'll just tak ye at your word,
   An' end this hurry-burry.'
So Robin an' our auld wife
   Agreed to creep thegither;
Now, I hae Robin Tamson's pet,
   An' Robin has my mither.

tyning losing   *girn'd* complained

William Tennant

1784–1848

FROM ANSTER FAIR

(Canto First XII-XXIII)

'Twas on a keen December night; John Frost
   Drove thro' mid air his chariot, icy-wheel'd,
And from the sky's crisp ceiling star-embost,
   Whiff'd off the clouds that the pure blue conceal'd;
The hornless moon amid her brilliant host
   Shone, and with silver sheeted lake and field;
'Twas cutting cold; I'm sure, each trav'ller's nose
Was pinch'd right red that night, and numb'd were all
     his toes.

Not so were MAGGIE LAUDER'S toes, as she
   In her warm chamber at her supper ate
(For 'twas that hour when burgesses agree
   To eat their suppers ere the night grows late):
Alone she sat, and pensive as may be
   A young fair lady, wishful of a mate;
Yet with her teeth held now and then a-picking,
Her stomach to refresh, the breast-bone of a chicken.

She thought upon her suitors, that with love
   Besiege her chamber all the livelong day,
Aspiring each her virgin heart to move
   With courtship's every troublesome essay –
Calling her angel, sweeting, fondling, dove,
   And other nicknames in love's friv'lous way;

While she, though their addresses still she heard,
Held back from all her heart, and still no beau preferr'd.

'What, what!' quo' MAG, 'must thus it be my doom
   To spend my prime in maidhood's joyless state,
And waste away my sprightly body's bloom
   In spouseless solitude without a mate –
Still toying with my suitors, as they come
   Cringing in lowly courtship to my gate?
Fool that I am, to live unwed so long!
More fool, since I am woo'd by such a clam'rous throng!

For was e'er heiress with much gold in chest,
   And dowr'd with acres of wheat-bearing land,
By such a pack of men, in amorous quest,
   Fawningly spaniel'd to bestow her hand?
Where'er I walk, the air that feeds my breast
   Is by the gusty sighs of lovers fann'd;
Each wind that blows wafts love-cards to my lap;
Whilst I – ah stupid MAG! – avoid each am'rous trap!

Then come, let me my suitors' merits weigh,
   And in the worthiest lad my spouse select:–
First, there's our ANSTER merchant, Norman Ray,
   A powder'd wight with golden buttons deck'd,
That stinks with scent, and chats like popinjay,
   And struts with phiz tremendously erect:
Four brigs has he, that on the broad sea swim; –
He is a pompous fool – I cannot think of him.

Next is the maltster Andrew Strang, that takes
   His seat i' the bailie's loft on Sabbath-day,
With paltry visage white as oaten cakes,
   As if no blood ran gurgling in his clay;
Heav'ns! what an awkward hunch the fellow makes,
   As to the priest he does the bow repay;

phiz bearded chin

Yet he is rich – a very wealthy man, true –
But, by the holy rood, I will have none of Andrew!

Then for the lairds – there's Melvil of Carnbee,
  A handsome gallant, and a beau of spirit;
Who can go down the dance so well as he?
  And who can fiddle with such manly merit?
Ay, but he is too much the debauchee –
  His cheeks seem sponges oozing port and claret;
In marrying him I should bestow myself ill –
And so, I'll not have you, thou fuddler, Harry Melvil!

There's Cunningham of Barns, that still assails
  With verse and billet-doux my gentle heart –
A bookish squire, and good at telling tales,
  That rhymes and whines of Cupid, flame, and dart;
But, oh! his mouth a sorry smell exhales,
  And on his nose sprouts horribly the wart;
What though there be a fund of lore and fun in him?
He has a rotten breath – I cannot think of Cunningham!

Why then, there's Allardyce, that plies his suit
  And battery of courtship more and more;
Spruce Lochmalonie, that with booted foot
  Each morning wears the threshold of my door;
Auchmoutie too and Bruce, that persecute
  My tender heart with am'rous buffets sore:–
Whom to my hand and bed should I promote! –
Eh-lah! what sight is this? – what ails my mustard-pot?'

Here broke the lady her soliloquy;
  For in a twink her pot of mustard, lo!
Self-moved, like Jove's wheel'd stool that rolls on high,
  'Gan caper on her table to and fro,
And hopp'd and fidgeted before her eye,
  Spontaneous, here and there, a wondrous show:
As leaps, instinct with mercury, a bladder,
So leaps the mustard-pot of bonny MAGGIE LAUDER.

Soon stopp'd its dance th' ignoble utensil,
    When from its round and small recess there came
Thin curling wreaths of paly smoke, that still,
    Fed by some magic unapparent flame,
Mount to the chamber's stucco'd roof, and fill
    Each nook with fragrance, and refresh the dame:
Ne'er smelt a Phoenix-nest so sweet, I wot,
As smelt the luscious fumes of MAGGIE's mustard-pot.

George Gordon Byron

1788–1824

LACHIN Y GAIR

Away, ye gay landscapes, ye gardens of roses!
   In you let the minions of luxury rove;
Restore me the rocks where the snow-flake reposes,
   Though still they are sacred to freedom and love;
Yet, Caledonia, beloved are thy mountains,
   Round their white summits though elements war;
Though cataracts foam 'stead of smooth-flowing fountains,
   I sigh for the valley of dark Loch na Garr.

Ah! there my young footsteps in infancy wander'd;
   My cap was the bonnet, my cloak was the plaid;
On chieftains long perish'd my memory pondor'd,
   As daily I strode through the pine-cover'd glade;
I sought not my home till the day's dying glory
   Gave place to the rays of the bright polar star;
For fancy was cheer'd by traditional story,
   Disclos'd by the natives of dark Loch na Garr.

'Shades of the dead! have I not heard your voices
   Rise on the night-rolling breath of the gale?'
Surely the soul of the hero rejoices
   And rides on the wind o'er his own highland vale;
Round Loch na Garr while the stormy mist gathers,
   Winter presides in his cold icy car:
Clouds there encircle the forms of my fathers;
   They dwell in the tempests of dark Loch na Garr.

'Ill-starr'd, though brave, did no visions foreboding
    Tell you that fate had forsaken your cause?'
Ah! were you destin'd to die at Culloden,
    Victory crown'd not your fall with applause;
Still were you happy in death's earthly slumber,
    You rest with your clan in the caves of Braemar;
The pibroch resounds to the piper's loud number,
    Your deeds on the echoes of dark Loch na Garr.

Years have roll'd on, Loch na Garr, since I left you,
    Years must elapse ere I tread you again:
Nature of verdure and flowers has bereft you,
    Yet still are you dearer than Albion's plain.
England! thy beauties are tame and domestic
    To one who has roved o'er the mountains afar;
Oh for the crags that are wild and majestic!
    The steep frowning glories of dark Loch na Garr.

FROM DON JUAN, CANTO FIRST
(Opening Stanzas)

I want a hero: an uncommon want,
    When every year and month sends forth a new one,
Till, after cloying the gazettes with cant,
    The age discovers he is not the true one;
Of such as these I should not care to vaunt,
    I'll therefore take our ancient friend Don Juan:
We all have seen him in the pantomime,
Sent to the devil somewhat ere his time.

Vernon, the Butcher Cumberland, Wolfe, Hawke,
    Prince Ferdinand, Granby, Burgoyne, Keppel, Howe,
Evil and good, have had their tithe of talk,
    And fill'd their sign-posts then, like Wellesley now:

pibroch a sonata-like composition for the bagpipe

Each in their turn, like Banquo's monarchs stalk,
　　Followers of fame 'nine farrow' of that sow:
France, too, had Buonaparte and Dumourier
Recorded in the *Moniteur* and *Courier*.

Barnave, Brissot, Condorcet, Mirabeau,
　　Petion, Clootz, Danton, Marat, La Fayette,
Were French, and famous people, as we know;
　　And there were others, scarce forgotten yet,
Joubert, Hoche, Marceau, Lannes, Dessaix, Moreau,
　　With many of the military set.
Exceedingly remarkable at times.
But not at all adapted to my rhymes.

Nelson was once Britannia's god of war,
　　And still should be so, but the tide is turn'd:
There's no more to be said of Trafalgar,
　　'Tis with our hero quietly inurn'd;
Because the army's grown more popular,
　　At which the naval people are concern'd:
Besides, the prince is all for the land service,
Forgetting Duncan, Nelson, Howe and Jervis.

Brave men were living before Agamemnon,
　　And since, exceeding valorous and sage,
A good deal like him too, though quite the same none
　　But then they shone not on the poet's page,
And so have been forgotten. I condemn none,
　　But can't find any in the present age
Fit for my poem (that is, for my new one);
So, as I said, I'll take my friend Don Juan.

Most epic poems plunge *in medias res*
　　(Horace makes this the heroic turnpike road),
And then your hero tells, whene'er you please
　　What went before – by way of episode,
While seated after dinner at his ease,
　　Beside his mistress in some soft abode,

Palace, or garden, paradise, or cavern,
Which serves the happy couple for a tavern.

That is the usual method, but not mine –
    My way is to begin with the beginning;
The regularity of my design
    Forbids all wandering as the worst of sinning.
And therefore I shall open with a line
    (Although it cost me half an hour in spinning)
Narrating somewhat of Don Juan's father,
And also of his mother, if you'd rather.

In Seville was he born, a pleasant city,
    Famous for oranges and women: he
Who has not seen it will be much to pity,
    So says the proverb – and I quite agree;
Of all the Spanish towns is none more pretty,
    Cadiz, perhaps – but that you soon may see.
Don Juan's parents lived beside the river,
A noble stream, and call'd the Guadalquivir.

His father's name was Jose – *Don*, of course,
    A true Hidalgo, free from every stain
Of Moor or Hebrew blood, he traced his source
    Through the most Gothic gentlemen of Spain;
A better cavalier ne'er mounted horse,
    Or, being mounted, e'er got down again,
Than Jose, who begot our hero, who
Begot – but that's to come – Well, to renew:

His mother was a learned lady, famed
    For every branch of every science known
In every Christian language ever named,
    With virtues equall'd by her wit alone.
She made the cleverest people quite ashamed;
    And even the good with inward envy groan,
Finding themselves so very much exceeded
In their own way, by all the things that she did.

Her memory was a mine; she knew by heart
  All Calderon and greater part of Lope,
So that if any actor miss'd his part,
  She could have served him for the prompter's copy;
For her Feinagle's were an useless art,
  And he himself obliged to shut up shop – he
Could never made a memory so fine as
That which adorned the brain of Donna Inez.

Her favourite science was the mathematical,
  Her noblest virtue was her magnanimity;
Her wit (she sometimes tried at wit) was Attic all,
  Her serious sayings darken'd to sublimity;
In short, in all things she was fairly what I call
  A prodigy: her morning dress was dimity,
Her evening silk, or, in the summer, muslin,
And other stuffs, with which I won't stay puzzling.

She knew the Latin – that is, 'the Lord's prayer',
  And Greek – the alphabet – I'm nearly sure;
She read some French romances here and there,
  Although her mode of speaking was not pure;
For native Spanish she had no great care,
  At least her conversation was obscure;
Her thoughts were theorems, her words a problem,
As if she deem'd that mystery would ennoble 'em.

She liked the English and the Hebrew tongue,
  And said there was analogy between 'em;
She proved it somehow out of sacred song,
  But I must leave the proofs to those who've seen 'em
But this I heard her say, and can't be wrong,
  And all may think which way their judgments lean 'em,
'Tis strange – the Hebrew noun which means 'I am,'
The English always use to govern d – n.'

Some women use their tongues – she *look'd* a lecture,
  Each eye a sermon, and her brow a homily

An all-in-all sufficient self-director,
　　Like the lamented late Sir Samuel Romilly.
The Law's expounder, and the State's corrector,
　　Whose suicide was almost an anomaly –
One sad example more, that 'All is vanity'
(The jury brought their verdict in 'Insanity').

In short, she was a walking calculation,
　　Miss Edgeworth's novels stepping from their covers,
Or Mrs Trimmer's books on education,
　　Or 'Coelebs' Wife' set out in quest of lovers;
Morality's prim personification,
　　In which not Envy's self a flaw discovers;
To others' share let 'female errors fall',
For she had not even one – the worst of all.

Oh! she was perfect, past all parallel –
　　Of any modern female saint's comparison;
So far above the cunning powers of hell,
　　Her guardian angel had given up his garrison:
Even her minutest motions went as well
　　As those of the best timepiece made by Harrison.
In virtues nothing earthly could surpass her,
Save thine 'incomparable oil', Macassar!

George Macdonald

1824–1905

ANE BY ANE

Ane by ane they gang awa',
The Gatherer gathers great an' sma',
Ane by ane mak's ane an' a'.

Aye when ane sets doun the cup,
Ane ahint maun tak it up,
Yet thegither they will sup.

Golden-heided, ripe an' strang,
Shorn will be the hairst ere lang,
Syne begins a better sang!

ane one   - *hairst* harvest
ahint behind

Alexander Smith

1830–67

GLASGOW

(Shortened version)

Sing, Poet, 'tis a merry world;
That cottage smoke is rolled and curled
   In sport, that every moss
Is happy, every inch of soil; –
Before *me* runs a road of toil
   With my grave cut across.
Sing, trailing showers and breezy downs –
I know the tragic hearts of towns.

City! I am true son of thine;
Ne'er dwelt I where great mornings shine
   Around the bleating pens;
Ne'er by the rivulets I strayed,
And ne'er upon my childhood weighed
   The silence of the glens.
Instead of shores where ocean beats,
I hear the ebb and flow of streets.

Black Labour draws his weary waves,
Into their secret-moaning caves;
   But with the morning light,
That sea again will overflow
With a long weary sound of woe,
   Again to faint in night.
Wave am I in that sea of woes,
Which, night and morning, ebbs and flows.

Draw thy fierce streams of blinding ore,
Smite on a thousand anvils, roar
    Down to the harbour-bars;
Smoulder in smoky sunsets, flare
On rainy night, with street and square
    Lie empty to the stars.
From terrace proud to alley base
I know thee as my mother's face.

When sunset bathes thee in his gold,
In wreaths of bronze thy sides are rolled,
    Thy smoke is dusky fire;
And, from the glory round thee poured,
A sunbeam like an angel's sword
    Shivers upon a spire.
Thus have I watched thee, Terror! Dream!
While the blue Night crept up the stream.

.   .   .

While o'er thy walls the darkness sails,
I lean against the churchyard rails;
    Up in the midnight towers
The belfried spire, the street is dead,
I hear in silence over head
    The clang of iron hours:
It moves me not – I know her tomb
Is yonder in the shapeless gloom.

.   .   .

But all these sights and sounds are strange;
Then wherefore from thee should I range?
    Thou has my kith and kin:
My childhood, youth, and manhood brave;
Thou has that unforgotten grave
    Within thy central din.
A sacredness of love and death
Dwells in thy noise and smoky breath.

Robert Louis Stevenson

1850–94

A MILE AN' A BITTOCK

A mile an' a bittock, a mile or twa,
Abune the burn, ayont the law
Davie an' Donal' an' Cherlie an' a',
    An' the mune was shinin' clearly!

Ane went hame wi' the ither, an' then
The ither went hame wi' the ither twa men,
An' baith wad return him the service again,
    An' the mune was shinin' clearly!

The clocks were chappin' in house an' ha',
Eleeven, twal' an' ane an' twa;
An' the guidman's face was turnt to the wa',
    An' the mune was shinin' clearly!

Noo, Davie was first to get sleep in his head,
'The best o' frien's maun twine,' he said;
'I'm weariet, an' here I'm awa' to my bed,'
    An' the mune was shinin' clearly!

bittock little bit   *twal'* twelve
abune above   *guidman* husband, householder
chappin' striking   *twine* separate

Twa o' them walkin' an' crackin' their lane,
The mornin' licht cam grey an' plain,
An' the birds they yammert on stick an' stane,
   An the mune was shinin' clearly!

O years ayont, O years awa',
My lads, ye'll mind whate'er befa' –
My lads, ye'll mind on the beild o' the law,
   When the mune was shinin' clearly.

ILLE TERRARUM

Frae nirly, nippin', Eas'lan' breeze,
Frae Norlan' snaw, an' haar o' seas,
Weel happit in your gairden trees,
    A bonny bit,
Atween the muckle Pentland's knees,
    Secure ye sit.

Beeches an' aiks entwine their theek,
An' firs, a stench, auld-farrant clique,
A' simmer day, your chimleys reek,
    Couthy and bien;
An' here an' there your windies keek
    Amang the green.

A pickle plats an' paths an' posies,
A wheen auld gillyflowers an' roses:
A ring o' wa's the hale encloses

crackin' gossiping	*theek* thatch
yammert clamoured	*auld-farrant* old-fashioned
beild shelter	*reek* smoke
law hillock	*couthy* cosy
nirly stunted	*bien* comfortable
haar cold mist	*pickle* few
happit covered	*plats* plots
aiks oaks	*hale* whole

Frae sheep or men;
An' there the auld housie beeks an' dozes,
A' by her lane.

The gairdner crooks his weary back
A' day in the pitaty-track,
Or mebbe stops awhile to crack
        Wi' Jane the cook,
Or at some buss, worm-eaten-black,
        To gie a look.

Frae the high hills the curlew ca's;
The sheep gang baaing by the wa's;
Or whiles a clan o' roosty craws
        Cangle thegether;
The wild bees seek the gairden raws,
        Weariet wi' heather.

Or in the gloamin' douce an' grey
The sweet-throat mavis tunes her lay;
The herd comes linkin doun the brae;
        An' by degrees
The muckle siller müne maks way
        Amang the trees.

Here aft hae I, wi' sober heart,
For meditation sat apairt,
When orra loves or kittle art
        Perplexed my mind;
Here socht a balm for ilka smart
        O' humankind.

beeks bakes	*cangle* wrangle
lane lone	*mavis* song-thrush
pitaty potato	*muckle* big
crack gossip	*orra* sundry
buss bush	*kittle* difficult
gang go	

Here aft, weel neukit by my lane,
Wi' Horace, or perhaps Montaigne,
The mornin' hours hae come an' gane
    Abüne my heid –
I wadnae gi'en a chucky-stane
    For a' I'd read.

But noo the auld city, street by street,
An' winter fu' o' snaw an' sleet,
Awhile shut in my gangrel feet
    An' goavin' mettle;
Noo is the soopit ingle sweet,
    An' liltin' kettle.

An' noo the winter winds complain;
Cauld lies the glaur in ilka lane;
On draigled hizzie, tautit wean
    An' drucken lads,
In the mirk nicht, the winter rain
    Dribbles an' blads.

Whan bugles frae the Castle rock,
An' beaten drums wi' dowie shock,
Wauken, at cauld-rife sax o'clock,
    My chitterin' frame,
I mind me on the kintry cock,
    The kintry hame.

neukit cornered	*tautit wean* untidy child
chucky-stane pebble	*blads* splashes
gangrel vagrant	*dowie* sad
goavin' staring	*cauld-rife* chilly
soopit swept	*chitterin'* shivering
glaur mud	*kintry* country
hizzie hussy	

I mind me on yon bonny bield;
An' Fancy traivels far afield
To gaither a' that gairdens yield
    O' sun an' Simmer:
To hearten up a dowie chield,
    Fancy's the limmer!

TO S. R. CROCKETT

(On receiving a Dedication)

Blows the wind today, and the sun and the rain are flying,
    Blows the wind on the moors today and now,
Where about the graves of the martyrs the whaups are crying,
    My heart remembers how!

Grey recumbent tombs of the dead in desert places,
    Standing-stones on the vacant wine-red moor,
Hills of sheep, and the howes of the silent vanished races,
    And winds, austere and pure.

Be it granted me to behold you again in dying,
    Hills of home! and to hear again the call;
Hear about the graves of the martyrs the peewees crying,
    And hear no more at all.

IN THE HIGHLANDS

In the highlands, in the country places,
Where the old plain men have rosy faces,
And the young fair maidens
    Quiet eyes;

bield hut, shelter	*whaups* curlews
chield fellow	*howes* hollows, glens
limmer flirt	*peewees* lapwings

Where essential silence cheers and blesses,
And for ever in the hill-recesses
Her more lovely music
    Broods and dies.

O to mount again where erst I haunted;
Where the old red hills are bird-enchanted,
And the low green meadows
    Bright with sward;
And when even dies, the million-tinted,
And the night has come, and planets glinted,
Lo, the valley hollow
    Lamp-bestarred!

O to dream, O to awake and wander
There, and with delight to take and render,
Through the trance of silence,
    Quiet breath;
Lo! for there, among the flowers and grasses,
Only the mightier movement sounds and passes;
Only winds and river,
    Life and death.

John Davidson

1857–1909

THE LAST JOURNEY

I felt the world a-spinning on its nave,
  I felt it sheering blindly round the sun;
I felt the time had come to find a grave:
  I knew it in my heart my days were done.
I took my staff in hand; I took the road,
And wandered out to seek my last abode.
      Hearts of gold and hearts of lead
        Sing it yet in sun and rain,
         'Heel and toe from dawn to dusk,
        Round the world and home again.'

Oh, long before the bere was steeped for malt,
  And long before the grape was crushed for wine,
The glory of the march without a halt,
  The triumph of a stride like yours and mine
Was known to folk like us, who walked about,
To be the sprightliest cordial out and out!
      Folk like us, with hearts that beat,
        Sang it too in sun and rain –
         'Heel and toe from dawn to dusk,
        Round the world and home again.'

My feet are heavy now, but on I go,
  My head erect beneath the tragic years.
The way is steep, but I would have it so;
  And dusty, but I lay the dust with tears,
Though none can see me weep: alone I climb

The rugged path that leads me out of time –
   Out of time and out of all,
      Singing yet in sun and rain,
      'Heel and toe from dawn to dusk,
      Round the world and home again.'

Farewell the hope that mocked, farewell despair
   That went before me still and made the pace.
The earth is full of graves, and mine was there
   Before my life began, my resting-place;
And I shall find it out and with the dead
Lie down for ever, all my sayings said –
      Deeds all done and songs all sung,
        While others chant in sun and rain,
        'Heel and toe from dawn to dusk,
        Round the world and home again.'

FROM A BALLAD IN BLANK VERSE:
GREENOCK

His father's house looked out across a firth
Broad-bosomed like a mere, beside a town
Far in the North, where Time could take his ease,
And Change hold holiday; where Old and New
Weltered upon the border of the world.

'Oh now,' he thought – a youth whose sultry eyes,
Bold brow and wanton mouth were not all lust,
But haunted from within and from without
By memories, visions, hopes, divine desires –
'Now may my life beat out upon this shore
A prouder music than the winds and waves
Can compass in their haughtiest moods. I need
No world more spacious than the region here:
The foam-embroidered firth, a purple path

For argosies that still on pinions speed,
Or fiery-hearted cleave with iron limbs
And bows precipitous the pliant sea;
The sloping shores that fringe the velvet tides
With heavy bullion and with golden lace
Of restless pebble woven and fine spun sand;
The villages that sleep the winter through,
And, wakening with the spring, keep festival
All summer and all autumn: this grey town
That pipes the morning up before the lark
With shrieking steam, and from a hundred stalks
Lacquers the sooty sky; where hammers clang
On iron hulls, and cranes in harbours creak
Rattle and swing, whole cargoes on their necks;
Where men sweat gold that others hoard or spend,
And lurk like vermin in their narrow streets:
This old grey town, this firth, the further strand
Spangled with hamlets, and the wooded steeps,
Whose rocky tops behind each other press,
Fantastically carved like antique helms
High-hung in heaven's cloudy armoury,
Is world enough for me. Here daily dawn
Burns through the smoky east; with fire-shod feet
The sun treads heaven, and steps from hill to hill
Downward before the night that still pursues
His crimson wake; here winter plies his craft,
Soldering the years with ice; here spring appears,
Caught in a leafless brake, her garland torn,
Breathless with wonder, and the tears half-dried
Upon her rosy cheek; here summer comes
And wastes his passion like a prodigal
Right royally; and here her golden gains
Free-handed as a harlot autumn spends;
And here are men to know, women to love.'

Charles Murray

1864–1941

DOCKENS AFORE HIS PEERS

(Exemption tribunal)

Nae sign o' thow yet. Ay, that's me, John Watt o' Dockenhill:
We've had the war throu' han' afore, at markets ower a gill.
O ay, I'll sit, birze ben a bit. Hae, Briggie, pass the snuff;
Ye winna hinner lang wi' me, an' speer a lot o' buff,
For I've to see the saiddler yet, an Watchie, honest stock,
To gar him sen' his 'prentice up to sort the muckle knock,
Syne cry upo' the banker's wife an' leave some settin' eggs,
An' tell the ferrier o' the quake that's vrang aboot the legs.
It's yafa wedder, Mains, for Mairch, wi' snaw an' frost an' win',
The ploos are roustin' i' the fur, an' a' the wark's ahin'.
Ye've grun yersel's an' ken the tyauve it is to wirk a ferm,
An' a' the fash we've had wi' fouk gyaun aff afore the term;
We've nane to spare for sojerin', that's nae oor wark ava',
We've rents to pey, an' beasts to feed, an' corn to sell an' saw;

thow thaw	*yafa* awful
birze ben press along	*ploos* ploughs
hinner hinder	*fur* furrow
speer inquire	*ahin'* behind
buff nonsense	*tyauve* struggle
stock fellow	*ferm* farm
gar cause	*fash* trouble
muckle knock big clock	*gyaun* going
syne then	*ava'* at all
quake heifer	*saw* sow

Oonless we get the seed in seen, faur will we be for meal?
An' faur will London get the beef they leuk for aye at Yeel?
There's men aneuch in sooters' shops, an' chiels in masons'
　　yards,
An' coonter-loupers, sklaters, vrichts, an' quarrymen, an'
　　cyaurds,
To fill a reg'ment in a week, withoot gyaun vera far,
Jist shove them in ahin' the pipes, an' tell them that it's War;
For gin aul' Scotland's at the bit, there's naething for't but
　　list.
Some mayna like it vera sair, but never heed, insist.
Bit, feich, I'm haverin' on like this, an' a' I need's a line
To say there's men that maun be left, an' ye've exemptit mine.
Fat said ye? Fatna fouk hae I enoo' at Dockenhill?
It's just a wastrie o' your time, to run them throu', but still –
First there's the wife – 'Pass her,' ye say. Saul! had she been a
　　lass
Ye hadna rappit oot saw quick, young laird, to lat her pass,
That may be hoo ye spak' the streen, fan ye was playin' cairds,
But seein' tenants tak' at times their menners fae their lairds,
I'll tell ye this, for sense an' thrift, for skeel wi' hens an' caur,
Gin ye'd her marrow for a wife, ye woudna be the waur.
Oor maiden's neist, ye've heard o' her, new hame fae buirdin'
　　squeel,
Faur she saw mair o' beuks than broth, an' noo she's never
　　weel,

seen soon	*maun* must
faur where	*fat* what
Yeel Yule	*fouk* folk
sooters shoemakers	*the streen* last night
chiels fellows	*fan* when
coonter-loupers shop assistants	*skeel* skill
cyaurds cards	*caur* calves
at the bit in trouble	*marrow* like
sair sore	*waur* worse
haverin' prattling	*buirdin' squeel* boarding school

But fan she's playin' ben the hoose, there's little wird o'
    dwaams,
For she's the rin o' a' the tunes, strathspeys, an' sangs an'
    psalms;
O' 'Evan' an' 'Neander' baith, ye seen can hae aneuch,
But 'Hobble Jennie' gars me loup, an' crack my thooms, an'
    hooch.
Weel, syne we hae the kitchie deem, that milks an' mak's the
    maet,
She disna aft haud doon the deese, she's at it ear' an' late,
She cairries seed, an' braks the muck, an' gies a han' to hyow,
An' churns, an' bakes, an' syes the so'ens, an' fyles there's
    peats to rowe.
An' fan the maiden's frien's cry in, she'll mask a cup o' tay,
An' butter scones, and dicht her face, an' cairry ben the tray,
She's big an' brosy, reid and roch, an' swippert as she's stoot,
Gie her a kilt instead o' cotts, an' thon's the gran' recruit.
There's Francie syne, oor auldest loon, we pat him on for
    grieve,
An' fegs, we would be in a soss, gin he should up an' leave;
He's eident, an' has lots o' can, an' cheery wi' the men,
An' I'm sae muckle oot aboot wi' markets till atten'.
We've twa chaps syne to wirk the horse, as sweir as sweir can
    be,

wird word	*mask* infuse
dwaams swoonings	*tay* tea
aneuch enough	*brosy* stout
loup leap	*roch* rough
thooms thumbs	*swippert* lithe, lissom
deem dame, young woman	*cotts* skirts
maet meat, food	*loon* boy
she disna, etc. she had little time to rest	*pat* put
muck dung	*grieve* foreman
hyow hoe	*fegs* faith
syes strains	*soss* mess
so'ens a kind of porridge	*eident* diligent
fyles whiles, at times	*can* know-how
rowe roll, stack	*sweir* lazy

They fussle better than they ploo, they're aul' an' mairret tee,
An' baith hae hooses on the ferm, an' Francie never kens
Foo muckle corn gyangs hame at nicht, to fatten up their
    hens.
The baillie syne, a peer-hoose geet, nae better than a feel,
He slivvers, an' has sic a mant, an' ae clog-fit as weel;
He's barely sense to muck the byre, an' cairry in the scull,
An' park the kye, an' cogue the caur, an' scutter wi' the bull.
Weel, that's them a' – I didna hear – the laadie i' the gig?
That's Johnnie, he's a littlan jist, for a' he leuks sae big.
Fy na, he isna twenty yet – ay, weel, he's maybe near't;
Ower young to lippen wi' a gun, the crater would be fear't.
He's hardly throu' his squeelin' yet, an' noo we hae a plan
To lat him simmer i' the toon, an' learn to mizzer lan'.
Fat? Gar him 'list! Oor laadie 'list? 'Twould kill his mither,
    that,
To think o' Johnnie in a trench awa' in fat-ye-ca't;
We would hae sic a miss at hame, gin he was hine awa',
We'd raither lat ye clean the toon o' ither twa;
Ay, tak' the wife, the dother, deem, the baillie wi' the mant,
Tak' Francie, an' the mairret men, but John we canna want.
Fat does he dee? Ye micht as weel speir fat I dee mysel',
The things he hisna time to dee is easier to tell;
He dells the yard, an' wi' the scythe cuts tansies on the brae,

fussle whistle	*cogue* feed
tee too	*scutter* mess about with
foo how	*gig* small cart
gyangs goes	*littlan* child
peer-hoose poor-house	*lippen* trust
geet bastard	*crater* creature
feel fool	*squeelin'* schooling
slivvers slavers	*mizzer* discern
mant stammer	*hine* far
clog-fit club-foot	*dother* daughter
byre cowshed	*dee* do
scull basket	*dells* delves
kye cattle	*tansies* weeds

An' fan a ruck gyangs throu' the mull, he's thrang at wispin'
    strae,
He sits aside me at the mart, an' fan a feeder's sell't
Tak's doon the wecht, an' leuks the beuk for fat it's worth fan
    fell't;
He helps me to redd up the dask, he tak's a han' at loo,
An' sorts the shalt, an' yokes the gig, an' drives me fan I'm fou'.
Hoot, Mains, hae mind, I'm doon for you some sma' thing wi'
    the bank;
Aul' Larickleys, I saw you throu', an' this is a' my thank;
An' Gutteryloan, that time ye broke, to Dockenhill ye cam' –
'Total exemption.' Thank ye, sirs. Fat say ye till a dram?

GIN I WAS GOD

Gin I was God, sittin' up there abeen,
Weariet nae doot noo a' my darg was deen,
Deaved wi' the harps an' hymns oonendin' ringin',
Tired o' the flockin' angels hairse wi' singin',
To some clood-edge I'd daunder furth an', feth,
Look ower an' watch hoo things were gyaun aneth.
Syne, gin I saw hoo men I'd made mysel'
Had startit in to pooshan, sheet an' fell,
To reive an' rape, an' fairly mak' a hell
O' my braw birlin' Earth, – a hale week's wark –

ruck mass	*deen* done	
mull mill	*deaved* deafened	
thrang busy	*hairse* hoarse	
wecht weight	*daunder* saunter	
redd clean, order	*gyaun* going	
dask desk	*aneth* beneath	
shalt pony	*syne* then	
fou drunk	*gin* if, given	
dram drink	*pooshan* poison	
abeen above	*sheet* shoot	
darg work	*reive* harry	

I'd cast my coat again, rowe up my sark,
An', or they'd time to lench a second ark,
Tak' bak my word an' sen' anither spate,
Droon oot the hale hypothec, dicht the sklate,
Own my mistak', an' aince I'd cleared the brod,
Start a'thing ower again, gin I was God.

sark shirt   *sklate* slate
lench launch   *brod* board
hypothec concern   *ower* over
dicht wipe

Marion Angus

1866–1946

THE LILT

Jean Gordon is weaving a' her lane
Twinin' the threid wi' a thocht o' her ain,
Hearin' the tune o' the bairns at play
That they're singin' amang them ilka day;
And saftly, saftly, ower the hill
Comes the sma', sma' rain.

Aye, she minds o' a simmer's nicht
Afore the waning o' the licht —
Bairnies chantin' in Lover's Lane
The sang that comes ower an' ower again,
And a young lass stealin' awa' to the hill,
In the sma', sma' rain.

Oh! lass, your lips were flamin' reid,
An' cauld, mist drops lay on yer heid,
Ye didna gaither yon rose yer lane
An yer he'rt was singin' a sang o' its ain,
As ye slippit hameward, ower the hill,
In the sma', sma' rain.

her lane alone   *ower* over
threid thread   *cauld* cold
bairns children

Jean Gordon, she minds as she sits her lane,
O' a' the years that's bye and gane,
And naething gi'en and a'thing ta'en
But yon nicht o' nichts on the smoory hill
In the sma', sma' rain –
And the bairns are singin' at their play
The lilt that they're liltin' ilka day.

ALAS! POOR QUEEN

She was skilled in music and the dance
And the old arts of love
At the court of the poisoned rose
And the perfumed glove,
And gave her beautiful hand
To the pale Dauphin
A triple crown to win –
And she loved little dogs
          And parrots
          And red-legged partridges
And the golden fishes of the Duc de Guise
And a pigeon with a blue ruff
She had from Monsieur d'Elbœuf.

Master John Knox was no friend to her;
She spoke him soft and kind,
Her honeyed words were Satan's lure
The unwary soul to bind.
'Good sir, doth a lissome shape
And a comely face
Offend your God His Grace
Whose Wisdom maketh these
Golden fishes of the Duc de Guise?'

smoory misty

She rode through Liddesdale with a song;
'Ye streams sae wondrous strang,
Oh, mak' me a wrack as I come back
But spare me as I gang.'
While a hill-bird cried and cried
Like a spirit lost
By the grey storm-wind tost.

Consider the way she had to go,
Think of the hungry snare,
The net she herself had woven,
Aware or unaware,
Of the dancing feet grown still,
The blinded eyes –
Queens should be cold and wise,
And she loved little things,
      Parrots
   And red-legged partridges
And the golden fishes of the Duc de Guise
And the pigeon with the blue ruff
She had from Monsieur d'Elbœuf.

Lewis Spence

1874–1955

THE PROWS O' REEKIE

O wad this braw hie-heapit toun
Sail aff like an enchanted ship,
Drift owre the warld's seas up and doun
And kiss wi' Venice lip to lip,
Or anchor into Naples Bay
A misty island far astray,
Or set her rock to Athens' wa',
Pillar to pillar, stane to stane,
The cruikit spell o' her backbane,
Yon shadow-mile o' spire and vane,
Wad ding them a'! Wad ding them a'!
Cadiz wad tine the admiralty
O' yonder emerod fair sea,
Gibraltar frown for frown exchange
Wi Nigel's Crags at elbuck-range,
The rose-red banks o' Lisbon make
Mair room in Tagus for her sake.

A hoose is but a puppet-box
To keep life's images frae knocks,
But mannikins scrieve oot their sauls

Reekie Edinburgh	*ding* beat, defeat
hie-heapit high-built	*tine* lose
owre over	*elbuck* elbow
cruikit crooked	*scrieve* write

Upon its craw-steps and its walls:
Whaur hae they writ them mair sublime
Than on yon gable-ends o' time?

Alexander Gray

1882–1968

SCOTLAND

Here in the uplands
The soil is ungrateful
The fields, red with sorrel,
Are stony and bare.
A few trees, wind-twisted –
Or are they but bushes?
Stand stubbornly guarding
A home here and there.

Scooped out like a saucer,
The land lies before me;
The waters, once scattered,
Flow orderly now
Through fields where the ghosts
Of the marsh and the moorland
Still ride the old marches,
Despising the plough.

The marsh and the moorland
Are not to be banished;
The bracken and the heather,
The glory of broom,
Usurp all the balks
And the field's broken fringes,
And claim from the sower
Their portion of room.

This is my country,
The land that begat me,
These windy spaces
Are surely my own.
And those who here toil
In the sweat of their faces
Are flesh of my flesh,
And bone of my bone.

Hard is the day's task
Scotland, stern Mother –
Wherewith at all times
Thy sons have been faced:
Labour by day,
And scant rest in the gloaming
With Want an attendant,
Not lightly outpaced.

Yet do thy children
Honour and love thee.
Harsh is thy schooling,
Yet great is the gain:
True hearts and strong limbs,
The beauty of faces,
Kissed by the wind
And caressed by the rain.

Andrew Young

1885–

THE FALLS OF GLOMACH

Rain drifts forever in this place
Tossed from the long white lace
The Falls trail on the black rocks below,
And golden-rod and rose-root shake
In wind that they forever make;
So though they wear their own rainbow
It's not in hope, but just for show,
For rain and wind together
Here through the summer make a chill wet weather.

CULBIN SANDS

Here lay a fair fat land;
  But now its townships, kirks, graveyards,
Beneath bald hills of sand
  Lie buried deep as Babylonian shards.

But gales may blow again;
  And like a sand-glass turned about
The hills in a dry rain
  Will flow away and the old land look out;

And where now hedgehog delves
  And conies hollow their long caves
Houses will build themselves
  And tombstones rewrite names on dead men's graves.

THE PAPS OF JURA

Before I crossed the sound
  I saw how from the sea
These breasts rise soft and round,
  Not two but three;

Now, climbing, I clasp rocks
  Storm-shattered and sharp-edged,
Grey ptarmigan their flocks,
  With starved moss wedged;

And mist like hair hangs over
  One barren breast and me,
Who climb, a desperate lover,
  With hand and knee.

Helen B. Cruickshank

1886–1975

A PRAYER

Oh, Thou who dost forbear
   To grant me motherhood,
Grant that my brow may wear
   Beneath its maiden's snood
Love to distressed Mankind,
   And helpful sympathy
For all whom Fate doth bind
   In Sorrow's company.

Help me always to choose,
   To comfort and to bless,
And in Man's service lose
   My fruitful barrenness;
So that my children may
   Succour and pity give
To sadder hearts. I pray
   O help me so to live.

THE PONNAGE

> .... *Sing*
> *Some simple silly sang*
> *O' willows or o' mimulus*
> *A river's banks-alang.'*
>
> Hugh MacDiarmid

I mind o' the Ponnage Pule,
The reid brae risin',
Morphie Lade,
An' the saumon that louped the dam,
A tree i' Martin's Den
Wi' names carved on it;
But I ken na wha I am.

Ane o' the names was mine,
An' still I own it.
Naething it kens
O' a' that mak's up me.
Less I ken o' mysel'
Than the saumon wherefore
It rins up Esk frae the sea.

I am the deep o' the pule,
The fish, the fisher,
The river in spate,
The broon o' the far peat-moss,
The shingle bricht wi' the flooer
O' the yellow mim'lus,
The martin fleein' across.

I mind o' the Ponnage Pule
On a shinin' mornin',
The saumon fishers

ponnage ferry   *louped* leaped.

Nettin' the bonny brutes –
I' the slithery dark o' the boddom
O' Charon's Coble
Ae day I'll faddom my doobts.

KEEPIT IN

O, fient a bit o' lear hae I,
It beats me hoo X equals Y,
An' nine times nine hooe'er I try
   I canna mind ava, sir.
But I ken whaur the yorline biggs,
An' peewits lay atween the rigs,
An' whaur the brock his burrow digs,
    An' moudiewarps an a', sir.

A squirrel nests in Jerrat's Wood,
An' on the dam an early brood
O' waterhennies has begood
   Amang the reeds tae steer, sir.
But I maun bide inside an' say
My Latin verbs an' trash like thae –
O' dinna keep me in the day,
    Indeed I'm feelin' queer, sir.

The keeper doon at Lowrie Mill
Is huntin' tods on Rossie Hill,
Were I ootside I'd no' feel ill

boddom bottom
coble dinghy
fient a bit devil the bit, none
lear learning
mind remember
ava at all

yorline yellowhammer
brock badger
moudiewarps moles
thae those
queer unwell
tods foxes

I ha'ena muckle doubt, sir.
My heid is bizzin' like a bee,
My een are het, I canna see,
Ye waste your time an' tawse on me!
  O, *please*, can I get oot, sir!

THERE WAS A SANG

There was a sang
That aye I wad be singin';
There was a star,
An' clear it used tae shine;
An' liltin' in the starlicht
Thro' the shadows
I gaed lang syne.

There was a sang;
But noo, I canna mind it.
There was a star;
But noo, it disna shine.
There was a luve that led me
Thro' the shadows –
And it *was* mine.

tawse belt   *lang syne* long since
gaed went

Edwin Muir

1887–1959

SCOTLAND 1941

We were a tribe, a family, a people.
Wallace and Bruce guard now a painted field,
And all may read the folio of our fable,
Peruse the sword, the sceptre and the shield.
A simple sky roofed in that rustic day,
The busy corn-fields and the haunted holms,
The green road winding up the ferny brae.
But Knox and Melville clapped their preaching palms
And bundled all the harvesters away,
Hoodicrow Peden in the blighted corn
Hacked with his rusty beak the starving haulms.
Out of that desolation we were born.

Courage beyond the point and obdurate pride
Made us a nation, robbed us of a nation.
Defiance absolute and myriad-eyed
That could not pluck the palm plucked our damnation.
We with such courage and the bitter wit
To fell the ancient oak of loyalty,
And strip the peopled hill and altar bare,
And crush the poet with an iron text,
How could we read our souls and learn to be?
Here a dull drove of faces harsh and vexed,
We watch our cities burning in their pit,
To salve our souls grinding dull lucre out,
We, fanatics of the frustrate and the half,
Who once set Purgatory Hill in doubt.

Now smoke and dearth and money everywhere,
Mean heirlooms of each fainter generation,
And mummied housegods in their musty niches,
Burns and Scott, sham bards of a sham nation,
And spiritual defeat wrapped warm in riches,
No pride but pride of pelf. Long since the young
Fought in great bloody battles to carve out
This towering pulpit of the Golden Calf,
Montrose, Mackail, Argyle, perverse and brave,
Twisted the stream, unhooped the ancestral hill.
Never had Dee or Don or Yarrow or Till
Huddled such thriftless honour in a grave.
Such wasted bravery idle as a song,
Such hard-won ill might prove Time's verdict wrong,
And melt to pity the annalist's iron tongue.

SCOTLAND'S WINTER

Now the ice lays its smooth claws on the sill,
The sun looks from the hill
Helmed in his winter casket,
And sweeps his arctic sword across the sky.
The water at the mill
Sounds more hoarse and dull.
The miller's daughter walking by
With frozen fingers soldered to her basket
Seems to be knocking
Upon a hundred leagues of floor
With her light heels, and mocking
Percy and Douglas dead,
And Bruce on his burial bed,
Where he lies white as may
With wars and leprosy,
And all the kings before
This land was kingless,
And all the singers before

This land was songless,
This land that with its dead and living waits the Judgement
    Day.
But they, the powerless dead,
Listening can hear no more
Than a hard tapping on the floor
A little overhead
Of common heels that do not know
Whence they come or where they go
And are content
With their poor frozen life and shallow banishment.

THE CASTLE

All through that summer at ease we lay,
And daily from the turret wall
We watched the mowers in the hay
And the enemy half a mile away.
They seemed no threat to us at all.

For what, we thought, had we to fear
With our arms and provender, load on load,
Our towering battlements, tier on tier,
And friendly allies drawing near
On every leafy summer road.

Our gates were strong, our walls were thick,
So smooth and high, no man could win
A foothold there, no clever trick
Could take us, have us dead or quick.
Only a bird could have got in.

What could they offer us for bait?
Our captain was brave and we were true . . .
There was a little private gate,

A little wicked wicket gate.
The wizened warder let them through.

Oh then our maze of tunnelled stone
Grew thin and treacherous as air.
The cause was lost without a groan,
The famous citadel overthrown,
And all its secret galleries bare.

How can this shameful tale be told?
I will maintain until my death
We could do nothing, being sold;
Our only enemy was gold,
And we had no arms to fight it with.

THE HORSES

Barely a twelvemonth after
The seven days war that put the world to sleep,
Late in the evening the strange horses came.
By then we had made our covenant with silence,
But in the first few days it was so still
We listened to our breathing and were afraid.
On the second day
The radios failed; we turned the knobs; no answer.
On the third day a warship passed us, heading north,
Dead bodies piled on the deck. On the sixth day
A plane plunged over us into the sea. Thereafter
Nothing. The radios dumb;
And still they stand in corners of our kitchens,
And stand, perhaps, turned on, in a million rooms
All over the world. But now if they should speak,
If on a sudden they should speak again,
If on the stroke of noon a voice should speak,
We would not listen, we would not let it bring
That old bad world that swallowed its children quick

At one great gulp. We would not have it again.
Sometimes we think of the nations lying asleep,
Curled blindly in impenetrable sorrow,
And then the thought confounds us with its strangeness.
The tractors lie about our fields; at evening
They look like dank sea-monsters couched and waiting.
We leave them where they are and let them rust:
'They'll moulder away and be like other loam',
We make our oxen drag our rusty ploughs,
Long laid aside. We have gone back
Far past our fathers' land.
                                    And then, that evening
Late in the summer the strange horses came.
We heard a distant tapping on the road,
A deepening drumming; it stopped, went on again
And at the corner changed to hollow thunder.
We saw the heads
Like a wild wave charging and were afraid.
We had sold our horses in our fathers' time
To buy new tractors. Now they were strange to us
As fabulous steeds set on an ancient shield
Or illustrations in a book of knights.
We did not dare go near them. Yet they waited,
Stubborn and shy, as if they had been sent
By an old command to find our whereabouts
And that long-lost archaic companionship.
In the first moment we had never a thought
That they were creatures to be owned and used.
Among them were some half-a-dozen colts
Dropped in some wilderness of the broken world,
Yet new as if they had come from their own Eden.
Since then they have pulled our ploughs and borne our loads,
But that free servitude still can pierce our hearts.
Our life is changed; their coming our beginning.

THE CONFIRMATION

Yes, yours, my love, is the right human face.
I in my mind had waited for this long,
Seeing the false and searching for the true,
Then found you as a traveller finds a place
Of welcome suddenly amid the wrong
Valleys and rocks and twisting roads. But you,
What shall I call you? A fountain in a waste,
A well of water in a country dry,
Or anything that's honest and good, an eye
That makes the whole world bright. Your open heart,
Simple with giving, gives the primal deed,
The first good world, the blossom, the blowing seed,
The hearth, the steadfast land, the wandering sea,
Not beautiful or rare in every part,
But like yourself, as they were meant to be.

THE FATHERS

Our fathers all were poor,
Poorer our fathers' fathers;
Beyond, we dare not look.
We, the sons, keep store
Of tarnished gold that gathers
Around us from the night,
Record it in this book
That, when the line is drawn,
Credit and creditor gone,
Column and figure flown,
Will open into light.

Archaic fevers shake
Our healthy flesh and blood
Plumped in the passing day

And fed with pleasant food.
The fathers' anger and ache
Will not, will not away
And leave the living alone,
But on our careless brows
Faintly their furrows engrave
Like veinings in a stone,
Breathe in the sunny house
Nightmare of blackened bone,
Cellar and choking cave.

Panics and furies fly
Through our unhurried veins,
Heavenly lights and rains
Purify heart and eye,
Past agonies purify
And lay the sullen dust.
The angers will not away.
We hold our fathers' trust,
Wrong, riches, sorrow and all
Until they topple and fall,
And fallen let in the day.

Hugh MacDiarmid

1892–1978

EMPTY VESSEL

I met ayont the cairney
A lass wi' tousie hair
Singin' till a bairnie
That was nae langer there.

Wunds wi' warlds to swing
Dinna sing sae sweet,
The licht that bends owre a' thing
Is less ta'en up wi't.

O WHA'S THE BRIDE?

O wha's the bride that cairries the bunch
O' thistles blinterin' white?
Her cuckold bridegroom little dreids
What he sall ken this nicht.

For closer than gudeman can come
And closer to'r than hersel',
Wha didna need her maidenheid
Has wrocht his purpose fell.

tousie tangled   *blinterin'* gleaming
bairnie baby   *dreids* dreads
a' thing the universe   *gudeman* husband
ta'en up concerned

O wha's been here afore me, lass,
And hoo did he get in?
    – A man that deed or I was born
This evil thing has din.
And left, as it were on a corpse,
Your maidenheid to me?
    – Nae lass, gudeman, sin' Time began
's had ony mair to gi'e.

But I can gi'e ye kindness lad,
And a pair o' willin hands,
And you sall ha'e my breists like stars,
My limbs like willow wands.

And on my lips ye'll heed nae mair,
And in my hair forget,
The seed o' a' the men that in
My virgin womb ha'e met. . . .

THE WATERGAW

Ae weet forenicht i' the yow-trummle
I saw yon antrin thing,
A watergaw wi' its chitterin' licht
Ayont the on-ding;
An' I thocht o' the last wild look ye gied
Afore ye deed!

There was nae reek i' the laverock's hoose
That nicht – an' nane i' mine;
But I hae thocht o' that foolish licht

mair more   *chitterin'* shivering
watergaw rainbow   *on-ding* storm
yow-trummle cold wind   *reek* smoke
antrin occasional, fleeting   *laverock* lark

Ever sin' syne;
An' I think that mebbe at last I ken
What your look meant then.

SUPPER TO GOD

S'ud ye ha'e to gi'e
His supper to God
What like fare
'Ud ye set on the brod?

Lint-white linen
And siller-ware
And a tassie o' floo'ers
In the centre there?

Pot-luck 'ud be best,
I need ha'e nae fear
Gin God s'ud come
To's supper here.

Deal scrubbed like snaw
And blue-and-white delf
And let ilk ane
Rax oot for hisself.

A' that I'd ask
Is no' to ken whan,
Or gin it's Him
Or a trev'lin man.

brod	board	*rax*	reach
tassie	glass, vase	*whan*	when

Wi' powsoudie or drummock,
Lapper-milk kebbuck and farle,
We can aye wecht the wame
O' anither puir carle.

GAIRMSCOILE

Aulder than mammoth or than mastodon
Deep i' the herts o' a' men lurk scaut-heid
Skrymmorie monsters few daur look upon.
Brides sometimes catch their wild een, scansin' reid,
Beekin' abune the herts they thocht to lo'e
And horror-stricken ken that i' themselves
A like beast stan's, and lookin' love thro' and thro'
Meets the reid een wi' een like seevun hells.
. . . Near the twa beasts draw, and, couplin' brak
The bubbles o' twa sauls and the haill warld gangs black.

Yet wha has heard the beasts' wild matin'-call
To ither music syne can gi'e nae ear.
The nameless lo'enotes haud him in a thrall.
Forgot are guid and ill, and joy and fear.
. . . My bluid sall thraw a dark hood owre my een
And I sall venture deep into the hills
Whaur, scaddows on the skyline, can be seen

powsoudie sheepshead broth   *skrymmorie* tail-lashing
drummock oatmeal and water   *scansin'* glancing
lapper-milk buttermilk   *beekin'* basking, showing
kebbuck cheese   *abune* above
farle oatcake   *een* eyes
wecht load   *brak* break
wame belly   *gangs* goes
puir poor   *syne* then
carle old man   *haud* hold
aulder older   *thraw* throw
scaut-heid scabbed-head

Twinin' the sun's brent broo wi' plaited horns
As gin they crooned it wi' a croon o' thorns –
The beasts in wha's wild cries a' Scotland's destiny thrills.

The lo'es o' single herts are strays; but there
The herds that draw the generations are,
And whasae hears them roarin', evermair
Is yin wi' a' that gangs to mak' or mar
The spirit o' the race, and leads it still
Whither it can be led, 'yont a' desire and will.
Wergeland, I mind o' thee – for thy bluid tae
Kent the rouch dirl o' an auld Scots strain,
– A dour dark burn that has its ain wild say
Thro' a' the thrang bricht babble o' Earth's flood.
Behold, thwart my ramballiach life again,
What thrawn and roothewn dreams, royat and rude,
Reek forth – a foray dowless herts condemn –
While chance wi' rungs o' sang or silence renshels them.

(A foray frae the past – and future tae
Sin Time's a blindness will thraw aff some day!)
. . . On the rumgunshoch sides o' hills forgotten
Life bears beasts rowtin' that it deemed extinct,
And, sudden, on the hapless cities linked
In canny civilisation's canty dance
Poor herds o' heich-skeich monsters, misbegotten,
. . . Streets clear afore the scarmoch advance:
Frae every winnock skimmerin' een keek oot

brent unfurrowed	*royat* riotous
whasae whoso	*reek* smoke
yin one	*dowless* imponderable
rouch rough	*renshels* drives
dirl thrill	*rumgunshoch* rocky
dour grim	*rowtin'* rooting
burn stream	*heich-skeich* skittish
thrang busy	*scarmoch* noisy
ramballiach stormy	*winnock* window
thrawn twisted	*skimmerin'* glancing

To see what sic camsteerie cast-offs are aboot.
Cast-offs – But wha mak's life a means to ony end?
This sterves and that stuff's fu', scraps this and succours that?
The best survive there's nane but fules contend.
Na! Ilka daith is but a santit need.
... Lo! what bricht flames o' beauty are lit at
The unco' een o' lives that Life thocht deid
Till winnock efter winnock kindles wi' a sense
O' gain and glee – as gin a mair intense
Starn nor the sun had risen in wha's licht
Mankind and beasts anew, wi' gusto, see their plicht.

Mony's the auld hauf-human cry I ken
Fa's like a revelation on the herts o' men
As tho' the graves were split and the first man
Grippit the latest wi' a freendly han'.
... And there's forgotten shibboleths o' the Scots
Ha'e keys to senses lockit to us yet
– Coorse words that shamble thro' oor minds like stots,
Syne turn on's muckle een wi' doonsin' emerauds lit.
I hear nae 'hee-haw' but I mind the day
A'e donkey strunted doon a palm-strewn way
As Chesterton has sung; nae wee click-clack
O' hoofs but to my hert at aince comes back
Jammes' Prayer to Gang to Heaven wi' the Asses;
And shambles-ward nae cattle-beast e'er passes
But I mind hoo the saft een o' the kine
Lichted Christ's craidle wi' their canny shine.

camsteerie irresponsible	*stots* oxen
cast-offs outcasts	*doonsin'* glinting
santit sainted	*strunted* strutted
starn star	*canny* careful

Hee-Haw! Click-Clack! And Cock-a-doodle-doo!
– Wull Gabriel in Esperanto cry
Or a' the warld's undeemis jargons try?
It's soon', no' sense, that faddoms the herts o' men,
And by my sangs the rouch auld Scots I ken
E'en herts that ha'e nae Scots'll dirl richt thro'
As nocht else could – for here's a language rings
Wi' datchie sesames, and names for nameless things.

Wergeland, my warld as thine 'ca' canny' cries,
And daurna lippen to auld Scotland's virr.
Ah, weel ye kent – as Carlyle quo' likewise –
Maist folk are thowless fules wha downa stir,
Crouse sumphs that hate nane 'bies wha'd wauken them.
To them my Pegasus tae's a crocodile.
Whummelt I tak' a bobquaw for the lift.
Insteed o' sangs my mou' drites eerned phlegm.
... Natheless like thee I stalk on mile by mile,
Howk'n up deid stumps o' thocht, and saw'in my eident gift.
Ablachs, and scrats, and dorbels o' a' kinds
Aye'd drob me wi' their puir eel-droonin' minds,
Wee drochlin' craturs drutling their bit thochts
The dorty bodies! Feech! Nae Sassunach drings
'll daunton me. – Tak' ye sic things for poets?

undeemis incredible	*drites* drips
soon' sound	*howk'n* digging
datchie subtle	*saw'in* sowing
sesames magic words	*eident* diligent
ca' canny go easy	*ablachs* dwarfs
lippen trust	*scrats* nonentities
virr virility	*dorbels* ugly creatures
thowless spiritless	*drob* prickle
downa daren't	*drochlin'* dwarfish
crouse smug	*drutling* shitting
sumphs idiots	*dorty* self-important
'bies except	*sassunach* saxon
whummelt overthrown	*drings* misers
bobquaw shaky bog	

Cock-lairds and drotes depert Parnassus noo.
A'e flash o' wit the lot to drodlich dings.
Rae, Martin, Sutherland – the dowless crew,
I'll twine the dow'd sheaves o' their toom-ear'd corn,
Bind them wi' pity and dally them wi' scorn.
Lang ha'e posed as men o' letters here,
Dounhaddin' the Doric and keepin't i' the draiks,
Drivellin' and druntin', wi' mony a datchie sneer
. . . But soon we'll end the haill eggtaggle, fegs!
. . . The auld volcanoes rummle 'neath their feet,
And a' their shoddy lives'll soon be drush,
Danders o' Hell! They feel th' unwelcome heat,
The deltit craturs, and their sauls are slush,
For we ha'e faith in Scotland's hidden poo'ers,
The present's theirs, but a' the past and future's oors.

CROWDIEKNOWE

Oh to be at Crowdieknowe
When the last trump blaws,
An' see the deid come loupin' owre
The auld grey wa's.

Muckle men wi' tousled beard$_f$
I grat at as a bairn
'll scramble frae the croodit clay
Wi' feck o' swearin'.

drotes conceited squires	*druntin'* drawling
depert leave	*eggtaggle* low company
drodlich useless rubbish	*drush* dross
dings knocks down	*danders* slag
Rae, Martin, etc. poetasters who attacked MacDiarmid	*deltit* petted
	loupin' leaping
toom-eared earless	*owre* over
Doric Scots dialect as 'language of slaves'	*grat* wept
	croodit crowded
draiks depressed state	*feck* a lot

An' glower at God an' a' his gang
O' angels i' the lift
– Thae trashy bleezin' French-like folk
Wha gar'd them shift!

Fain the weemun-folk'll seek
To mak' them haud their row
– *Fegs, God's no blate gin he stirs up*
The men o' Crowdieknowe!

COPHETUA

Oh! The King's gane gyte,
Puir auld man, puir auld man,
An' an ashypet lassie
Is Queen o' the lan'.
Wi' a scoogie o' silk
An' a bucket o' siller
She's showin' the haill coort
The smeddum intil her!

THE PARROT CRY

Tell me the auld, auld story
O' hoo the Union brocht
Puir Scotland into being
As a country worth a thocht.

glower glare
lift heavens
thae those
gar'd made
haud hold
blate afraid
gane gyte gone mad

ashypet lassie kitchen-maid
scoogie apron
smeddum drive
Union Treaty of Union with
    England 1707
puir poor

England, frae whom a' blessings flow
What could we dae withoot ye?
Then dinna threep it doon oor throats
As gin we e'er could doot ye!
　　My feelings lang wi' gratitude
　　Ha'e been sae sairly harrowed
　　That dod! I think it's time
　　The claith was owre the parrot!

Tell me o' Scottish enterprise
And canniness and thrift,
And hoo we're baith less Scots and mair
Than ever under George the fifth,
And hoo to 'wider interests'
Oor ain we sacrifice
And yet tine naething by it
As aye the parrot cries.
　　Syne gie's a chance to think it oot
　　Aince we're a' weel awaur o't,
　　For, losh, I think it's time
　　The claith was owre the parrot!

Tell me o' love o' country
Content to see't decay,
And ony ither paradox
Ye think o' by the way.
I doot it needs a Hegel
Sic opposites to fuse;
Oor education's failin'
And canna gie's the views
　　That were peculiar to us
　　Afore our vision narrowed
　　And gar'd us think it time
　　The claith was owre the parrot!

dae do	*tine* lose
threep force, preach	*syne* then
claith cloth	*gar'd* made

A parrot's weel eneuch at times
But whiles we'd leifer hear
A blackbird or a mavis
Singin' fu' blythe and clear.
Fetch ony native Scottish bird
Frae the eagle to the wren,
And faith! you'd hear a different sang
Frae this painted foreigner's then.
   The marine that brocht it owre
   Believed its every word
   – But we're a' deeved to daith
   Wi' his infernal bird.

It's possible that Scotland yet
May hear its ain voice speak
If only we can silence
This endless chatterin' beak.
The blessing wi' the black
Selvedge is the clout!
It's silenced Scotland lang eneuch,
Gi'e England turn aboot.
   For the puir bird needs its rest –
   Wha else'll be the waur o't?
   And it's lang past the time
   The claith was owre the parrot.

And gin that disna dae, lads,
We e'en maun draw its neck
And heist its body on a stick
A' ither pests to check.
I'd raither keep't alive, and whiles
Let bairns keek in and hear

eneuch enough
leifer rather
mavis song-thrush
deeved deafened

blessing wi' the black selvedge the
   Treaty of Union
waur worse
maun must
heist hoist

What the Balliol accent used to be
Frae the Predominant Pairtner here!
 – But save to please the bairns
I'd absolutely bar it
For fegs, it's aye high time
The claith was owre the parrot!

PRAYER FOR A SECOND FLOOD

There'd ha'e to be nae warnin'. Times ha'e changed
And Noahs are owre numerous nooadays,
(And them the vera folk to benefit maist!)
Knock the feet frae under them, O Lord, wha praise
Your unsearchable ways sae muckle and yet hope
  To keep within knowledgeable scope!

Ding a' their trumpery show to blauds again.
Their measure is the thimblefu' o' Esk in spate.
Like whisky the tittlin' craturs mete oot your poo'ers
Aince a week for bawbees in the kirk-door plate,
 – And pit their umbrellas up when they come oot
  If mair than a pulpitfu' o' You's aboot!

O arselins wi' them! Whummle them again!
Coup them heels-owre-gowdy in a storm sae gundy
That mony a lang fog-theekit face I ken
'll be sooked richt doon under through a cundy
In the High Street, afore you get weel-sterted
  And are still hauf-herted!

Balliol pun on the Oxford Col-
  lege and John Balliol the 13th
  century Scots quisling king
ding strike
blauds pieces
tittlin' prattling
bawbees coppers

whummle turn them head over
  heels
coup overturn
gundy wild
fog-theekit moss-grown
cundy grating

Then flush the world in earnest. Let yoursel' gang,
Scour't to the bones, and mak' its marrow holes
Toom as a whistle as they used to be
In days I mind ere men fidged wi' souls,
But naething had forgotten you as yet,
  Nor you forgotten it.

Up then and at them, ye Gairds o' Heaven.
The Divine Retreat is owre. Like a tidal bore
Boil in among them; let the lang lugs nourished
On the milk o' the word at last hear the roar
O' human shingle; and replenish the salt o' the earth
  In the place o' their birth.

DEPTH AND THE CHTHONIAN IMAGE

On looking at a ruined
mill and thinking of
the greatest

Absolvitur ab instantia is decreed
In every case against you men array.
Yours is the only nature stiflin' nocht,
Meetin' a' the experiences there are to ha'e
And never meetin' ane o' them raw-edged.
Ripe, reconcilin' mind, sublimely gauged,
Serene receptiveness, nae tongue can speak
Your fair fey form felicitously enow,
Nae subtle mind seek your benmaist howe
And gar your deepest implications beek.

gang go	*fey* supernatural
scour scrub	*benmaist* innermost
toom empty	*howe* hollow
fidged bothered	*gar* make
lugs ears	*beek* show

The mills o' God grind sma', but they
In you maun crumble imperceptibly tae.
Nor shadowed nor lit up by ony thocht,
Nae perfect shinin' o' a simmer's day
Vies wi' your ark's assopat speed
In its pure task engaged.
Time and Eternity are no' at odds
In you as in a' that's Man's – and God's,
For nane can look through you as through the sun and see
Some auld adhantare wi' neuked bonnet there,
Urphanömen – o' what? Ah, no, alluterlie
You deal afflufe wi' a' that's fordel and nae gair
In your allryn activity lets kyth
    The faur-side o' your sneith.

As life to death, as man to God, sae stands
This ruined mill to your great aumrie then,
This ruined mill – and every rinnin' mill?
The awte or bait o' everything you ken
And tak' it quicker than a barber's knife
Wi' nocht aclite. There is nae chance o' strife.
Micht a' the canny your abandon see!
Nor ony din they mak' let them forget
Their generations tae and creeds'll yet
Crine to a sic-like laroch while the lets-a-be
O' a' your pairts as eidently agree.
Nocht needs your wa's mair audience to gi'e.
Forever ample baith in scouth and skill,
Watchin' your aws by nicht it seems to me

maun must	*aumrie* pantry
tae too	*awte* grain of material
assopat drudging	*bait* ditto
adhantare phantom	*aclite* one-sided
afflufe offhand	*crine* wither
fordel progressive	*laroch* heap of ruins
gair greedy	*eidently* diligently
allryn weird	*scouth* range
kyth reveal	*aws* windmill sails
sneith smoothness	

The stars adreigh mimic their drops and 'mang hands
There is nae nearer image gi'en to life
O' that conclusive power by which you rin
Even on, drawin' a' the universe in,
Than this loose simile o' the heavenly hosts
Vainly prefigurin' the unseen jaups
Roond your vast wheel – or mair waesome ghosts
O' that reality man's pairt o' and yet caps
Wi' Gods in his ain likeness drawn
    – Puir travesties o' your plan.

To picture the invisible via the stars
Is the least boutgate that man's speech can gang,
As for your speed and your boon millin, – no, even the lang
Processes o' metamorphosis in rock
Can fetch that ben to him like the shadowy flock
O' atoms in himsel' precariously seen,
Queer dirlin' o' his cells at sic an 'oor,
He whiles can note wha hasna else the poo'er,
Laichest Brownian movements swarmin' to his een
As neath a microscope – a deemless thrang,
To catch their changin' time, and get the hang
O' a' their swift diminishments doon the steep
Chutes o' dissolution, as he lay amang
The mools already, and watched the maggots' wars
Upon his flesh, and sune its finitude mock
Their midgeswarm jaws until their numbers fa'
To a'e toom mou', the fremit last o' a'
The reelin' corruption, its vain mudgeons there
Wi' motions that nae measure can seize on
As micht the sun to earth's last look appear

adreigh distant	*thrang* crowd
jaups jolts, waves	*mools* graves
boutgate deceitful course	*sune* soon
boon excellent	*toom* empty
dirlin' jolting	*fremit* strange
deemless uncritical	*mudgeons* sneers

Like yon cart-wheel that raxes to a cone
Afore the spider lets its anchorage slip,
     An insect in its grip.

Nae knowledge its ain offices here
Can seek to magnify and ithers suppress.
An arbiter frae corruption free hauds sway
Unlike man's mind that canna ken unless
It decks its data wi' interpretation
To try to mak' a rational creation.
Hence a' men see contains faur mair than's seen,
Remembrance o' the past, fancy o' the future.
To memory and imagination you stand neuter
As 'twere a scientist confrontin' the gi'en
That nae logical, *a priori*, or ither reasons confess
And yet are carriers o' value that redress
His rational world frae bein' senseless tae,
Tho' here, as in sma'er things, nae inspired guess,
Teleological reasonin' or rapport sheer,
Gi'es minds like his sic valuable dilation.
You're no' its meanin' but the world itsel'.
Yet let nae man think he can see you better
By concentratin' on your aneness either.
He pits his mind into a double fetter
Wha hauds this airt or that, no baith thegither.
You are at aince the road a' croods ha' gane
     And alane wi' the alane.

Alane wi' the alane, yet let us no' forget
Theistic faiths but, extrapolate, plottin' on
The curve o' sae-ca'd knowledge science had made
– Science and theism ha'e their roots in common
(Tho' few can credit sic a teachin' noo!) –
And needs the same redress as sciences do
To say the least. Alane wi' the alane remains
A relative conception as self-betrayed

raxes reaches   *airt* direction

As heidstrang science dispensin' wi' sic aid
As frae the world's allogic, kept in mind, it gains.
Nae mutual justice, undue claims foregone,
Sympathy wi' divers ootlooks and endeavours shown,
Union o' knowledge's kingdoms piously prayed,
Is less a movement leadin' awa' frae you
Than ony in the opposite airt to it,
Nor can a poet as I am cease to con,
Heedless o' baith, your prime significance
To lead his muse a needle-angel's dance
By hailin' truth a mathematical point
Wi' nae relation to the ooter world,
Whether the times are in or oot o' joint
O' scant concern since a'thing earthly's hurled
– You tae – indifferent, *adiaphora*, faur alow
      Ocht this taks' heed o'.

Aye balk and burral lie the fields o' life.
It fails to acresce a kennin' frae the past,
In a' its fancied contacts wi' what's meant
When it seems shairest in worst backspangs cast;
Its heritage but a bairn's pairt o' gear,
A puir balapat at hairst its fingers speir
And often mairket a toom barley-box;
Aye in bad breid despite their constant toil,
As bairns in their bairnliness, a cursed coil
Hauds men content wi' casual sweetie-pokes
O' a' creation's gear; and little is amassed
Maist folk can life-rent – nocht hain at last.
Yet o' the way-drawn profit what tak's tent?
The feast is spread yet helplessly they fast,

ocht anything	*balapat* family pot
balk and burral high-furrowed and deep-hollowed	*hairst* harvest
	speir search
kennin' knowledge	*pokes* bags
shairest surest	*hain* safe
backspangs recoils	*tent* heed
gear possessions	

Aye win an Irishman's rise wi' unco strife,
Cast oot frae a' their dues by the silly fear
That hauds them in habits o' poortith still,
While by them brim the torrents to your mill,
The vast way-drawing that denies mankind
Or pairt or parcel in science or in art
Till bare as worms the feck o' them we find.
Each generation at zero still maun start
And's doomed to end there, wi' a' that they forgaed
    Caught in the suction o' your lade.

Or pairt or parcel in science or in art.
– Or even in life! Hoo few men ever live
And what wee local lives at best they ha'e.
Sirse, science and art might weel rin through the sieve,
Or jow like backfa's when the mill is set.
If maist folk through nae elf-bores dribbled yet
But in some measure lived to a' life is.
Wad that their latent poo'ers 'ud loup alist,
Kyth suddenly a' their wasted past has missed,
And nae mair leave their lives like languages,
– Mere leaks frae streamin' consciousness as if
Thocht roon' itsel' raised wa's prohibitive
O' a' but a fraction o' its possible sway –
But rax in freedom, nocht inhibitive,
In fearless flourishin' amidwart,
Fed by the haill wide world and feedin' it,
Universal life, like an autonymous tongue
In which some vision o' you micht be sung,
Let us remove a' lets and hindrances then
Even as the principle o' limitation, God,
Packed wi' posterity, silent like the deid,

Irishman's rise dismissal	*backfa's* side-sluices of mill
feck most	*elf-bores* holes left by knots in
lade mill-stream	wood
sirse exclamation of surprise	*loup* leap
jow jolt	*alist* come to life

And aye respondin' to a lesser need,
Has vanished like a clood that weighed on men
Owre-lang – till your pure radiance glowed.

Ein Mann aus dem Volke—weel I ken
Nae man or movement's worth a damn unless
The movement 'ud gang on withoot him if
He de'ed the morn. Wherefore in you I bless
My sense o' the greatest man can typify
And universalise himsel' maist fully by.
Nocht ta'en at second-hand and nocht let drift,
Nae bull owre big to tackle by the horns,
Nae chance owre sma' for freedom's sake he scorns,
But a' creation through himsel' maun sift
Even as you, nor possible defeat confess,
Forever poised and apt in his address;
Save at this pitch nae man can truly live.
Hence to these ruins I maun needs regress
– As to the facts o' death and a' the past again,
Beast life, plant life, minerals, water, sky,
A' that has been, is, is to be – frae you
Clear seen, still clearer sicht to pursue.
Similia similibus rotantur, a' facts amang
I seek the *Ereigniswerden*'s essence then
That shows a' that seems kent in it wrang
And gars a' else point back to it again,
Their worth to guide wha can use them hence
      To your fulfillin' experience.

Elschaddai. Emelachan. We only want
The world to live and feel its life in us?
But the world lives whether we dae' or no',
A's vice that abates life or can blin' us
To your final epopteia – contents us with
The hearin' o' the ear, no' the vision swith,
The life o' shadows, mere tautology,
Ony curious fig-leaf o' the mind whereby
Humanity has socht to hide its sin,

Portentuous prison-hooses o' fause thocht we see
'Science' big heicher daily – a' that can pin us
To the spectral frae the live world, come atween us
And the terrible crystal, the ineffable glow.
Diseases o' the will that needs maun fin' us
Less potent to act, and a' the cliches and cant,
Limitations o' personality, pap for pith,
Robotisation, feminism, youth movements,
A' the super-economic programme's intents
Set grey, a hellish parody (oot there
Forenenst your blazin' energy), and its
Perpetual fause alarms, shams o' seemin' fair,
Fixed fallacies auld as man, sheer waste o' wits
– Oh, you are no' the glory mankind desires
        Yet naething else inspires!

The recurrent vividness o' licht and water
Through every earthly change o' mood or scene
Puirly prefigures you – a' Nature's dreamt,
And no' dune, thrang wi' 'ither plans, has been
A fog twixt you and us. It's nocht to ken
Something has happened – save only when
'Mang mony alternatives sic choice was ta'en.
You aye exclude a' ither possibilities.
A'e voice may cry alood: 'Wha ever sees
You to hairy goon and mossy cell has gane.'
Anither proclaim the vital vision gi'en
'Ud move to deeds frae care o' consequences clean.
But baith are wrang – the reckless and the fremt.
And in your radiant licht man's first truth's seen
– Tho' still the last and least to matter
In a' their fond affairs to the mass o' men –
The love o' economics is the mainspring
O' a' the virtues. Eternity like a ring,

thrang busy   *fremt* foreign
goon gown

Virile, masculine, abandoned at nae turn
To enervatin' luxury
Aboot me here shall ever clearer burn,
And in its licht perchance at last men'll see
Wi' the best works o' art, as wi' you tae,
    Chance can ha's nocht to dae!

Joe Corrie

1894–1968

MINERS' WIVES

We have borne good sons to broken men,
    Nurtured them on our hungry breast,
And given them to our masters when
    Their day of life was at its best.

We have dried their clammy clothes by the fire,
    Solaced them, cheered them, tended them well,
Watched the wheels raising them from the mire,
    Watched the wheels lowering them to Hell.

We have prayed for them in a Godless way
    (We never could fathom the ways of God),
We have sung with them on their wedding day,
    Knowing the journey and the road.

We have stood through the naked night to watch
    The silent wheels that raised the dead;
We have gone before to raise the latch,
    And lay the pillow beneath their head.

We have done all this for our masters' sake,
    Did it in rags and did not mind;
What more do they want? what more can they take?
    Unless our eyes and leave us blind.

THE IMAGE O' GOD

Crawlin' aboot like a snail in the mud,
    Covered wi' clammy blae,
ME, made after the image o' God –
    Jings! but it's laughable, tae.

Howkin' awa' 'neath a mountain o' stane,
    Gaspin' for want o' air,
The sweat makin' streams doon my bare back-bane
    And my knees a' hauckit and sair.

Strainin' and cursin' the hale shift through,
    Half-starved, half-blin', half-mad;
And the gaffer he says, 'Less dirt in that coal
    Or ye go up the pit, my lad!'

So I gi'e my life to the Nimmo squad
    For eicht and fower a day;
Me! made after the image o' God –
    Jings! but it's laughable, tae.

clammy blae blue mud	*hale* whole
howkin' digging	*gaffer* foreman
hauckit hacked	

William Jeffrey

1896–1946

STONES

The stones in Jordan's stream
Perceived the dove descend
In its lily of light:
That glory entered
Their interminable dream.

The stones in Edom's wilderness
Observed the fiend
Take five of their number
And build a cairn thereof,
And beckoning to Jesus
He pointed to the stones and said:
Make bread.
But because of his great love
For the uniqueness of created things,
The confraternity in disparity
Of plant and rock, of flesh and wings,
Jesus would not translate the stones
Out of their immobile immortality
Into that dynasty of death,
Decaying bread:

The stones upon Golgotha's hill
Took the shadow of the cross
Upon them like the scorch of ice:

And they felt the flick of dice
And Jesus' blood mingling with his mother's tears;
And these made indelible stains:
And some of them were taken up
And with curses thrown
At that rejected throne,
And others felt the clamorous butts of Roman spears:
And the pity, horror, and love within them pent
Welled out and shook the earth.
And the veil was rent.

The great stones of the tomb
Enfolded Jesus' body
In silence and deep gloom.
They had him to themselves alone,
That shard of him, sinew and bone,
Transient dust on their immortality.
And now their inanimate heart
Yearned over that shrouded form:
And while three midnights passed
They made of that tomb
A womb:

The fragile bones renewed their strength,
The flesh trembled and moved,
The glory of the dove
Re-descended from above
And with the break of day
The door was rolled away:
The function of the stones was done:
His second birth
Achieved on earth,
Jesus walked into the sun.

William Soutar

1898–1943

THE TRYST

O luely, luely, cam she in,
and luely she lay doun:
I kent her by her caller lips
and her breists sae smaa and round.

Aa throu the nicht we spak nae word
nor sindered bane frae bane:
aa throu the nicht I heard her hert
gang soundin wi my ain.

It was about the waukrif hour
whan cocks begin to craw
that she smooled saftly throu the mirk
afore the day wad daw.

Sae luely, luely cam she in,
sae luely was she gane;
and wi her aa my simmer days
like they had never been.

luely lovely	*smooled* glided
caller fresh-cool	*mirk* dark
smaa small	*simmer* summer
waukrif wakeful	

THE AULD HOUSE

There's a puckle lairds in the auld house
   wha haud the waas thegither:
there's no muckle graith in the auld house
   nor smeddum aither.

It was aince a braw and bauld house
   and guid for onie weather:
kings and lords thranged in the auld house
   or it gaed a'smither.

There were kings and lords in the auld house
   and birds o monie a feather:
there were sangs and swords in the auld house
   that rattled ane anither.

It was aince a braw and bauld house
   and guid for onie weather:
but it's noo a scruntit and cauld house
   whaur lairdies forgaither.

Lat's caa in the folk to the auld house,
   the puir folk aa thegither:
it's sunkit on rock is the auld house,
   and the rock's their brither.

It was aince a braw and bauld house
   and guid for onie weather:
but the folk maun funder the auld house
   and bigg up anither.

puckle good number of	*thranged* thronged
lairds squires	*a'smither* to pieces
haud hold	*scruntit* stunted
graith furniture	*funder* wreck
smeddum gumption	*bigg* build
bauld bold	

THE MAKAR

Nae man wha loves the lawland tongue
but warstles wi the thocht –
there are mair sangs that bide unsung
nor aa that hae been wrocht.

Ablow the wastery o the years
the thorter o himsel,
deep buried in his bluid he hears
a music that is leal.

And wi this lealness gangs his ain;
and there's nae ither gait
though aa his feres were fremmit men
wha cry: *Owre late, owre late.*

SONG

Whaur yon broken brig hings owre,
Whaur yon water maks nae soun',
Babylon blaws by in stour:
Gang doun wi a sang, gang doun.

Deep, owre deep, for onie drouth,
Wan eneuch an ye wud droun,
Saut, or seelfu', for the mouth:
Gang doun wi a sang, gang doun.

lawland tongue lowland Scots　　　*brig* bridge
warstles wrestles　　　　　　　　　*stour* dust
thorter frustration　　　　　　　　*gang* go
leal true　　　　　　　　　　　　　*saut* salt
gait way　　　　　　　　　　　　　*seelfu'* sweet
fremmit alienated

Babylon blaws by in stour
Whaur yon water maks nae soun':
Darkness is your only door;
Gang doun wi a sang, gang doun.

Robert Garioch

1908–

EMBRO TO THE PLOY

In simmer, whan aa sorts foregether
in Embro to the ploy,
folk seek out friens to hae a blether,
or faes they'd fain annoy;
smorit wi British Railways' reek
frae Glesca or Glen Roy
or Wick, they come to hae a week
of cultivated joy

                              or three,
In Embro to the Ploy.

Americans wi routh of dollars,
wha drink our whisky neat,
wi Sasunachs and Oxford Scholars
are eydent for the treat
of music sedulously high-tie
at thirty-bob a seat;
Wop opera performed in Eyetie

simmer summer   *reek* smoke
ploy festival   *routh* plenty
blether gossip   *Sasunachs* saxons, English
faes foes   *eydent* eager
smorit smothered *Eyetie* Italian

to them's richt up their street,
                          they say,
in Embro to the ploy.

Furthgangan Embro folk come hame
for three weeks in the year,
and find Auld Reekie no the same,
fu sturrit in a steir.
The stane-faced biggins whaur they froze
and suppit puirshous lear
of cultural cauld-kale and brose
see cantraips unco queer
                          thae days
in Embro to the ploy.

The tartan tred wad gar ye lauch;
nae problem is owre teuch.
Your surname needna end in *-och*;
they'll cleik ye up the cleuch.
A puckle dollar bills will aye
preive Hiram Teufelsdröckh
a septary of Clan McKay,
it's maybe richt eneuch,
                          verflüch!
in Embro to the ploy.

The auld High Schule, whaur monie a skelp
of triple-tonguit tawse
has gien a heist-up and a help

furthgangan emigrant	*thae* those
Auld Reekie Edinburgh	*tred* trade
sturrit in a steir stirred in	*gar* make
confusion	*teuch* tough
biggins buildings	*cleik* claw (deceive you)
puirshous lear poor-house	*cleuch* the Castle-rock
learning	*preive* prove
cauld-kale yesterday's cabbage	*skelp* blow
soup	*tawse* belt
cantraips tricks, capers	*heist-up* lift-up

towards Doctorates of Laws,
nou hears, for Ramsay's cantie rhyme,
loud pawmies of applause
frae folk that pey a pund a time
to sit on wudden raws
                          gey hard
in Embro to the ploy.

The haly kirk's Assembly-haa
nou fairly coups the creel
wi Lindsay's Three Estaitis, braw
devices of the Deil.
About our heids the satire stots
like hailstanes till we reel;
the bawrs are in auld-farrant Scots,
it's maybe jist as weill,
                          imphm,
in Embro to the ploy.

The Epworth Haa wi wonder did
behold a pipers' bicker;
wi *hadarid* and *hindarid*
the air gat thick and thicker.
Cumha na Cloinne pleyed on strings
torments a piper quicker
to get his dander up, by jings,
than thirty u.p. liquor,
                          hooch aye!
in Embro to the ploy.

The Northern British Embro Whigs
that stayed in Charlotte Square,
they fairly wad hae tined their wigs

cantie merry	*bawrs* jokes
pawmies blows on the palms	*auld-farrant* old-fashioned
pey pay	*bicker* competition
raws rows	*dander* temper, mettle
coups the creel upsets the basket	*tined* lost
stots bounces	

to see the Stuarts there,
the bleeding Earl of Moray and aa
weill-pentit and gey bare;
Our Queen and Princess, buskit braw,
enjoyed the hale affair
                    (see Press)
in Embro to the ploy.

Whan day's anomalies are cled
in decent shades of nicht,
the Castle is transmogrified
by braw electric licht.
The toure that bields the Bruce's croun
presents an unco sicht
mair sib to Wardour Street nor Scone,
wae's me for Scotland's micht,
                    says I
in Embro to the ploy.

A happening, incident, or splore
affrontit them that saw
a thing they'd never seen afore –
in the McEwan Haa:
a lassie in a wheelie-chair
wi naething on at aa;
jist like my luck! I wasna there,
it's no the thing ava,
                    tut-tut,
in Embro to the ploy.

The Cafe Royal and Abbotsford
are filled wi orra folk
whas stock-in-trade's the scrievit word,

gey rather   *ava* at all
cled clad   *orra* strange
bields shelters   *scrievit* written
splore spree, revel

or twicet-scrievit joke.
Brains, weak or strang, in heavy beer,
or ordinary, soak.
Quo yin: This yill is aafie dear,
I hae nae clinks in poke
                                nor fauldan-money,
in Embro to the ploy.

The auld Assembly-rooms, whaur Scott
foregethert wi his fiers,
nou see a gey kenspeckle lot
ablow the chandeliers.
Til Embro drouths the Festival Club
a richt godsend appears;
it's something new to find a pub
that gaes on serving beers
                                eftir hours
in Embro to the ploy.

Jist pitten-out, the drucken mobs
frae howffs in Potterraw,
fleean, to hob-nob wi the Nobs,
ran to this Music Haa.
Register Rachel, Cougait Kate,
Nae-neb Nellie and aa
stauchert about amang the Great,
what fun! I never saw
                                the like,
in Embro to the ploy.

They toddle hame doun lit-up streets
filled wi synthetic joy;
aweill, the year brings few sic treats

yill ale		*howffs* pubs
aafie awful		*fleean* drunk
clinks coins		*nae-neb* noseless
kenspeckle notable		*stauchert* staggered

and muckle to annoy.
There's monie hartsom braw high-jinks
mixed up in this alloy
in simmer, whan aa sorts foregether
in Embro to the ploy.

Kathleen Raine

1908–

FROM EILEANN CHANAIDH

—

THE ANCIENT SPEECH

A Gaelic bard they praise who in fourteen adjectives
Named the one indivisible soul of his glen;
For what are the bens and the glens but manifold qualities,
Immeasurable complexities of soul?
What are these isles but a song sung by island voices?
The herdsman sings ancestral memories
And the song makes the singer wise,
But only while he sings
Songs that were old when the old themselves were young,
Songs of these hills only, and of no isles but these.
For other hills and isles this language has no words.

The mountains are like manna, for one day given,
To each his own:
Strangers have crossed the sound, but not the sound of the
    dark oarsmen
Or the golden-haired sons of kings,
Strangers whose thought is not formed to the cadence of
    waves,
Rhythm of the sickle, oar and milking pail,
Whose words make loved things strange and small,
Emptied of all that made them heart-felt or bright.
Our words keep no faith with the soul of the world.

eileann Chanaidh isle of Canna (Inner Hebrides)

HIGHLAND GRAVEYARD

Today a fine old face has gone under the soil;
For generations past women hereabouts have borne
Her same name and stamp of feature.
Her brief identity was not her own
But theirs who formed and sent her out
To wear the proud bones of her clan, and live its story,
Who now receive back into the ground
Worn features of ancestral mould.

A dry-stone wall bounds off the dislimned clay
Of many an old face forgotten and young face gone
From boundless nature, sea and sky.
A wind-withered escalonia like a song
Of ancient tenderness lives on
Some woman's living fingers set as shelter for the dead, to tell
In evergreen unwritten leaves,
In scent of leaves in western rain
That one remembered who is herself forgotten.

Many songs they knew who now are silent.
Into their memories the dead are gone
Who haunt the living in an ancient tongue
Sung by old voices to the young,
Telling of sea and isles, of boat and byre and glen;
And from their music the living are reborn
Into a remembered land,
To call ancestral memories home
And all that ancient grief and love our own.

George Bruce

1909–

INHERITANCE

This which I write now
Was written years ago
Before my birth
In the features of my father.

It was stamped
In the rock formations
West of my hometown,
Not I write,

But, perhaps, William Bruce,
Cooper,
Perhaps here his hand
Well articled in his trade.

Then though my words
Hit out
An ebullition from
City or flower,

There not my faith,
These the paint
Smeared upon
The inarticulate,

The salt-crusted sea-boot,
The red-eyed mackerel,
The plate shining with herring,
And many men,

Seamen and craftsmen and curers,
And behind them
The protest of hundreds of years,
The sea obstinate against the land.

Norman MacCaig

1910–

SPARROW

He's no artist.
His taste in clothes leans towards
the dowdy and second hand.
And his nest – that blackbird, writing
pretty scrolls on the air with the gold nib of his beak
would call it a slum.

To stalk solitary on lawns,
to sing solitary in midnight trees,
to glide solitary over gray Atlantics –
not for him: he'd rather
a punch-up in a gutter.

He carries what learning he has
lightly – it is, frankly, based
on the usefulness whose result
is survival. A proletarian bird.
No scholar.

But when the winter soft-shoes in,
and these other birds –
ballet dancers, pedants, architects –
die in the snow
and freeze to branches,
watch him happily flying
on the O-levels and A-levels
of the air.

GOLDEN CALF

If all the answer's to be the Sinai sort
The incorruptible lava of the word
Made alphabetic in a stormspout, what
Mere human vocabies you've ever heard,
Poor golden calf, could overbear, I wonder,
    The magniloquence of thunder?

You're for another flame. The Moses in me
Looks with a stone face on our gaudy lives.
His fingers, scorched with godhead, point, and loose
An influence of categorical negatives
That make an image of love, a trope of lover.
    Our dancing days are over.

The buckles tarnish at the thought of it.
The winecup shatters. The bragging music chokes
To the funeral silence it was awkward in.
And before the faggot of salvation smokes,
Your knees are loosed, your wreathed neck bows lowly
    In presence of the holy.

What's a disgruntled cloud to you or me?
Listen to my multitudes, and beam for them,
Making a plinth of this dark wilderness.
Utter such rigmaroles an apothegm,
Doing its head-stroke, drowns in such wild water
    And proves itself no matter.

Or where's the desert cat, or hunching shade
That ambles hugely in the dark outside,
Or hospitable anguish beckoning
To its foul ceremony a sorry bride
Could bear the darts struck from your hide by torches
    That guard our pleasure's marches?

Forty years. Small wilderness to unravel
Such an unknotted thread of wandering.
The desert is in Moses' skull, the journey
To the white thalamus whose cradling
Enfolds the foetus of the law – gestation
  Of Moses as a nation.

A chosen people, since they have no choice,
The doors are locked, the flesh-pots on the shelves,
And a long line of lamentation moves
Led by the nose through their own better selves
To buy with blood a land of milk and honey
  Where's no need of money.

The smoke and thunder die. And here I stand
Smelling of gunpowder and holiness.
The great fire does its belly-dance and in it
You shine unharmed, not knowing what's to confess;
And the desert, seeing the issue grows no clearer,
  Takes one long slow step nearer.

VISITING HOUR

The hospital smell
combs my nostrils
as they go bobbing along
green and yellow corridors.

What seems a corpse
is trundled into a lift and vanishes
heavenward.

I will not feel, I will not
feel, until
I have to.

Nurses walk lightly, swiftly,
here and up and down and there,
their slender waists miraculously
carrying their burden
of so much pain, so
many deaths, their eyes
still clear after
so many farewells.

Ward 7. She lies
in a white cave of forgetfulness.
A withered hand
trembles on its stalk. Eyes move
behind eyelids too heavy
to raise. Into an arm wasted
of colour a glass fang is fixed,
not guzzling but giving.
And between her and me
distance shrinks till there is none left
but the distance of pain that neither she nor I
can cross.

She smiles a little at this
black figure in her white cave
who clumsily rises
in the round swimming waves of a bell
and dizzily goes off, growing fainter,
not smaller, leaving behind only
books that will not be read
and fruitless fruits.

NOVEMBER NIGHT, EDINBURGH

The night tinkles like ice in glasses.
Leaves are glued to the pavements with frost.
The brown air fumes at the shop windows,
Tries the door, and sidles past.

I gulp down winter raw. The heady
Darkness swirls with tenements.
In a brown fuzz of cottonwool
Lamps fade up crags, die into pits.

Frost in my lungs is harsh as leaves
Scraped up on paths. – I look up, there,
A high roof sails, at the mast-head
Fluttering a grey and ragged star.

The world's a bear shrugged in his den.
It's snug and close in the snoring night.
And outside like Chrysanthemums
The fog unfolds its bitter scent.

Douglas Young

1913–73

LAST LAUCH

The Minister said it wad dee,
the cypress bush I plantit.
But the bush grew til a tree,
naething dauntit.

Hit's growin, stark and heich,
derk and straucht and sinister,
kirkyairdie-like and dreich.
But whaur's the Minister?

lauch laugh   *dreich* grim
heich high

G. S. Fraser

1915–1980

LEAN STREET

Here, where the baby paddles in the gutter,
    Here in the slaty greyness and the gas,
Here where the women wear dark shawls and mutter
    A hasty word as other women pass,

Telling the secret, telling, clucking and tutting,
    Sighing, or saying that it served her right,
The bitch! – the words and weather both are cutting
    In Causewayend, on this November night.

At pavement's end and in the slaty weather
    I stare with glazing eyes at meagre stone,
Rain and the gas are sputtering together
    A dreary tune! O leave my heart alone,

O leave my heart alone, I tell my sorrows,
    For I will soothe you in a softer bed
And I will numb your grief with fat to-morrows
    Who break your milk teeth on this stony bread!

They do not hear. Thought stings me like an adder,
    A doorway's sagging plumb-line squints at me,
The fat sky gurgles like a swollen bladder
    With the foul rain that rains on poverty.

W. S. Graham

1915–

FIVE VISITORS TO MADRON

1

In the small hours on the other side
Of language with my chair drawn
Up to the frightening abstract
Table of silence, taps. A face
Of white feathers turns my head
To suddenly see between the mad
Night astragals her looking in
Or wanted this to happen. She
Monster muse old bag or. Something
Dreamed is yes you're welcome always
Desired to drop in. It was your bleached
Finger on the pane which startled me
Although I half-expected you
But not you as you are but whoever
Would have looked in instead, another
More to my liking, not so true.

He realized it was a mistake. Closing
The door of the tomb afterwards
Secretly he thanked whoever
He could imagine to thank, some quick
Thought-up thankable god of the moment.

2

As slow as distant spray falling
On the nether rocks of a headland never
Encountered but through the eye, the first

Of morning's ghost in blue palely
Hoisted my reluctant lid.
Watch what you say I said and watched
The day I uttered taking shape
To hide me in its bright bosom.

Like struck flints black flocking jack
Daws wheel over the Madron roofs.

3

I am longing not really longing
For what don't tell me let me think.
Or else I have to settle for
That step is that a step outside
At my back a new eddy of air?

And left these words at a loss to know
What form stood watching behind me
Reading us over my shoulder. I said
Now that you have come to stand
There rank-breathed at my elbow I will
Not be put off. This message must
Reach the others without your help.

4

And met the growing gaze willing
To give its time to me to let
Itself exchange discernments
If that surely it said is what
I wanted. Quick panics put out
A field of images round me to
Look back out at it from and not
Be gazed out of all composure.

And found my research ridiculously
Ending forced to wear a mask
Of a held-up colander to peer

Through as the even gaze began
Slowly to abate never having asked
Me if I had recognized an old
Aspect of need there once my own.

Terror-spots itch on my face now.
My mind is busy hanging up
Back in their places imagination's
Clever utensils. I scratch my cheek.

5

When the fifth came I had barely drawn
A breath in to identify who
I newly am in my new old house
In Madron near the slaughterhouse.

The hint was as though a child running
Late for school cried and seemed
To have called my name in the morning
Hurrying and my name's wisp
Elongated. Leaves me here
Nameless at least very without
That name mine ever to be called
In that way different again.

Sydney Goodsir Smith

1915–75

THE MITHER'S LAMENT

What care I for the leagues o sand,
The prisoners and the gear they've won?
My darlin liggs amang the dunes
Wi mony a mither's son.

Doutless he deed for Scotland's life;
Doutless the statesmen dinna lee;
But och tis sair begrutten pride
And wersh the wine o victorie!

COKKILS

Doun throu the sea
Continuallie
A rain o cokkils, shells
Rains doun
Frae the ceaseless on-ding
O' the reefs abune –
Continuallie.

liggs lies   *on-ding* tumult
begrutten bewept   *abune* above
wersh tasteless

Slawlie throu millennia
Biggan on the ocean bed
Their ain subaqueous Himalaya
Wi a fine white rain o shells
Faa'an continuallie
    Wi nae devall.

Sae, in my heid as birdsang
Faas throu simmer treen
Is the thocht o my luve
Like the continual rain
O' cokkils throu the middle seas
    Wi nae devall –
The thocht o my true-luve
    Continuallie.

FROM UNDER THE EILDON TREE

—

23RD ELEGY: FAREWELL TO CALYPSO

The time is come, my luve,
    My luve, whan I maun gae –
The sevin-pinioned bird is gyran
    Outowre the muir o winds;
Aneath the hills the gigants turn
    In their ayebydan dwaum –
Finn under Nevis, the great King
Under Arthur's Seat, True Tammas
    Neth the Eildons steers again;
As the sand rins i the gless, aince mair
    Tannhäuser, blae and wan as sin –

biggan	building	*dwaum*	sleep
faa'an	falling	*steers*	stirs
devall	stop	*blae*	blue
gigants	giants		

As I, depairts frae Horselberg,
Lane and weirdless, nou aince mair
Ulysses bids his Calypso fareweill ...
                    Fareweill!
Defeatit by his ain back-slitherin
Efter lang strauchle wi the serpent slee,
Lea him at least outgang wi mockerie,
        The Makar macironical!
        A sang on his perjurit lips
        And naething i the pouch
            – Or i the hert, for that!
                        Music, maestro!
Bring on the Dancing Girls!
Vauntie i the muslins o Cos,
Wreathit wi hibiscus and bearan
Amphorae o the richt Falernian!
– O, let there be nae girnin at the Bar!
            – Chi ha vissuto per amore
            Per amore si mori.

strauchle struggle   *lea* leave
slee subtle   *outgang* go out

George Campbell Hay

1915–

FLOOER O THE GEAN

Flooer o the gean,
yere aefauld white she wore yestreen.
Wi gentle glances aye she socht me.
Dwell her thochts whaur dwalt her een?

Flooer o the broom,
gowden abune the thicket's gloom,
I canna see ye as I pu' ye.
My een are fu', my hert is toom.

Flooeran slae,
white ye are, untried, in May.
When Simmer's gane, an' hard days rock ye,
yere fruit is black an' bitter tae.

Bloom o the whin,
born frae the stabs an' still their kin,
the een that seek her beauty yearn for
a flooer that wounds are dernan in.

gean wild cherry   *slae* sloe
aefauld unified   *dernan* hiding
toom empty

Flooer o the briar,
the haund that socht ye throbs wi fire.
The hert that socht her tholes its searan
tae see her mood grow sweir an' tire.

Flooer o the thorn,
the haund that plucked at ye is torn.
Is anger's edge in ane sae gracious?
Can thon sweet face be sherp wi scorn?

Spray o the pine,
that never fades nor faas tae crine,
green I pu' ye, leal I ken ye.
I'll weir the green I winna tine.

*Fior di mento,
la roba vien e va come va il vento.
La bella donna fa l'uomo contento.*

Flooer o the mint,
lik wund the warld's goods come an' are tint.
Wumman's beauty gies man true content.

tholes suffers	*weir* wear
sweir unwilling	*tine* lose
crine wither	*tint* lost
leal true	

Maurice Lindsay

1918–

FARM WIDOW

She moved among the sour smell of her hens' droppings,
her cheeks rubbed to a polish, her skirts bustled
with decent pride; alone since the day the tractor
hauled itself up the field on the hill and toppled

her man away from her. Around her feet
her daughter played, the face of innocence puckered
with the solemn self-importance of being alone
in a grown-up world; her friends, the hens that speckled

her mother's allotment. Some of the weekly folk
who came to buy their eggs, had watched her counting
their change from the money smooth in her purse, and given
her
silent pity, then sensed that she wasn't wanting

in anything they could offer; that she seemed
like one whom life had used too soon for writing
some sort of purpose with, her gestures economies
spelling completeness; gone beyond our waiting

for times and places to happen, beyond the will,
to where time and place lie colourless and still.

Tom Scott

1918–

FERGUS*
(shortened version)

I look back doun my centuries o life
   To see the freindly grip
o Pict and Scot, when Kenneth and his wife
   Plattit this kingrik up,
And whaur was desart, gart the gress grouw green.
   And on Iona's isle
The white monks o Columcill I've seen,
   And the santit bard himsel.

Sae mony lives I'd lived and dee'd afore
   Big-heidit Malcolm brocht
His Celtic-hatan Margaret til the door
   o the ae house we'd wrocht:
Heard Deirdre murn her love, to be unduin
   On Erin's traitor shore:
Seen the saumon that Mungo clawcht, like Finn –
   The plaid MacLir ance wore.

Alexander daed, our ship wrackt on yon sand,
   The rule o bairns begun . . .
Wallace an ae-man fortress, fully manned . . .
   Bruis the embattled sun . . .

santit sainted

*The title refers to the first king of Scots, from A.D. 501. The poem
uses him as symbol of the eternal Scot, and posits the eternal Scots
problem, the integration of Scottish historical experience into a
civilized nation.

Strang airms bluid-red on mony a groanan field . . .
   Berwick a butcherie . . .
Mony sic broken and tormentit bield
   There kyths afore my ee.

Upon sic anvils Edward hammered out
   Our nationhood and saul,
Seasoned the stentit bow til it could shoot
   Doun meteors as they fall,
And gart our noble dogs come in til heel
   Ahent King Bruis's tairge,
Temperan Scottish spines til swippert steel
   In his smiddy's brim forge.

Hou mony things throu thae years I hae been,
   Hou mony trades I kent!
As scholar, merchant, sodger, and marine
   I becam acquent
Wi the haill o Europe, say frae Unst til Kerch,
   Lisbon til Kazan,
For syne we were as het-fuit on the mairch
   As the hounds o Mananan.

Wi Henrysoun I beikit by the fire
   On dowie winter nichts,
And watched the gentry dansan, wi Dunbar,
   Under the Palace lichts.
I stilpt aboard the Caravel wi Wood,
   Saw Oslo and Belgrade,
And murned wi Scotland in her sairest mood
   Owre the Flodden daed.

bield	image	*brim*	fierce
kyths	looms up	*beikit*	warmed
stentit	stretched tight	*dowie*	dreary
swippert	supple	*stilpt*	strode

And in sic style our Reformation cam:
  As weed that chokes the grain.
The unicorn was chased by a hell-bleck ram,
  The garth made a pen.
Hae I no seen frae Solway Firth til Wick
  The white witch Beautie brunt?
It wes our saul they seared at ilka stake,
  That reekt frae ilka lunt.

O white Sanct-Aundraes, bein inben your bay,
  I've seen them stane by stane
Tak doun your braw cathedral on the brae
  And leave it bare as bane;
On mony a muir and hag I've seen douce men
  Huntit like the tod,
And Murder turn the land a bluid-soakt fen
  To spread the love o God.

They made His day a rookery o kirks,
  His pulpit nests o craws,
And lowsed on us a herd o lowan stirks
  Wi iron hoofs and jaws
To trample owre the green and bairgean fields,
  Makan them bogs o sharn,
Imprisonan the fowk inben their beilds,
  And reivan ilka barn.

They kaad doun Woman frae the throne and skies,
  And even frae the chair,
Hapt her beautie in a dow disguise
  And sat her on the fluir.

garth garden
lunt flame
bein snug
inben inside
douce decent
tod fox
stirks steers

bairgean burgeoning (with the
  Renaissance)
sharn shit
reivan robbing
kaad drove
dow mournful

Degradan her, they undermined theirsels
  Wi casuistic laws,
And brutalised their future in the schuils
  Wi never idle taws.

Syne a Prince cam sailan frae the Wast
  To claim a perjured croun,
And rackt the Sudron wi a nordren blast
  Afore *his* house gaed doun.
But he tae by our nobles wes betrayed
  In sicht o victorie:
Culloden smoored for aye a broken blade
  And sent him owre the sea.

The lave's suin telt. Wi Mungo Park I've seen
  The lordly Niger flow,
Wi Murray, Bruce, Mackenzie, I hae been
  In lands o sun and snow.
Ither fires nor Beltane's lit our hills
  When Danu's Bairns were 'cleared',
And ither lands hae reapt the Celtic skills
  Our Sudron neibours feared.

I ken the iron forests on the Clyde,
  The bothybields o Burns;
I've seen the reekan chimneys come to bide,
  The deer amang the ferns;
I've read the secret name o Knox's God,
  The gowd calf 'Getting On':
Ranged Newfoundland Banks to fish for cod,
  Strippit saumon o their spawn.

In laboratories I hae wrocht aa nicht
  Like Vulcan at his forge,
To bring our race mair comfort and licht,

taws strap
smoored smothered
lave remainder

bothybields farm-servants'
  quarters

To fecht ilk human scourge.
The warld weill kens hou guid my labours were,
  Hou usefu my inventions:
But the name and race o the labourer
  The warld seldom mentions.

Hou sall aa the fowk I've been ere meet
  And bide in yae wee house?
Knox wi Burns and Mary, Wishart and Beaton
  Aa be snod and crouse?
Campbell and MacDonald be guid feirs,
  The Bruis sup wi Comyn?
By God, I dout afore sic love appears,
  Nae man sall kiss a woman!

snod snug, agreeable   *feirs* comrades
crouse content

Modern Folk Songs

JOHNNIE LAD

I bought a wife in Edinburgh for ae baw-bee,
I got a farthing back again to buy tobacco wi,
And wi' you, and wi' you, and wi' you Johnnie lad,
I'll drink the buckles o' my shoon wi' you my Johnnie lad.

When auld King Arthur ruled this land
  He was a thieving King.
He stole three bolls o' barley meal
  To make a white pudding.

An' wi' you, and wi' you, and wi' you Johnnie lad,
We'll drink the Bauchles aff wur feet wi you my Johnnie lad.

The pudding it was awfu' guid,
  'Twas weel mixed up wi' plumes;
The lumps o' suet into it
  Were big as baith ma thooms.

  An' wi' you, and wi' you, etc.

Samson was a michty man
  Wha focht wi' cuddies' jaws;
He focht a score o' battles,
  Wearing crimson flannel drawers.

  An' wi' you, and wi' you, etc.

baw-bee halfpenny   *wur* our

Napoleon was an Emperor,
   And ruled by land and sea,
He was King of France and Germany
   But he never ruled Polmadie.

    An' wi' you, and wi' you, etc.

On the royal tour ti Glesca,
   Ye should hae seen the Queen
Playin, a gemme o' fitba',
   Wi' the lads on Glesca Green.

    An' wi' you, and wi' you, etc.

The Captain of the other side
   Was scoring in such style,
The Queen cried owre a polisman,
   And clapped him in the jyle.

    An' wi' you, and wi' you, etc.

The Queen wis in her Parlour,
   Suppin' Cream and Honey,
The Knave wis in the Coontin'-Hoose,
   Fiddling Scotland's Money.

    An' wi' you, and wi' you, etc.

Bit Johnnie wis a raucle boy,
   He gied the Knave a fricht,
And fotch back Scotland's money
   And the people danced aa nicht.

    An' wi' you, and wi' you, etc.

gemme game   *raucle* brash
jyle jail   *fotch* fetched

Johnnie is a bonnie lad,
  He is a lad o' min:
I never had a better lad,
  An' I've had twenty-nine.

  An' wi' you, and wi' you, etc.

COME A' YE TRAMPS AN' HAWKERS

Come a' ye tramps and Hawker lads, ye gaitherers o' blaw,
That tramps the country roon an' roon, come listen een an' a'.
I'll tell tae ye a rovin' tale, an' sichts that I hae seen
Far up intae the snawy north or sooth by Gretna Green.

I've seen the high Ben Nevis, awa' toorin tae the mune,
I've been by Crieff an' Callander an' roon by bonnie Doon;
I've been by Nethy's silvery tides and places ill tae ken,
Far up intil the stormy north lies Urquhart's fairy glen.

Aft times I've lauched untae mysel' when trudgin on the road,
Wi' a bag o' blaw upon my back, my face as broon's a toad,
Wi' lumps o' cake and tattie scones, an' cheese an' braxie ham,
It's nae thinking faur I'm comin' frae nor faur I'm gyaun tae
  gan.

But I'm happy in the summer time beneath the bright blue
  sky,
Nae thinking in the morning at nicht whaur I'm tae lie,
Bothies or Byres or anywhaur, or oot amang the hay,
And if the weather does permit I'm happy a' the day.

blaw oatmeal	*toad* fox
een one	*faur* where
toorin towering	*gyaun tae gan* going to go
Nethy a tributary of the Spey	

Loch Catrine an' Loch Lomond hae a' been seen by me,
The Dee, the Don, the Deveron that flows intae the sea,
Dunrobin Castle by the way I nearly had forgot,
And aye the Rickle o' Carlin marks the Hoose o' John O'
    Groat.

I'm often roon by Galloway and doon aboot Stranraer,
My business leads me anygates, for I travel near and far,
I've got the rovin' notion, there's naething fae't I loss,
And a' my day is my daily fare, an' what'll pay my doss.

I think I'll go tae Paddy's land, I'm makin' up my mind,
For Scotland's greatly altered noo – sure I canna raise the
    wind,
But I will trust in Providence, if Providence will prove true,
And I will sing o' Erin's Isle when I come back to you.

As sung by Jimmie MacBeath

THE BARNYARDS O DELGATIE

As I cam in by Turra market, Turra market for to fee,
It's I fell in wi a wealthy fairmer, the Barnyards o Delgatie.
    Linten adie, toorin adie, linten adie, toorin ee;
    Linten lowrin, lowrin, lowrin the Barnyards o Delgatie.

    He promised me the twa best horse
        That wis in aa the kintra roun,
    But fan I wan tae the barnyards,
        Wis naething there but skin and bone.

anygates everywhere	*kintra* countryside
fae't from it	*fan* when
Turra Turriff	*wan* won, reached
to fee to engage as farm-worker for a year	

It's Jean MacPherson maks ma bed,
    Ye'll see the marks upon ma shins;
For she's the coorse ill-tricket jaud
    That fills ma bed wi prickly whins.

When I gae to the kirk on Sunday,
    Mony's the bonnie lass I see
Sittin by her faither's side,
    And winkin owre the pews at me.

Some can drink and no get drunken,
    Some can fecht and no get slain;
I can kiss anither loon's lass
    And aye be welcome tae ma ain.

My caunle it is near brunt oot,
    The snotter's fairly on the wane;
Sae fare ye weel, ye Barnyards,
    Yc'll never find me here again.

coorse coarse   *caunle* candle
loon lad   *snotter* candle-wax

Alexander Scott

1920–

CONTINENT O VENUS

She lies ablow my body's lust and love,
A country dearly-kent, and yet sae fremd
That she's at aince thon Tir-nan-Og I've dreamed,
The airt I've lived in, whar I mean tae live,
And mair, much mair, a mixter-maxter warld
Whar fact and dream are taigled up and snorled.

I ken ilk bay o aa her body's strand,
Yet ken them new ilk time I come to shore,
For she's the uncharted sea whar I maun fare
To find anither undiscovered land,
To find it fremd, and yet to find it dear,
To seek for't aye, and aye be bydan there.

ablow below   *airt* quarter of compass
fremd foreign   *bydan* staying
Tir-nan-Og land-of-youth, Gaelic
    paradise

Edwin Morgan

1920–

THE SHEAF

My life, as a slant of rain
on the grey earth fields
is gathered in thirsty silence, disappears.
I cannot even guess
the roots, but feel them sighing
in the stir of the soil I die to. Let this rain
be on the children of my heart,
I have no other ones.
          On the generations,
on the packed cells and dreaming shoots,
the untried hopes, the waiting good
I send this drop to melt.

George Mackay Brown

1927–

THE OLD WOMEN

Go sad or sweet or riotous with beer
Past the old women gossiping by the hour,
They'll fix on you from every close and pier
An acid look to make your veins run sour.

'No help,' they say, 'his grandfather that's dead
Was troubled with the same dry-throated curse,
And many a night he made the ditch his bed.
This blood comes welling from the same cracked source.'

On every kind of merriment they frown.
But I have known a gray-eyed sober boy
Sail to the lobsters in a storm and drown.
Over his body dripping on the stones
Those same old hags would weave into their moans
An undersong of terrible holy joy.

Burns Singer

1928–64

STILL AND ALL

I give my word on it. There is no way
Other than this. There is no other way
Of speaking. I am my name. I find my place
Empty without a word, and my word is
Given again. It is nothing less than all
Given away again, and all still truly
Returned on a belief. Believe me now.
There is no other. There is no other way.

These words run vertical in their slim green tunnels
Without any turning away. They turn into
The first flower and speak from a silent bell.
But underneath it is as always still
Truly awakening, slowly and slowly turning
About a shadow scribbled down by sunlight
And turning about my name. I am in my
Survival's hands. I am my shadow's theme.

My shadow's ground feeds me with roots, and rhymes
My statement over. Its radius feeds my flames
Into a cool tunnel. And I who find your ways
About me (In every part I find your ways
Of speech.) pierce ground and shadow still. The light
Is struck. Its definition makes me my quiet
Survival's answer. All still and all so truly
Wakening underneath me and turning slowly.

It's all so truly still. I'll take you into
The first statement. I'll take you along cool tunnels
That channelled light and petalled an iridescent
Symmetry over my bruised shadow. And yes
I'll take you, and your word will follow me,
Till definitions gather distilled honey
And make their mark the fingerprints of light.
I am, believe me then, the name I write.

I lie here still. Yes, truly still. And all
My deliberate identities have fallen
Away with the word given. I find my place
In every place, in every part of speech,
And lie there still. I let my statements go.
A cool green tunnel has stepped in the light of my shadow
There is no way round it. It leads to the flower
Bell – that swings slowly and slowly over.

Iain Crichton Smith

1928-

JOHN KNOX

That scything wind has cut the rich corn down –
the satin shades of France spin idly by –
the bells are jangled in St Andrew's town –
a thunderous God tolls from a northern sky.
He pulls the clouds like bandages awry.
See how the harlot bleeds below her crown.
This lightning stabs her in the heaving thigh –
such siege is deadly for dallying gown.

A peasant's scythe rings churchbells from the stone.
From this harsh battle let the sweet birds fly,
surprised by fields, now barren of their corn.
(Invent, bright friends, theology, or die.)
The shearing naked absolute blade has torn
through false French roses to her foreign cry.

CULLODEN AND AFTER

You understand it? How they returned from Culloden
over the soggy moors aslant, each cap
at the low ebb no new full tide could pardon:
how they stood silent at the end of the rope
unwound from battle: and to the envelope
of a bedded room came home, polite and sudden.

And how, much later, bards from Tiree and Mull
would write of exile in the hard town
where mills belched English, anger of new school:
how they remembered where the sad and brown
landscapes were dear and distant as the crown
that fuddled Charles might study in his ale.

Acknowledgements

For permission to publish the poems in this anthology acknowledgement is made to the following:

For Marion Angus, 'The Lilt', 'Alas! Poor Queen', from *The Turn of the Day*, 1931, to Faber & Faber Ltd; for George Bruce, 'Inheritance', from *Selected Poems*, published by The Saltire Society 1947, to the author; for George Campbell Hay, 'Flooer o The Gean', from *The Wind on Loch Fyne*, published by Oliver & Boyd 1948, to the author; for Joe Corrie, 'Miners' Wives', 'The Image o' God' from *The Image o' God*, published by Faber & Faber 1930, to Mrs M. Corrie; for I. Crichton Smith, 'Culloden and After', 'John Knox', from *Thistles and Roses*, 1961, to Eyre & Spottiswoode, and to the author; for Helen Cruickshank, 'A Prayer', 'The Ponnage', 'Keepit In', 'There was a Sang', from *The Ponnage Pool*, published by M. MacDonald, 1968, to the author; for G. S. Fraser, 'Lean Street', from *Home Town Elegy*, published by Nicholson & Watson, 1944, to the author; for Robert Garioch, 'Embro to the Ploy', from *Collected Poems*, published by M. MacDonald, 1967, to the author; for Sidney Goodsir Smith, 'Cokkils', 1953, 'The Mither's Lament', 'Under the Eildon Tree', from *The Eildon Tree*, published by Serif Books, 1948, and for the use of the edited texts from 'The Merry Muses of Caledonia', 1959, to the author; for W. S. Graham, 'Five Visitors to Madron', 1959, to the author; for Alexander Gray, 'Scotland', from *Gossip*, published by Faber & Faber, 1928, to the Executors of the Estate of the late Sir Alexander Gray; for William Jeffrey, 'Stones', from *Selected Poems of William Jeffrey*, published by Serif Books, 1951, to Mrs M. Jeffrey; for Maurice Lindsay, 'Farm Widow', from *One Later Day* published by Brookside Press, 1964, to the author; for Norman MacCaig, 'Golden Calf', 'November Night, Edinburgh', from *The Sinai Sort*, to the Hogarth Press Ltd, 1957, and for 'Visiting Hour', to the author; for Hugh MacDiarmid, 'Empty Vessel', 'O Wha's the Bride, 'The Watergaw', 'Supper to God', 'Gairmscoile', 'Crowdieknowe', 'Cophetua', 'The Parrot Cry', 'Prayer for a Second Flood', 'Depth and the Chthonian Image', from *Collected Poems*, 1962, to the

Macmillan Company, New York; for George Mackay Brown, 'The Old Women', from *Loaves and Fishes*, 1959, to the Hogarth Press Ltd; for Edwin Morgan, 'The Sheaf', from *A Second Life*, published by Edinburgh University Press, 1968, to the author; for Edwin Muir, 'Scotland, 1941', 'Scotland's Winter', 'The Castle', 'The Horses', 'The Confirmation', 'The Fathers' from *Collected Poems* 1921-1958, 1960, to Faber & Faber; for Charles Murray, 'Dockens afore his Peers', 'Gin I was God', from *Hamewith*, 1909, to Constable & Co. Ltd; for Kathleen Raine, from 'Eileann Chanaidh', 'The Ancient Speech', 'Highland Graveyard', from *The Hollow Hill*, 1965, to Hamish Hamilton Ltd; for Alexander Scott, 'Continent o Venus', from *Latest in Elegies*, published by Caledonian Press, 1949, to the author; for Tom Scott, 'Fergus', from *The Ship and Ither Poems*, 1963, to Oxford University Press; for Burns Singer, 'Still and All', from *Still and All*, 1957, to Secker & Warburg Ltd; for William Soutar, 'The Tryst', 'The Auld House', 'The Makar', 'Song', from *Collected Poems*, published by Andrew Dakers, 1948, to the Trustees of the National Library of Scotland; for Lewis Spence, 'The Prows o' Reekie', from *Plumes of Time*, published by Allen & Unwin, 1926, to Miss Rhoda Spence; for Andrew Young, 'The Falls of Glomach', 'Culbin Sands', 'The Paps of Jura', from *Collected Poems*, 1950, to Rupert Hart-Davis Ltd; for Douglas Young, 'Last Lauch', from *A Braird of Thistles*, published by Wm MacLellan, 1947, to the author.

Indexes

Index of First Lines

Index of Authors

FOR THE BEST IN PAPERBACKS, LOOK FOR THE 🐧

In every corner of the world, on every subject under the sun, Penguin represents quality and variety – the very best in publishing today.

For complete information about books available from Penguin – including Puffins, Penguin Classics and Arkana – and how to order them, write to us at the appropriate address below. Please note that for copyright reasons the selection of books varies from country to country.

In the United Kingdom: Please write to *Dept E.P., Penguin Books Ltd, Harmondsworth, Middlesex, UB7 0DA.*

If you have any difficulty in obtaining a title, please send your order with the correct money, plus ten per cent for postage and packaging, to *PO Box No 11, West Drayton, Middlesex*

In the United States: Please write to *Dept BA, Penguin, 299 Murray Hill Parkway, East Rutherford, New Jersey 07073*

In Canada: Please write to *Penguin Books Canada Ltd, 2801 John Street, Markham, Ontario L3R 1B4*

In Australia: Please write to the *Marketing Department, Penguin Books Australia Ltd, P.O. Box 257, Ringwood, Victoria 3134*

In New Zealand: Please write to the *Marketing Department, Penguin Books (NZ) Ltd, Private Bag, Takapuna, Auckland 9*

In India: Please write to *Penguin Overseas Ltd,. 706 Eros Apartments, 56 Nehru Place, New Delhi, 110019*

In the Netherlands: Please write to *Penguin Books Netherlands B.V., Postbus 195, NL–1380AD Weesp*

In West Germany: Please write to *Penguin Books Ltd, Friedrichstrasse 10–12, D–6000 Frankfurt/Main 1*

In Spain: Please write to *Longman Penguin España, Calle San Nicolas 15, E–28013 Madrid*

In Italy: Please write to *Penguin Italia s.r.l., Via Como 4, I-20096 Pioltello (Milano)*

In France: Please write to *Penguin Books Ltd, 39 Rue de Montmorency, F-75003 Paris*

In Japan: Please write to *Longman Penguin Japan Co Ltd, Yamaguchi Building, 2–12–9 Kanda Jimbocho, Chiyoda-Ku, Tokyo 101*

FOR THE BEST IN PAPERBACKS, LOOK FOR THE 🐧

PENGUIN INTERNATIONAL WRITERS

Titles already published or in preparation

Gamal Al-Ghitany	**Zayni Barakat**
Isabel Allende	**Eva Luna**
Wang Anyi	**Baotown**
Joseph Brodsky	**Marbles: A Play in Three Acts**
Doris Dörrie	**Love, Pain and the Whole Damn Thing**
Shusaku Endo	**Scandal**
	Wonderful Fool
Ida Fink	**A Scrap of Time**
Daniele Del Giudice	**Lines of Light**
Miklos Haraszti	**The Velvet Prison**
Ivan Klíma	**My First Loves**
	A Summer Affair
Jean Levi	**The Chinese Emperor**
Harry Mulisch	**Last Call**
Cees Nooteboom	**The Dutch Mountains**
	A Song of Truth and Semblance
Milorad Pavić	**Dictionary of the Khazars**
Luise Rinser	**Prison Journal**
A. Solzhenitsyn	**Matryona's House and Other Stories**
	One Day in the Life of Ivan Denisovich
Tatyana Tolstoya	**On the Golden Porch and Other Stories**
Elie Wiesel	**Twilight**
Zhang Xianliang	**Half of Man is Woman**

FOR THE BEST IN PAPERBACKS, LOOK FOR THE 🐧

PLAYS IN PENGUIN

Edward Albee   **Who's Afraid of Virginia Woolf?**

Alan Ayckbourn   **The Norman Conquests**

Bertolt Brecht   **Parables for the Theatre (The Good Woman of Setzuan/The Caucasian Chalk Circle)**

Anton Chekhov   **Plays (The Cherry Orchard/Three Sisters/Ivanov/The Seagull/Uncle Vanya)**

Henrik Ibsen   **Hedda Gabler/The Pillars of the Community/The Wild Duck**

Eugène Ionesco   **Absurd Drama (Rhinoceros/The Chair/The Lesson)**

Ben Jonson   **Three Comedies (Volpone/The Alchemist/Bartholomew Fair)**

D. H. Lawrence   **Three Plays (The Collier's Friday Night/ The Daughter-in-Law/The Widowing of Mrs Holroyd)**

Arthur Miller   **Death of a Salesman**

John Mortimer   **A Voyage Round My Father/What Shall We Tell Caroline?/ The Dock Brief**

J. B. Priestley   **Time and the Conways/I Have Been Here Before/An Inspector Calls/The Linden Tree**

Peter Shaffer   **Lettice and Lovage/Yonadab**

Bernard Shaw   **Plays Pleasant (Arms and the Man/Candida/The Man of Destiny/You Never Can Tell)**

Sophocles   **Three Theban Plays (Oedipus the King/Antigone/Oedipus at Colonus)**

Arnold Wesker   **Plays, Volume 1: The Wesker Trilogy (Chicken Soup with Barley/Roots/I'm Talking about Jerusalem)**

Oscar Wilde   **Plays (Lady Windermere's Fan/A Woman of No Importance/ An Ideal Husband/The Importance of Being Earnest/Salome)**

Thornton Wilder   **Our Town/The Skin of Our Teeth/The Matchmaker**

Tennessee Williams   **Sweet Bird of Youth/A Streetcar Named Desire/The Glass Menagerie**

FOR THE BEST IN PAPERBACKS, LOOK FOR THE 🐧

PENGUIN POETRY LIBRARY

Arnold Selected by Kenneth Allott
Blake Selected by W. H. Stevenson
Browning Selected by Daniel Karlin
Burns Selected by W. Beattie and H. W. Meikle
Byron Selected by A. S. B. Glover
Coleridge Selected by Kathleen Raine
Donne Selected by John Hayward
Dryden Selected by Douglas Grant
Hardy Selected by David Wright
Herbert Selected by W. H. Auden
Keats Selected by John Barnard
Kipling Selected by James Cochrane
Lawrence Selected by Keith Sagar
Milton Selected by Laurence D. Lerner
Pope Selected by Douglas Grant
Shelley Selected by Isabel Quigley
Tennyson Selected by W. E. Williams
Wordsworth Selected by W. E. Williams

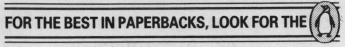

FOR THE BEST IN PAPERBACKS, LOOK FOR THE 🐧

PENGUIN BOOKS OF POETRY

American Verse
British Poetry Since 1945
Caribbean Verse in English
A Choice of Comic and Curious Verse
Contemporary American Poetry
Contemporary British Poetry
English Christian Verse
English Poetry 1918–60
English Romantic Verse
English Verse
First World War Poetry
Greek Verse
Irish Verse
Light Verse
Love Poetry
The Metaphysical Poets
Modern African Poetry
New Poetry
Poetry of the Thirties
Post-War Russian Poetry
Scottish Verse
Southern African Verse
Spanish Civil War Verse
Spanish Verse
Women Poets